Sex, Violence and the Body

Also by Viv Burr

AN INTRODUCTION TO SOCIAL CONSTRUCTIONISM

GENDER AND SOCIAL PSYCHOLOGY

INVITATION TO PERSONAL CONSTRUCT PSYCHOLOGY (*with Trevor W. Butt*)

THE PERSON IN SOCIAL PSYCHOLOGY

Also by Jeff Hearn

BIRTH AND AFTERBIRTH: A Materialist Account

'SEX' AT 'WORK': The Power and Paradox of Organisation Sexuality (*with Wendy Parkin*)

THE GENDER OF OPPRESSION: Men, Masculinity and the Critique of Marxism

MEN, MASCULINITIES AND SOCIAL THEORY (*co-editor with David Morgan*)

MEN IN THE PUBLIC EYE: The Construction and Deconstruction of Public Men and Public Patriarchies

THE VIOLENCES OF MEN: How Men Talk about and How Agencies Respond to Men's Violence to Women

CONSUMING CULTURES: Power and Resistance (*co-editor with Sasha Roseneil*)

TRANSFORMING POLITICS: Power and Resistance (*co-editor with Paul Bagguley*)

GENDER, SEXUALITY AND VIOLENCE IN ORGANIZATIONS: The Unspoken Forces of Organization Violations (*with Wendy Parkin*)

ENDING GENDER-BASED VIOLENCE: A Call for Global Action to Involve Men (*with Harry Ferguson et al.*)

INFORMATION SOCIETY AND THE WORKPLACE: Spaces, Boundaries and Agency (*co-editor with Tuula Heiskanen*)

GENDER AND ORGANISATIONS IN FLUX? (*co-editor with Päivi Eriksson et al.*)

HANDBOOK OF STUDIES ON MEN AND MASCULINITIES (*co-editor with Michael Kimmel and R. W. Connell*)

MEN AND MASCULINITIES IN EUROPE (*with Keith Pringle et al.*)

EUROPEAN PERSPECTIVES ON MEN AND MASCULINITIES: National and Transnational Approaches (*with Keith Pringle and members of CROME*)

Sex, Violence and the Body

The Erotics of Wounding

Edited by

Viv Burr
University of Huddersfield, UK

Jeff Hearn
University of Huddersfield, UK, Linköping University, Sweden and Swedish School of Economics, Finland

palgrave
macmillan

Softcover reprint of the hardcover 1st edition 2008 978-0-230-54934-0

First published 2008 by
PALGRAVE MACMILLAN

Palgrave Macmillan in the UK is an imprint of Macmillan Publishers Limited, registered in England, company number 785998, of Houndmills, Basingstoke, Hampshire RG21 6XS.

Palgrave Macmillan in the US is a division of St Martin's Press LLC, 175 Fifth Avenue, New York, NY 10010.

Palgrave Macmillan is the global academic imprint of the above companies and has companies and representatives throughout the world.

Palgrave® and Macmillan® are registered trademarks in the United States, the United Kingdom, Europe and other countries.

ISBN 978-1-349-36182-3　　ISBN 978-0-230-22839-9 (eBook)
DOI 10.1057/9780230228399

This book is printed on paper suitable for recycling and made from fully managed and sustained forest sources. Logging, pulping and manufacturing processes are expected to conform to the environmental regulations of the country of origin.

A catalogue record for this book is available from the British Library.

Library of Congress Cataloging-in-Publication Data

Sex, violence, and the body : the erotics of wounding / [edited by]
Viv Burr, Jeff Hearn.
p. cm.
Includes bibliographical references and index.

1. Sadomasochism. 2. Wounds and injuries—Erotic aspects. I. Burr, Viven. II. Hearn, Jeff, 1947

HQ79.S49 2008
306.77′5—dc22　　2008024580

10 9 8 7 6 5 4 3 2 1
17 16 15 14 13 12 11 10 09 08

Transferred to Digital Printing 2009

In memory of Gem and Spot who, although not troubled by the questions addressed in this book, happily accompanied me on many walks while I pondered them.

And for Hans, for still talking, walking and singing.

Contents

Figures and Table

Notes on Contributors

Jenny Alexander wrote her PhD on nineteenth-century anarchism and political autobiography. She was a lecturer at the University of Sussex in the Department of Media and Film from 2003 to 2006 where she helped set up the Gender Studies MA and BA Programmes. She specialises in gender and media, political autobiography and the media and advertising. At present she is working as an Investigative Researcher at the Advertising Standards Authority in London.

Viv Burr is Reader in Psychology, University of Huddersfield, UK. Her main research interests are social constructionism, gender and cultural studies. Her books include *Invitation to Personal Construct Psychology* (with Trevor Butt, Whurr Publishers, 1992; 2nd edition, 2003), *An Introduction to Social Constructionism* (Routledge, 1995), *The Person in Social Psychology* (Routledge, 2002), *Gender and Social Psychology* (Routledge, 1998) and *Social Constructionism* (Psychology Press, 2003).

Tim Edwards is Senior Lecturer in Sociology at the University of Leicester and has taught and published widely on matters relating to masculinity, sexuality and sexual politics. His recent works include *Cultures of Masculinity* (Routledge, 2006), 'Sex, booze and fags' in Bethan Benwell (ed.) *Masculinity and Men's Lifestyle Magazines* (Blackwell, 2003), *Contradictions of Consumption* (Open University Press, 2000), *and Men in the Mirror: Men's Fashion, Masculinity and Consumer Society* (Cassell, 1997).

Jeff Hearn is Professor, University of Huddersfield, UK; Linköping University, Sweden; and Swedish School of Economics, Helsinki, Finland. His books include *The Gender of Oppression* (Wheatsheaf/St. Martin's, 1987), *'Sex' at 'Work'* (with Wendy Parkin, St. Martin's/Prentice Hall, 1987/1995), *The Sexuality of Organization* (co-editor, Sage, 1989), *Men in the Public Eye* (Routledge, 1992), *The Violences of Men* (Sage, 1998), *Consuming Cultures* (co-editor, Macmillan, 1999), *Gender, Sexuality and Violence in Organizations* (with Wendy Parkin, Sage, 2001), *Information Society and the Workplace* (co-editor, Routledge, 2004), *Handbook of Studies on Men and Masculinities* (co-editor, Sage, 2005), *and European Perspectives on Men and Masculinities* (with Keith Pringle and CROME, Palgrave Macmillan, 2006). His current research interests include men's relations to ageing, virtuality and transnationalisation.

Sheila Jeffreys is Professor in the School of Social and Political Sciences at the University of Melbourne where she teaches sexual politics, international feminist politics, and lesbian and gay politics. She has written six books on the history and politics of sexuality, on prostitution and beauty practices. Her most recent book is *Beauty and Misogyny: Harmful Cultural Practices in the West* (Routledge, 2005). In addition, she has just completed a book for Routledge on the international sex industry, provisionally entitled *The Industrial Vagina,* and is writing a book on the politics of transgenderism with Lorene Gottschalk of Ballarat University. She has been involved in feminist activism since 1973, mostly against sexual violence and pornography, and in lesbian feminism since 1978, through the London Lesbian Archive and the Lesbian History Group. She moved to Melbourne in 1991, where she was a founding member (in 1994) of the Australian branch of the Coalition against Trafficking in Women. She works both within Australia and internationally against commercial sexual violence.

Michelle Jones completed her PhD at the University of Adelaide examining public, professional and private constructions of domestic violence. Michelle's undergraduate degree is in social work. She has worked in both academia and as a social work practitioner. As a practitioner, she has worked in the fields of women's reproductive health, and rape and sexual assault. Michelle has combined research and practice interests and is employed in practice-based evaluation positions within the area of men's violence evaluating men's sex and violent offender treatment programmes, and currently in health promotion evaluating childhood obesity programmes. Her research interests include men's violence against women, women's health and health promotion.

Ulla Angkjær Jørgensen is Associate Professor of Art History at the Norwegian University of Science and Technology (NTNU), Trondheim. Her research interests focus on twentieth-century art, contemporary art, art theory, feminism and gender perspectives on art history. She is the author of *Kropslig kunst: kunstanalyse, køn og æstetisk erfaring* (Bodily art: Art Analysis, Gender, and Aesthetic Experience) (Museum Tusculanum Press, University of Copenhagen, 2007). She has written articles on contemporary art, film, body and gender, curated several exhibitions and written for exhibition catalogues.

Taina Kinnunen works as a University Lecturer of Cultural Anthropology at the University of Oulu, Finland. Her recent projects are a monograph on embodied meanings of cosmetic surgery (2008) and a co-edited book on sexuality and the body (2006), both published in Finnish. She completed her PhD in 2001 on extreme bodybuilding interpreted as a communal identity sacralising technique, and has co-authored a book on winter swimming. As regards bodily issues, she also has written articles examining representations of the ideal male body in sport journalism and gendered meanings of food in women's magazines. In addition, she has researched the body centredness of new religious movements and the gendering of bodies and places in fitness sports.

Mona Livholts, PhD, is Senior Lecturer in Social Work and Postdoctoral Fellow, Department of Social Work, Mid Sweden University, where she is also active at the Centre for Gender Studies. She is a Virtual Fellow, Centre for Narrative and Auto/Biographical Studies, University of Edinburgh, and Coordinator of the Network for Reflexive Academic Writing Methodologies (RAW). Her research concerns feminist theorising, categorisation, social change, and textual and visual methodologies. A new research area concerns the telephone as a meeting place for people in sparsely populated areas. In Swedish, she is author of *'As normal as water': Masculinity and Normality in Media Representations of Rape* (Gleerups, 2007) and co-editor of *Gender and Forms of Academic Writing* (Studentlitteratur, 2007).

Anthony McCosker, PhD, has taught sociology at the University of Newcastle, Australia, and cultural studies in the School of Culture and Communication at the University of Melbourne where he is currently a Research Fellow. His recent work on issues of bodily pain and visual culture has appeared in the journals *Continuum, Scope* and *Sexualities*. As well as the culture and politics of bodily pain, his research interests include the cultural production of illness, forms of media censorship and the production of public and private in everyday life.

Ani Ritchie is Senior Lecturer in Media and Cultural Studies, Southampton Solent University, UK. She lectures on cultural identity with a particular focus on gender and sexualities. Her current research interests are on the role of representations in the construction of non-normative identities such as SM. Forthcoming projects include analysis of representations of consent in hardcore film and an ethnographic study exploring the uses of pornography by lesbians.

Victoria Robinson is Senior Lecturer in Sociology, University of Sheffield, UK. With Jenny Hockey and Angela Meah, she has published *Mundane Heterosexualities: From Theory to Practices* (Palgrave Macmillan,

2007); has co-edited, with Diane Richardson, *Introducing Gender and Women's Studies* (3rd edition, Palgrave Macmillan, 2008); and is author of *Everyday Masculinities and Extreme Sport: Male Identity and Rock-Climbing* (Berg, 2008). She has published widely on gender/women's studies, men and masculinities, and heterosexuality.

1
Introducing the Erotics of Wounding: Sex, Violence and the Body

Jeff Hearn and Viv Burr

Sex, violence, the body

Sex, violence, the body – any one of these alone alerts complex emotions, questions of power, feelings around vulnerability, even awareness of existence, mortality and life themselves. Put together, various connections and permutations of sex, violence and the body suggest further challenges and indeed often considerable uncertainties, contestations and ambivalences. For example, sexual violences, such as rape and sexual assault, can be understood, from one point of view, as specific forms of (often male) sexuality, and then, from another point of view, not as sexuality, but rather as forms of violence.[1]

There is a vast literature, and a large set of public debates, on the relations of sex and violence – in pornography, prostitution, the sex trade more generally, sexual violence and abuse, eroticisation of violence, sadomasochism (S&M), bondage and dominance (B&D),[2] visual media, censorship and so on. However, the extent to which commentaries on such political matters are explicitly embodied varies considerably; even if they are clearly matters of the body, they are not always located within an explicit politics of the body and body power. The reference to 'the body' here is necessarily broad and open ended. This is not least because different contributors address very different bodily practices, social relations and representations, and different practices, social relations and representations of the body/bodies. Suffice it to say at this stage, we take a social view of the body and embodiment, but that does not suggest a social essentialism, as in some constructionist and postmodernist versions: bodies do exist, are matter, and do matter; they can be and are violated and damaged.

In this book the sex-violence-body nexus is approached through a specific focus on the erotics of wounding, breaking skin and injuring bodies. While wounding, and potential wounding, is our primary concern, it is not always possible to make clear distinctions from violence and violation more generally. This introductory chapter seeks to synthesise some of the main ideas in the book, clarify conceptual issues and articulate some of the debates and challenges.

Wounding and its erotics

In this book we present a range of contributions that examine the relations between sexuality, violence and the body, by way of the erotics of wounding. When we began this project focusing on wounding some years ago, it seemed at times a somewhat specialist concern. The social and psychological significance of wounding and injury has been studied in relation to a variety of phenomena, for example S&M practices, sex crimes, body modification, cosmetic surgery, pornography, self-mutilation and self-injury (for example, Babiker and Arnold, 1997). At the same time, in many anthropological studies there is extensive research on scarification, tattooing and forms of wounding, often as part of initiation or generational rites of passage. In some such contexts wounding may have positive connotations, often with clear gendered meanings, sometimes overtly sexual meanings.

However, the more we, as editors, explored these concerns, with the inspiration of colleagues and contributors, the more we realised that the erotics of wounding are widely pervasive and embedded within many general and pervasive cultural forms – in war, militarism, surgery and medicine, film, fantasy, religion, art, aesthetics, beauty, fashion, sport, 'ordinary' sexual practice and imagery, and not least in the recurrent relation of sex and death. Wounding is a central feature of various religious and spiritual traditions (Glucklich, 1999; Loughlin, 2004), not least in the idea of 'Christ's wounds'. Penance and bodily self-mortification recur in many religions traditions, for example in Muslim self-flagellation of the back or chest[3] and in the use of the cilice[4] by Opus Dei Catholic numeraries.

Importantly, transgression is a major theme in constructions of erotics and sexuality (Bataille, 1985, 2006; Kaite, 1988; Nead, 1992; Denman, 2006): 'Is not the most erotic portion of a body where *the garment gapes*? . . . it is intermittence . . . which is erotic' (Barthes, 1976: 9–10, emphasis in original); wounding is one form of transgression. We see the specific focus on wounding as a productive approach partly because it makes the embodied nature of the relations of sex and violence more explicit, more speakable, more fully articulated for interrogation. To put this differently, attending to wounding, breaking skin and injuring bodies, along with their erotics, impels clearer confrontation with embodiment. Despite the assertion that 'human sex takes place mainly in the head' (Stone, 1977: 483), the doing of the relations of sex and violence produce, perform, 'do', invoke and represent the body, and bodies. The sexual body is constituted in the intersection of corporeality, cultural discourses and institutions (cf. Frank, 1995; Grosz, 1995; Williams and Bendelow, 1998; Weiss, 1999).

These social relations are typically intensely gendered, and subject to and part of gender and intersectional power relations. These gendered relations occur not only in particular, individual and interpersonal bodily events and practices but also at cultural, structural and societal levels. These latter social processes are also increasingly transnational and transsocietal in character, as in the spread of pornography and the sex trade through information and communication technology (Hughes, 1999, 2002; Hearn and Parkin, 2001; Hearn, 2006).

The concept of 'wounding' – used here as a shorthand for bodily wounding, breaking skin and the injuring of bodies – deserves some further analytical and conceptual attention. We see the cutting or breaking of skin as a prime concern, as in some legal definitions of 'Wounding'.[5] This may be with or without 'consent', a term that raises multiple legal and ethical complications.[6] However, it is also necessary to use the term at times in a broader way in some chapters. In particular, there is the question of the relations of the direct physical wounding of the body, through breaking of the skin, however accomplished, and less specific forms of wounding, as in emotional and psychological wounding. Thus how the boundaries around the topic are discussed and defined deserve close attention.

A number of dimensions can readily be seen as relevant: degree of damage or injury; whether injury is self-inflicted, other-inflicted or naturally occurring (for example, is body piercing wounding or adornment?); the boundary between breaking of the skin and wounding through bruising; the extent to which the damage or injury carries what are principally sexual or non-sexual (for example, aesthetic or medical) meanings; whether any sexual meanings are almost entirely personal (for example, self-harm) or culturally shared (for example, circumcision); and the relations between physical wounding and non-physical wounding.

While most chapters attend primarily to physical wounding, this is not always so, and indeed the separation of physical and 'non-physical' wounding may be problematic. The chapter by Michelle Jones and Jeff Hearn on women's experiences of violence from male partners and ex-partners is especially relevant here, as is Mona Livholts's chapter on textual representation by journalists and researchers of rape, sexual assault and attempted murder. Such violence, whether by known assailants or strangers, can mean both physical and non-physical damage. Psychological violence, control and wounding, particularly in long-term relationships, can have dire effects on those victimised and their sense of self. Textual violence both builds on these relations and has its own power dynamics. In a different way, the broad phenomenon of wounding can include risk or threat of being wounded, as discussed in Victoria Robinson's chapter on rock climbing and extreme sports (see Palmer, 2004).

What this brief discussion illustrates is that there is a need for some precision in distinguishing between wounding as a general and sometimes extended social process of temporary or permanent damage; the wounder; the wounded; the wound(s) produced; and the wound(s) 'healed' (as in cosmetic surgery or healed wounds after scarification in initiation). In some contexts wounds are best understood as a process, at other times as an object of attention, a thing, even a fetish, that comes to be eroticised.

In terms of sexual desire, a considerable number of connections with wounding are possible; these include desire of/for the wounder, desire of/for the wounded and desire for the wound. There are of course possible in-between positions between desire 'of' and desire 'for', in terms of ambiguities and changing positions in sexual and related relations, over time or across biographies. In addition, and perhaps more controversially, the wound itself or the production of the wound may, for some, be constitutive of sexuality and erotics.

Sexualised (or sexualed)[7] relations to wounding may be from the perspective of the wounder – whether the self, mutually, by proxy or others (for example, the sadistic) – or those wounded (for example, the masochistic) or others as 'observers'. More specifically, and as represented simply in Table 1.1, *the wounder* or *the wounded* (or indeed others)

Table 1.1 Sexually positive and negative positions of the wounder and the wounded

	Sexually positive	***Sexually negative***
Wounder	Sadistic position	Regretful position
Wounded	Masochistic position	Violated position

can relate to wounding in *sexually positive* or *sexually negative* terms (or indeed ambiguously).

For some or in some situations, wounds and wounding may be given meaning as (sexually) positive, may be celebrated, sometimes aggressively so. (Sexual) Identification may take place with this position, as when wounds are signs of sexual initiation and maturity or as in sexual arousal by wounds in rape or other sexual crimes. Another example is the sexualisation of more institutional practices, such as corporal punishment (Butt and Hearn, 1998). Alternatively, those who are wounded may be identified with, in seeing their wounds, and wounding as negative, damaging and something to be condemned, but still as sexually relevant. In this, sexual experience or identification is with the sufferer. Indeed the wounded 'hero', the damaged victim, the wounded self may be or in turn may become desirable. This is not necessarily a masochistic position or identification; rather it may draw on associations of care, comfort and sex, and in that sense it can be compatible with non-violent sexualities. Such interlinking constructions of 'erotic wounds', identities and subjectivities may often be structured in terms of dichotomies, for example heterosexual/non-heterosexual and reproductive/non-reproductive sex and sexualities.

Sexuality can relate to wounding for those directly involved, and for others not so directly implicated. For example, there are those identifying with one or more parties; such identifications are especially important in understanding representations of wounding, and viewers' and other users' relations thereto. Further complex positionings may also be elaborated, for example, within mutual S&M, interlinked matrices of subjectivities, changing sexual preferences across biographies or paradoxical psychoanalytics. All these positions are used in visual media, film, television, video and pop culture.

As regards those who are less directly involved in doing wounding or being wounded, there is a range of possibilities. Such observers can include those who are directly, less directly or indirectly involved; they may be actively involved or passively uninvolved; they can be analysts or actors, for example, as medical or legal actors. The wounding may be done by proxy, as discussed by Sheila Jeffreys in her chapter on bodily mutilation and modification, including 'cosmetic surgery', in relation to postmodernism and feminism. Taina Kinnunen addresses similar questions, more specifically from the viewpoint of the women seeking such surgeries. These kinds of proxy wounding are seen by some, probably an increasing number, as 'respectable' and have become remarkably popular in recent years. They are also strongly international in their appeal, with the greatest concentrations of activity in the US, Spain, Mexico, Argentina and Brazil, with the UK not far behind with 577,000 cosmetic treatments in 2007 (Bindel, 2008). Spain boasts the headquarters of Corporación Dermoestética, the first plastic surgery company in Europe trading on the stock exchange. Plastic surgery is also popular in Iran; Turkey is becoming a lead country in botox treatments. In some contexts such wounding interventions are given liberatory meanings, as signs of sexual 'freedom', by the wounders or the wounded. According to some commentators, this can even be seen as a reaction to previous political authoritarianism, as in the Spanish case (see Fuchs, 2006). From a very different perspective, others stress the 'humane' benefits of such surgical interventions, as part of advocacy for individual control and conventional, often 'white', beauty ideals (Lewis, 2007).

Social practices and social representations

The book covers a range of forms of damage and injury, both in concrete social practices and in representations. It seeks to contribute to long-established general discussions on the relations of 'the real' and 'representational', and to recent debates on the relations of the social/human and the biological/human, and of things (such as weapons and texts) and people (such as wounders and wounded). In particular, it operates across the border of analyses of social practices and analyses of social representations. In this regard, an interesting contrast can be made between Ani Ritchie's chapter on SM social practices, and fictional writing and representations on BDSM, discussed in Jenny Alexander's chapter.

This quickly brings us to some complex debates. On the one hand, there are real differences between direct wounding of real flesh – of you or me – and representations of wounding, which may, or may not, be representations of previous or real-time actual wounding. On the other hand, there are, to complicate matters, all sorts of connections and crossovers between wounding practices and representations of wounding. For a start, representations are practices and are the result of practices. Representations can have very harmful effects and effects that are experienced as harmful, as in the production of pornography and consequent degradations, the use of the 'N word' or cartoons of the divine. However, a further important point is context. Sentences like 'He wounded her and she enjoyed it' and 'He was wounded and he enjoyed it' can have very different meanings and effects depending on context.

Slippages around these questions of practice-representation are one, but not the only, reason for the degree of disagreements between analysts and commentators on these issues, including between some of our contributors. Divergences in approach build on established and related differences around pornography and prostitution, even though these debates have their own specific character. Displaying the suffering and wounding of others is not straightforward, not least because of the existence of 'already well-worn, predictable forms of representation' (Rossi, 1995: 36).[8] Or, to put it differently, 'the assimilation of violent erotic images with violent erotic acts creates moral and methodological confusions which do not necessarily strengthen critiques of either violence or representation. On the contrary, such assimilations may indicate a collusion between viewer and viewed to the extent that "the official version of things has become reality"' (Heathcote, 1994a: 156).[9]

Let us take just one example of these linkages across practices and representations, that of pain. While pain is highly medicalised in modern society, beliefs about pain are deeply socially and culturally embedded. Illness narratives have elaborated pain experiences by focusing on the person and using concepts such as biographical disruption, narrative reconstruction and illness adjustment (Williams, 1984; Bury, 1991; Greenhalgh and Hurwitz, 1998), thus allowing for emotional and cultural frameworks. However, visual imagery and the complex rapport between art and pain (Morris, 1991; Spivey, 2001) also have a key role: links between pain and emotional suffering have long had erotic overtones, as in the relations between martyrdom and sadomasochism. These various perspectives on wounding can thus overlap and interconnect in representations and social practices (Bendelow, 1998).

Many genres and traditions engage with violence and wounding. A great number of classical, often firmly patriarchal, texts and works of art have shown complex links between sex, violence and wounding. These range from the conjunction of sex and death, for example Eros and Thanatos in classical Greek drama and Abrahamic religious texts, to grand opera, for example Puccini's *Tosca* (1900) and Strauss's *Salome* (1905). Many visual artists have engaged heavily in this terrain (Lucie-Smith, 1972) – from Bosch in his mediaeval horrors to Caravaggio in *The Flagellation* (1606–7) and his erotic mixing of armoured bodies and naked bodies, to Max Ernst in *The Blessed Virgin Chastising the Infant Jesus before Three Witnesses* (1926).

Beliefs about pain and suffering linked to sexuality and wounding are represented in the iconic images of pain, such as Gerrit von Honthorst's *San Sebastian* (1590) and Frida Kahlo's *The Broken Column* (1944).[10] In particular, various Renaissance depictions of St Sebastian and other martyred saints were spawned by a small industry of artists, and since then supplemented by imitators and commentators, attesting its painful, homoerotic allure. Andrea Mantegna painted St Sebastian c. 1457–8, with arrows entering his head from opposite directions and with another aimed at his groin. Tanzio da Varallo depicted the saint tended by angels c. 1620–30 in an ambiguous masochistic rapture of emotion and pain (Lucie-Smith, 1972: 217). These images remain highly resonant today.

With reference back to St Sebastian, and drawing on the works of Yukio Mishima and Eric Jourdan, Owen Heathcote (1994b) has analysed links between martyrdom, masochism, sadism and homotextuality. In this he 'exposes and magnifies homosexual exposure and homosexuality as exposure' (p. 176), for example, 'the masochistically aestheticized theme of containment and concealment in the narrative' (p. 178). This kind of exploration interrogates the complex relations between desire, violence and literature and between the violence *of* representation and violence *in* representation (Armstrong and Tennenhouse, 1989; Heathcote, 1994a).

The male gaze upon women and the feminine has been well charted (Mulvey, 1975); less explored is the gaze upon men and the masculine. A number of writers in the visual media, for example war photography (Vettel-Becker, 2002), fine art (Greer, 2003), literature (Slattery, 1999) and film studies (Neale, 1983; Tasker, 1993b), have noted that the naked and wounded (generally male) body is offered as 'spectacle' and carries sexual/gender meanings. But the focus has been principally upon the construction of masculinity, dynamics of the male gaze and the possibilities for a 'female gaze' (de Beauvoir, 1953; Gamman and Marchment, 1988; Doane, 1990; Waterhouse, 1993; Goddard, 2000). These questions are taken up, in different ways, in the chapters here by Viv Burr on *Buffy the Vampire Slayer* and Tim Edwards on masochism in the movies.

Interestingly, the idea of 'the Wound' or the 'wounding' of men has been taken up by a surprisingly diverse collection of mainly male writers in recent years, including Robert Bly (1990, 'father wound'), Victor Seidler (1997, 'wounds from both hegemonic forms of men's identities and from feminism'), and Michael Kaufman and Michael Kimmel (1993, 'mother wound') (also see Carrera, 2002; Ashe, 2008). They argue, in different ways and with less or more sympathies with feminisms, that men are damaged, wounded, by gender arrangements or patriarchal relations, in terms of their relations with men, women, mothers, fathers, self. Kaja Silverman (1992), drawing on the work of Leo Bersani (1987), has taken these critiques further, arguing for the subversive potential of masochistic wounding, through a fragmentation of the dominant male subject, focusing her attention on cultural products, notably films. Calvin

Thomas (2002), also developing Bersani, extends this approach both to the medium of writing and to what this means in social practice more generally, arguing that penetration *of* men is key for 'anti-patriarchal' identity and social change.

Film provides a rich set of traditions. According to Anneke Smelik (1999), in Hollywood, '[t]he denial of the homoeroticism of looking at images of men constantly involves sado-masochistic themes, scenes and fantasies. . . . the highly ritualized scenes of male struggle . . . deflect[s] the look away from the male body to the scene of the spectacular fight'. Gangster films routinely deploy violent heterosex, with blood, guns and weapons added none too subtly, and often phallically, into the concoction; horror and slasher genres, threaten vampiric bitings and monstrous woundings on the pure(r), usually female, victim(s), with its own replications of whore/virgins (Cherry, 1995). Special film favourites among both the viewing public and eager analysts are *Alien* (1979), *Fatal Attraction* (1987) and *The Silence of the Lambs* (1991) (and indeed their sequels, such as *Red Dragon* (2002) and *Hannibal Rising* (2007)), with sex, violence and wounding (actual, threatened, imagined) never far from the scene. The names of Peckinpah and Tarantino have become almost synonymous with the power of wounding; Michael Haneke's films, such as *Funny Games* (1997), *The Piano Teacher* (2001) and *Funny Games US* (2007), also explore sex, violence and S&M. The film *Crash* (1996), the subject of Anthony McCosker's chapter, is iconic of the erotics of wounding in the relations of body and technology.

Some of these representations thrive on intertextualities. Multiple links between sex (as an alien divine force within the body), violence and religion have been charted in film genres (Loughlin, 2004). In this view, divine Eros is always other; God is infinitely alien, yet intimate to ourselves: a sacred eroticism. And in a different approach crossing social practice and representation, Stephen Eisenman (2007) has shown the meaningful links between images from paintings of the grand masters and photographic images from Abu Ghraib. Meanwhile, contemporary mainstream television, *inter alia, Dexter, Grey's Anatomy, House, Nip/Tuck,* seems to delight in broadcasting wounds, nonchalantly.

Similar themes have also been taken up in various forms of body art and performance art (Vergine, 2000; Miglietta, 2003). In recent years there has been a pronounced tendency for some artists to use their own bodies as a medium for their art. In some cases, body art has been linked to feminist politics or clear gender themes, as in the works of Matthew Barney, Helen Chadwick, Sarah Lucas, Nan Goldin[11] and Carolee Schneeman; in others, different personal and political projects are emphasised, sometimes with nihilistic or negativistic aspects; either way, the artist's 'model' is the artist's body itself (Warr, 2000).

In *Extreme Bodies: The Use and Abuse of the Body in Art*, Francesca Alfano Miglietti (2003) builds on multiple examples from both classical and contemporary art to discuss 'About wounds'. She reviews the works of the photographer Rudolf Schwarzkogler, who inflicted wounding and mutilation, including symbolic castration, on himself; Gina Pane, who, through photography and film, used burning, cutting and thorns to link religious iconography and the exhibiting cut exposures of her body; and Franko B., who also used his body and blood in his performance art to overcome the separation of reality and representation. This is the arena explored by Ulla Angkjær Jørgensen in her chapter, 'Cut Pieces: Self-Mutilation in Body Art'. Her chapter illustrates the need to think across practice-representation. In this practice is representation, and vice versa (also see Spector, 2007).[12]

Wounds and wounding can carry multiple symbolic sexual meanings. Wounds wound flesh, human 'meat', which itself may sometimes become a sexual fetish. Cuts and cutting may signify loss (Lemaire, 1977: 196): 'the "erotic" may be assumed to arise in gaps, overlaps, contrasts, ambiguities between other elements that are split, as signs' (Hearn, 1992: 224). The arrows afflicting St Sebastian may be phallic or the slashing wound itself; the slashed wound may be the vaginal or anal 'slit', or again phallic; the blood may be menstrual, anal or seminal. The wound and wounding in representation is that extra notch of violence that may seem much more violent than the physical attack with fists or head or feet or even weapons (that brings heavy bruising or internal bleeding). It is, or pretends to be, the peak (visual) experience – the breaking of the skin membrane container and the letting out of flesh and blood within – perhaps equivalent to the pornographic 'money shot'. There are also many art house examples – most famously, Luis Buñuel and Salvador Dalí's iconic cutting of the eye in *Un Chien Andalou* (1929).

Theoretical, ethical and political issues

Thinking about sex and violence in wounding and embodied contexts raises many methodological and theoretical questions. Though our prime concern here is exploration rather than explanation, we might consider how to explain wounding – as an individual, interpersonal, group, cultural, societal or transsocietal phenomenon. The answer to such questions must of course depend on the specific forms of violence being addressed. Some examples of wounding are mass market, as in cosmetic surgery; others are more minority pursuits, such as ritual group S&M. Different practices are more or less readily understandable in relation to historical processes of capitalist marketisation of the body, heteropatriarchal gender power relations, imperialist and postcolonial ethnic othering and other structural power relations. Even so, the nature of the relationship between wounding and eroticism is often taken for granted. Where it has been given more focused attention (for example, Silverman, 1992), its theoretical analysis has been largely limited to a psychodynamic framework. Perhaps significantly and despite their critiques (Denman, 2006), psychoanalytic approaches sometimes seem hard to avoid totally in discussing these matters, not least through the return to the relations of sex and death.

Thinking about sex, violence, the body and wounding is instructive for thinking and acting on general methodological and epistemological concerns, for example the relations of materiality and discourse. Theoretical, and sometimes abstracted, debates on relations of the material and the discursive, the macro and the micro, and structure and agency become especially important as the context of research and intervention on these embodied matters (Hearn, 1998). They point to the significance of diverse theoretical traditions, including feminism, materialism, structuralism, post-structuralism and social constructionism, deconstruction, as well as psychoanalytics.

Violence and wounding are both simultaneously material and discursive: simultaneously painful, full of pain, and textual, full of text. They are matters of experience of change in bodily matter, and matters of change in discursive constructions. Wounding, and what is meant by wounding, is historically, socially and culturally constructed; this is a matter of material discourse. Talk and text about wounding is not just representation, it is also (creation of) reality in its own right. The whole complex of wounding, talk about wounding and responses thereto is a cultural phenomenon that is both material and discursive.

In this complex theoretical universe it might be appropriate to talk of 'post-poststructuralism' in emphasising materiality and bodily effects, especially of sexually violent acts and sexually violent words. There are possible misuses of 'discourse' and deconstruction in addressing wounding. They may divert attention from the body and the bodily materiality of violence, even if viewing the body as materialisation of discourse. There are certainly problems with apolitical uses of deconstruction, whether through confusion with 'destruction' or engulfment within the pleasure of the text. Deconstruction does not delete ethico-political concerns, as with the reappropriation, even revalidation, of the abject in 'wounding chic'.

In all this it is important to remember that a key focus of this work on wounding is on *violence*; as such, being against wounding in real life, that is wounding as violence, is part of stopping violence. At the same time, wounding, and thus its erotics, remains a broad concept. In some definitions, it might range from, for example, unwanted splitting of skin in consensual anal penetration to fatal wounding in sexual crime. Thus, the erotics of wounding raise many ethico-political concerns, contingent partly on what is being meant by wounding and partly on different ethical and political positions and standpoints. This is no more clear than in the contested arena of S&M sexual practice, especially more violent forms of S&M. One major issue is the status of 'consent' in such contexts. There is much room for disagreements among commentators here. For some, adults are able to announce their own consent unqualified and be beyond critique; for others, announced consent is no different from other social constructions within sexual, gendered and other power relations, including constructions of 'consent' within (gender) hegemony.

A crucial question remains the gendered/sexual/violent relations of talk/text on wounding and actions on wounding and the body. This is not to suggest that there is any fixed set of relations, but these questions do seem especially persistent in critically studying men and masculinities, where close relations of sexuality and violence often seem to inhabit the same bodies, times and places. Such gendered/sexual/violent relations also intersect with other social divisions in constructions of erotics of wounding.

Significantly, recent decades have seen important moves from dramatic or 'art' uses of wounding or wounding as a minority representational practice to the mass reproduction of such images, in mass market media. Rapid changes in modes of cultural reproduction, with virtuality, replication and construction of persons (Lury, 1993), have coupled with processes of pornographisation (Hearn and Jyrkinen, 2007). A recent mainstream magazine advertisement for Diesel clothing featured a topless man with whip marks on his back in the shape of a game of noughts and crosses; in this case of 'wounding chic', the complaint against it was upheld by the UK Advertising Standards Authority (Smithers, 2007).

This volume

This book necessarily brings together a range of issues around sexuality, gender, power, violence and representations. It straddles several disciplinary areas – cultural and media studies, sociology, psychology, social psychology, as well as studies on gender, sexuality and violence. It brings together contributions – from Australia, Finland, Norway, Sweden and the UK – on both social practices and representations in film and other media. The book acts on long-running preoccupations with the relations of sex and violence and seeks to contribute to general debates on the relationship between sexuality, violence and gender, as well as on more focused concerns. The cultural significance of the erotics of wounding has implications for sexuality, violence and gender more generally. The variety of the relations between wounding and sexuality is a key focus of this book.

Following this Introduction, the next five chapters address social sites where real bodily wounding and injury may take place. These examine body mutilation and cosmetic surgery (Sheila Jeffreys; Taina Kinnunen), domestic violence and bodily marking (Michelle Jones and Jeff Hearn), S&M and self-injury (Ani Ritchie), extreme sports and risk (Victoria Robinson). The next four chapters are more concerned with specific forms and examples of representation, focusing on the David Cronenberg film *Crash* (Antony McCosker), fan fiction (Jenny Alexander), *Buffy the Vampire Slayer* (Viv Burr) and men in the movies (Tim Edwards). While in some senses all the chapters deal with the interrelations of the real and the representational, this complex matter of the crossover between the real and the representational is highlighted in the last two chapters. These chapters are thus on performance art using the body as an art resource through injury (Ulla Angkjær Jørgensen) and researchers and journalists writing on rape, violence and wounding (Mona Livholts).

Notes

We are grateful to Trevor Butt and Wendy Parkin for previous collaborations on some of these questions, to Gillian Bendelow for her involvement in the early planning of this book, and to Alp Biricik for comments on an earlier version of this chapter.

1. Interestingly, the concept of 'sexual violence' is much more frequently used than that of 'violent sexuality'.
2. Various alternative abbreviations include SM, S/M, s/m, BD and BDSM, each sometimes with different connotations.
3. Shia Muslim men's self-flagellation while processioning is well known, though there are other examples of both women's and men's self-flagellation in different Muslim traditions.
4. A spiked chain worn around the upper thigh for two hours each day, except for Church feast days, Sundays and certain times of the year.

5. In British law, wounding means the breaking of the continuity of the whole of the outer skin, or the inner skin within the cheek or lip, but does not include the rupturing of internal blood vessels (Offences Against the Person Act 1861, Section 20 (Archbold 19–212)).
6. This was aptly illustrated in the 1990 UK case, *R.* v. *Brown* ('The Spanner case'), in which five men, including Anthony Joseph Brown, were convicted of assault occasioning actual bodily harm, even though the harms resulted from consensual S&M. The five appealed in 1992, contending that a person cannot be guilty of assault regarding acts that are consensual and not in the public domain. In 1993, the House of Lords affirmed the Court of Appeal's decision. There is an extensive legal secondary literature on this (cf. Athanassoulis, 2002; Markwick, 1992).
7. 'Sexualed' refers to having or being given meaning *in relation to* sexuality, including asexual meanings; 'sexualisation' refers to deliberate and explicit attempts to give, produce and heighten sexual meaning and attraction often for other instrumental purposes (Hearn and Parkin, 1987/1995).
8. Citing Minha, 1991: 191.
9. Citing Jolly, 1992: 172.
10. We are grateful to Gillian Bendelow for drawing our attention to the significance of these latter images in this specific way.
11. Nan Goldin (2003) has completed long-term photography and videoing of her life, her family and friends, including her sexual relations, the visible results of interpersonal violence on her and her own self-harm using cigarettes.
12. Matthew Barney explores 'how an action can become a proposal, rather than an overdetermined form. . . . [T]here was the possibility that it [an art performance] was all an imagined activity, that it never happened' (quoted in interview with Barney in Goodeve, 1995: 69, cited in Trotman, 2007: 146).

2
Body Modification as Self-Mutilation by Proxy

Sheila Jeffreys

Forms of cutting up the human body from piercing to leg amputation have become market opportunities in the West in the present stage of consumer capitalism. These are boom times. A variety of perpetrators, that is those carrying out the mutilations on aspirants, are presently making profits from these activities. Piercers and tattooists operate from high street shopfronts putting in nipple rings and doing scarification on the side. Surgeons carry out a range of forms of cutting from cosmetic surgery to transgender surgery, and in some cases, these days, voluntary limb amputation. The practices are escalating in their severity. Those engaging in them are largely drawn from socially despised constituencies, women, lesbians and gay men, the disabled, men and women who have experienced severe sexual and physical abuse or bullying. There is a medical literature which sees these practices as exhibiting an individual pathology, and which links them to suicidal ideation and practice (Favazza, 1996; First, 2004). The most common approach in the burgeoning popular and academic literature that has accompanied the boom is liberal individualist, however, often in its postmodern variety, stressing agency and transgression and explicitly rejecting the medical approach as stigmatising (Camphausen, 1997; McCorquodale, 1996; Sullivan, 2004, 2006). These practices are rarely addressed from either a critical economic perspective or a political perspective that considers the ways that social status may influence choices to mutilate (Jeffreys, 2000; Strong, 2000; Shaw, 2002).

In this chapter I shall suggest that the boom in cutting, rather than deserving the celebratory literature presently emerging from cultural studies and queer theory (Balsamo, 1996; Pitts, 2003; Sullivan, 2001), does need to be situated politically. Though the celebratory literature does not mention self-mutilation in private, or expressly repudiates any link between this private practice and its commercial form (Pitts, 2000b), I shall examine the ways in which public and commercial cutting and private self-mutilation are connected. Private self-mutilation has been overwhelmingly associated with girls and women, and with abuse and body hatred in the broad literature on this subject (Shaw, 2002; Strong, 2000; Kilby, 2001). I shall suggest, in contradiction to the celebratory literature (Sullivan, 2000), that public cutting, except in its mildest fashion-related forms, needs to be understood as a form of *self-mutilation by proxy*, engaged in mostly by persons of subordinate or stigmatised social status. The fact that women, lesbians and gay men, and transgenders form the largest proportion of the body modification movement is affirmed by the theorists and aficionados themselves (Pitts, 2003: 19).

Self-mutilation by proxy is a useful term to apply to a range of practices in which another person is employed, such as a top in sadomasochism, a cosmetic surgeon, a piercing practitioner or a surgeon who performs transsexual surgery or voluntary limb amputation, to perform the mutilation desired by the victim. Though the cutting in these contexts is carried out under the aegis of medicine or beauty, entertainment, or even sexual liberation, it often replicates quite precisely the techniques employed by solitary self-mutilators. Self-mutilation by proxy is linked to self-mutilation in private, by the fact that it is practised overwhelmingly by groups within society with unequal access to power or influence as a result of their sex, their sexuality or disability, or by those men who are unable to live up to the requirements of manhood. The proxies, generally for profit, though in the case of sadomasochism it may be simply for personal gratification, re-enact upon the bodies of their victims the violence that many of them suffered in childhood or adulthood from male perpetrators.

In the sections that follow, I shall consider the approach to body modification in the celebratory literature and the radical feminist response to this. From the necessity of limiting the range of self-mutilatory practices to be covered in this chapter, I shall omit any serious consideration of cosmetic surgery, though I consider that it fits into the framework of self-mutilation by proxy well, because there is, fortunately, a critical and feminist literature in existence elsewhere (Haiken, 1997; Jeffreys, 2005). I shall confine myself to self-mutilation in private and to those public practices which I argue most directly derive from it, in the forms of commercial piercing and cutting, voluntary limb amputation and transgender surgery, because there is little or no critical feminist literature on them.

Postmodern and liberal explanations for self-mutilation by proxy

There is an extensive celebratory or, as I would name it, an apologist literature on public or commercial body modification, some of which claims to be informed by various forms of postmodern, post-structuralist, or queer feminism, which approaches the practices as expressions of individual choice and agency, as transgressive, as creative, as positive ways to combat the norms of beauty practices, as ways to 'reclaim' the body after sexual violence, as being beyond meaning (Sullivan, 2001; Balsamo, 1996; Pitts, 2000a, 2000b, 2003; Atkinson, 2003). Nikki Sullivan, for instance, who reveals her own tattoos on her university website and organises academic conferences in Australia on body modification, argues that it is wrong to look for any kind of meaning in the practice beyond an individual's right to freedom of expression, saying, 'I do not want to make homogenizing and silencing pronouncements about modificatory practices' (Sullivan, 2004: 3). The search for meaning is pointless because marking and being 'marked' are not merely intentional acts, but 'an integral aspect of the inter-subjective and/or intertextual character of what we might call existence and existents – ineffable forms of (un)becoming that are beyond being or essence' (Sullivan, 2001: 113). Ineffable means 'That cannot be expressed in words; unutterable, unspeakable, inexpressible' (*The Shorter Oxford Dictionary*, 1990: 1062).

The writings of body modification apologists tend to include caveats as to the necessity of retaining an understanding of how body projects are embedded in political realities of class, race and gender and sexuality (Pitts, 2000, 2003). However, paying attention to race, sex and class seems restricted to arguing that the practices allow practitioners to transcend, defy or rebel against the restrictions that racism, male dominance and economic class create (Pitts, 2000b). Specifically Pitts argues that the women she interviewed in her study of lesbian sadomasochist body modifiers, who spoke of overcoming their severe experiences of child abuse and violent male partners, are engaged in the positive process of reclaiming their bodies and in forms of resistance to power, by scarification and breast tattoos. These latter practices are clearly distinguished from self-mutilation in private, she says, because only the positive public affirmation of cutting has such transformative effect (Pitts, 2003). The politics of race are usually only mentioned by writers on body modification in warnings against the appropriation of tribal forms of skin decoration as a form of neocolonialism (Klesse, 2000).

Some of the postmodern/queer literature in this area goes so far as to argue that 'gender' has already disappeared as a significant category. Thus in writing about the cosmetic surgery performance artist, Orlan, who engages in extreme procedures such as implantation of objects into her face by surgeons in public and on film, Julie Clarke tells us, 'We are living at a time in which the perceived boundaries between genders, the self and its image, real and virtual, synthetic and organic, interior and exterior, public and private space, past and future, have been all but erased' (Clarke, 2000: 185). The male performance artist, Stelarc, when asked in an interview, if his work addresses 'racial and gender difference in any way?', replies that 'one has to realize in a world of ambiguous gender . . . gender becomes a blur of lots of shades of subtle distinctions rather than a male and a female' (Farnell, 2000: 143). The supposed 'blurring' of gender makes the concerns of feminist critics conveniently irrelevant. Women's oppression has been effectively made to disappear, and disaggregation, for instance, of participants and their motives in body modification by sex is unnecessary, or may, in this understanding, be impossible.

The most common justification of self-mutilation by proxy in the form of the cutting and piercing that takes place in high-street studios is that these practices are exercises in agency by mostly girls and young women who engage in them. According to this approach, those getting themselves pierced are empowered individuals making their own choices. Her determination that body modifiers are expressing their free will and agency appears to make Victoria Pitts at odds with those media interpretations of the practice that present it as abuse (Pitts, 2000b: 297). She castigates the media for 'raising the spectre of suicide' in relation to the practice (ibid.). Such coverage 'casts doubt on Kate and Mandy's [two lesbian practitioners] status as 'consenting' adults free to make intentional choices' (p. 297). The critical mental health approach, she says, 'renders body modifiers' agency illegitimate' (Pitts, 2000: 300). Postmodern ebullience can make inequality and oppression disappear from view through a positive enthusiasm for body modification which goes far beyond the language of choice. Thus Bryan Turner, for instance, argues that 'body marks', in which he includes 'tattooing, piercing, cicatrisation, painting and so forth' (Turner, 2000), rather than indicating status as they did in the past, have, in the present, 'become optional, playful and ironic' (p. 41). This idea that body modification practices are 'playful' may be usefully tested against the details of such practices I shall provide in this chapter.

Radical feminist approaches to self-mutilation

Radical feminist approaches to body modification are distinguished from the celebratory literature by making connections between violence against women by male perpetrators, self-mutilation in private and self-mutilation by proxy (Jeffreys, 2000). Violence against women has been a particular focus of radical feminist theory, and analysis of self-mutilation has concentrated on the way this practice relates to the post-traumatic stress that commonly follows male violence and sexual abuse (Herman, 1992; Kilby, 2001). Critical feminist literature on self-mutilation by proxy has mainly been confined to cosmetic surgery and does not deal with commercial cutting and piercing or tattooing. It points out that, as an aspect of their subordinate status, women are expected to carry out painful practices upon their bodies, to suffer to be beautiful and fulfil the requirements of the 'sexual corv'ee' (Dworkin, 1974; Jeffreys, 2005). In stark contrast to liberal individualist and postmodern approaches to what women do to their bodies, whether in the form of cutting, make-up and beauty practices or sex and sexual exploitation, radical feminists problematise the notion of 'agency'. They are critical of the language of choice and agency that has become pervasive in many areas of feminist theory and research, particularly in media and cultural studies, seeing cutting practices as being the lot of women as a sex class under conditions of male domination (Thompson, 2001; Winter, Thompson and Jeffreys, 2002).

Rosalind Gill points out the problems with the individual agency approach in an article expressing frustration with such language in relation to young women's clothing 'choices'. She says, 'I want to problematize the terms "agency", "autonomy" and "choice" that are mobilized so frequently . . . and to ask how well such terms serve contemporary feminism' (Gill, 2007: 72). She associates this language with neoliberalism, and in relation to consumerism the adoption of 'choice' language can be seen as an adaptation to the dictates of a consumer culture. Gill explains that an approach which focuses on 'autonomous choices', 'remains complicit with, rather than critical of, postfeminist and neoliberal discourses that see individuals as entrepreneurial actors who are rational, calculating and self-regulating' (Gill, 2007: 74). She explains that 'neoliberalism requires individuals to narrate their life story as if it were the outcome of deliberative choices . . . ' (ibid.). This requirement is certainly clear in the words of body modifiers, interviewed by researchers who celebrate the practice, about their choices (Pitts, 2000a; Atkinson, 2004). Gill asks why it is that so much feminist theory has taken up choice language and suggests that it is because a post-feminist perspective no longer allows recognition of the oppression of women, 'Is there a subtext to this? A postfeminist subtext that no longer views women as oppressed' (ibid.). Her critique applies very well to the majority of the writing that is currently being produced about body modification.

Kathy Miriam offers a useful way of looking at the language of 'agency' (Miriam, 2007). Under male domination women 'negotiate' their 'own subordination', she says, and this is their experience of agency (Miriam, 2007: 221). She explains that 'Only by critically describing this reality can we truly distinguish an agency defined by choosing the terms of a given historical/sexual situation (defined by women's subordination) from a freedom defined by women's ability to co-create and transform this historical/sexual situation' (p. 225). She suggests that two kinds of agency should be recognised and differentiated. One kind of agency is that expressed by women within and shaped by the confines and limitations of living under male dominance. This kind of agency may help women to survive and gain some benefits, but though it deserves recognition, it does not deserve celebration. It can include participation in 'raunch' culture, for instance, and apparent enthusiasm for anticipating the demands of the pornographised male sexual imagination (Levy, 2005). The other kind of agency, Miriam suggests, is 'transformative' agency. If this idea is applied to self-mutilation by proxy, then it can be recognised that the agency expressed by women who get pierced, tattooed and cosmetically enhanced is far from being transformative as they are snared within a template of fashion, and sex industry demands that they fulfil their sexual corv'ee and excite male sexual response. 'Agency' can be expressed even in the cutting, burning and other forms of self-harm that women have recourse to in private as a response to the violence, abuse, constraints and assaults to their pride that they experience under male dominance (Shaw, 2002). This is 'agency' to the extent that they are taking action and seeking to assuage their distress, but it is not an agency worth celebrating.

Self-mutilation in private

That which is generally referred to as self-mutilation in mental health literature comprises attacks on the skin or bodily organs such as eyes or genitals, usually conducted in private and with the object of alleviating some mental distress (Favazza, 1996). It can include head-banging, hitting and self-biting, 'enucleation, castration, and limb amputation' but most commonly 'refers to acts such as hair-pulling, skin scratching and nail-biting . . . as well as to skin-cutting, carving, burning, needle sticking, bone breaking, and interference with wound healing, which comprise the episodic and repetitive subtypes' (ibid.: x). In psychiatric literature these practices are seen as symptoms or features of 'a number of mental disorders such as borderline, histrionic, and antisocial personality disorders' (ibid.). The psychiatric literature, however, does not generally mention that self-mutilation is overwhelmingly a behaviour of girls and young women, and treats the practice as representing individual mental health problems rather than social and political ones.

The feminist approach places self-mutilation in private in the context of women's subordination and relates it to child sexual abuse. Jane Kilby states, 'It is important to note that self-harm can be understood more generally as a form of posttraumatic distress syndrome which will signal other known and unknown histories of trauma' (Kilby, 2001: 141). Interestingly she offers an explanation for the difficulty that observers have in making sense of the practice: 'It would seem that the act of harming one's own skin by cutting it up and tearing it apart speaks with a "voice" so sheer that it is virtually impossible for anyone to bear witness to it' (Kilby, 2001: 124). Sarah Shaw also relates self-mutilation to childhood abuse: 'Studies abound linking childhood sexual and physical abuse and emotional neglect to the later development of self-injuring behavior' (Shaw, 2002: 193). It is a common behaviour. Marilee Strong (2000) estimates that two million young women in the US regularly self-mutilate.

Feminist analysis of women's self-injury suggests that it is engaged in to relieve the painful feelings associated with 'trauma, violations and silencing in a culture that fails to provide adequate opportunities for women's development, healing and expression' (Shaw, 2002: 201). The overwhelming majority of women in the ranks of self-injurers suggests that self-injury is associated with women's low status. Girls and women who have no outlet for the rage and pain they experience from male violence and abuse and from the other injuries of a male dominant culture attack their own bodies. Often they are emotionally disassociated from their bodies, having learnt this technique to survive abuse. Self-mutilation breaches the barriers they have created and allows them to 'feel'. An increasing frequency of self-mutilation by young women fits into a context of increasing mental and physical health problems in teenage girls. There is a good deal of research to suggest that sexualisation of girls in contemporary culture is leading to an unhealthy 'self-objectification' of the body which leads to depression, body shame and disordered eating (Zubriggen et al., 2007).

The creation of a commercial cutting and piercing industry operating from high-street studios has enabled the private distress of self-mutilators to be translated into the public realm in a way which makes a profit for the perpetrators of body mutilation and provides a respectable ideology and rationale for the cutting activities (Jeffreys, 2000). The celebratory literature firmly repudiates any such connections. Thus Victoria Potts, who calls self-mutilation in private 'delicate self-harm syndrome', explains that any association of body modification with this practice, by mental health practitioners for instance, is 'pathologising' and 'makes the prospect of agency dubious or theoretically impossible' (Pitts, 2000b: 296). However, she dedicates one whole chapter of her book to interviews with lesbian sadomasochists who are very open about the severe male violence they have suffered but argue that cutting and branding are a form of therapy for their experience (Pitts, 2003). The distinction lies, in her opinion, in the fact that the mutilations are conducted in rituals, and sometimes the scarification is done by a friend in a circle of women. This renders the same acts that women might carry out upon themselves in 'self-harm' into forms of resistance and reclamation of the abused body. She is critical of radical feminists, such as myself, who argue, in her words, 'that the practices violate the body and reproduce oppressive relations of power by echoing patriarchal violence' (ibid.: 73).

Girls and women form the majority of those accessing the commercial industry (Carroll et al., 2002), but boys and men are involved too. The studio cutters and tattooists are overwhelmingly male. Many of these men and boys are likely to be drawn from other despised constituencies, gay men, men confused about 'gender' and disabled men. Indeed the development of a commercial cutting industry arose from gay sadomasochism, a practice which reveals the connections between the abuse, bullying and oppression that gay men experience and the propensity towards self-harm.

Gay sadomasochism

Since the 1960s parts of the male gay community have developed sadomasochism as the focus of their sexual practice and given it a politics and a spirituality that render SM distinctively gay (Woods, 1995). Though private self-mutilation is overwhelmingly a behaviour of girls, self-mutilation in the form of sadomasochism is not. Gay men, a despised category in heteropatriarchal societies whose masculine status is denied or derided (Plummer, 1999), have made sadomasochism symbolic of gayness. The sociologist Martin Levine attributed the development of gay sadomasochism to the cult of gay masculinity that developed in response to the 'butch shift' in the 1970s (Levine, 1998). Sadomasochism was adopted as the ultimate in masculine sexual practice which would demonstrate that gay men were not nellies, that is effeminate, but 'real men'. Research from gay psychologists and therapists suggests that though both male children who will grow up to be gay and those who will grow up to be heterosexual are sexually abused by men in childhood, the numbers of those who will grow up to be gay are higher and they experience some particular difficulties in overcoming the distress that they experience (Cassese, 2000). Some gay men may have difficulty separating out the facts of their abuse from their homosexuality and find themselves locked into forms of adult sexuality that rely on dissociating mind from body, engaging in anonymous contacts and seeing their bodies and selves as deserving of punishment. The results can include ultramasculine acting out in the form of sadomasochist behaviour. Lesbians involved in sadomasochism can be quite open about seeing this practice as enabling the repeated acting out of abuse by fathers or other males (Jeffreys, 2003). Cutting, piercing, branding and scarification are all practices integral to gay sadomasochism, and gay cutting practitioners such as Fakir Musafar (Musafar, 1996) are pioneers of the body modification movement.

Victoria Pitts has interviewed six 'queer' body modifiers to show the practices they engage in and the explanations they give (Pitts, 2000a). The men in her study get extreme body modifications in the form of branding and scarification for masochistic sexual pleasure, and, interestingly, choose to be mutilated by lesbian sadomasochists or at the bidding of such. Submission to a female may be a more subordinating experience and offer extra masochistic enjoyment. One of her interviewees, Dave, who is transgender and disabled, 'was branded with thirteen strikes of hot metal at an event sponsored by a pro-sex women's bookstore' (ibid.: 449). Rachel branded him and 'warned the audience that if she held the metal on his skin too long, Dave's flesh and muscle would melt under its heat' (ibid.). Dave commented, 'She's a really tough woman and she's going to brand you, and you feel very submissive at that moment.' Branding is a way of 'affirming' his SM and transgendered identity in front of a 'supportive community' (ibid.). Dave expresses his self-injury as 'my choice and my body'. He is also disabled and his blindness is a crucial factor in his 'choosing' the practice. He sees his body modification as a way of acting against the 'social denial of the disabled sexual body' (p. 450). Another of her interviewees, Mark, was also branded by a 'lesbian body modification artist' in an SM club (p. 451).

He expressed his motivation as, 'claiming your body and your right to do this'. Mark and his partner, Shawn, saw their self-mutilation behaviour as transgressive and as marking them as 'queer'. They understand themselves as, 'set apart by their branded, colored, stretched and scarred bodies as sexual minorities who are not only homosexual but also queer and deviantly pleasured' (p. 452).

Though Pitts's interviewees spoke in positive terms about their experience, a rather different perspective emerges from a man interviewed by Chris Woods from the UK, in a critical commentary on the gay community's relationship with sadomasochism (Woods, 1995). A leading defendant in the Spanner case, in which gay male sadomasochists were found guilty of causing actual bodily harm in the practice of branding, talked of his psychotherapy and the fact that he was doing SM 'due to a painful relationship with my father . . . At one point I even got into the idea of being tortured to death. At the back of my mind I knew that wasn't natural'. The interviewee commented: 'If you meet someone who's mentally fucked up, then torturing them is only going to make things worse. One of X's boys was quite mixed up. He didn't need torturing, he needed help' (p. 53).

Sadomasochism and other forms of self-harm can, therefore, be seen as the result of oppressive forces such as sexual abuse, bullying, physical violence, hatred and contempt rather than celebrated as 'transgressive' or 'agentic'. Chris Woods sees SM as reflecting the damage suffered by gay men and lesbians from the 'hypocrisy and hostility of society'. In the 1970s, he says, it was understood that people could suffer 'internalised homophobia, self-hatred brought on people both by the horrors of external oppression and the requirements of an often-brutal scene' (p. 54). It became taboo to suggest that role playing and the 'scene' both arose from and reinforced the harm suffered from the oppression of homosexuality. The result is that 'as an antidote to our communities' failings, or as a badge of political nous, we encourage the pursuit of pain and abuse' (ibid.).

The damage of gay male sadomasochism did not remain confined to a gay constituency, but spread in the 1990s to heterosexual young women and, to a lesser extent, young men. Gay male fashion designers placed pierced models on their catwalks, and helped to inscribe a practice that had symbolised gayness, onto the bodies of conventional young women and some young men. The practices were enveloped in new age philosophy, said to be 'tribal' in their reflection of the practices of African and other non-Western peoples, and carried out by 'modern primitives' (Camphausen, 1997). The propensity of young women to self-mutilate in private and for some gay men and lesbians to perform self-mutilation in rituals came together to form the basis for this new industry.

Piercing and cutting

The private self-mutilation born of despair and self-directed rage at abuse and oppression was exploited by piercing entrepreneurs in the piercing industry. Piercing studios were set up in cities throughout the Western world offering various forms of self-injury to make a profit for the perpetrators of such practices. The forms of injury provided by these studios and independent operators ranged from bellybutton piercings to the extremes of spearing straight through the torso as carried out by the Californian ex-advertising executive and gay sadomasochist, Fakir Musafar (Musafar, 1996). One study of college students found that though piercing was becoming a cultural norm, with 25 per cent having been pierced, those with body modifications still reported more depression and anxiety than those without (Roberti and Storch, 2005). Some young people who are likely to already be self-mutilating in private are clearly attracted to more than just multiple piercings. They graduate to the extreme forms of what are now called 'body modification', such as tongue splitting, suspension and castration, and become participants in what has come to be called the body modification movement (Hicinbothem, et al., 2006).

Despite the rejection of the mental health approach to body modification as 'pathologising' (Pitts, 2000b), this literature does provide a useful counterweight to the celebratory literature of writers such as Pitts (2000b), Sullivan (2001) and Atkinson (2003). In response to the recent phenomenon of mass body modification among young people there has been a good deal of research from a medical or counseling perspective on whether there is a correlation between piercing and tattooing and indicators of poor mental health. Carroll et al.'s (2002) study of girls, for instance, who attended an Adolescent Clinic residential programme for those 'at risk' found that tattoos and/or body piercing were linked with risk-taking behaviours such as 'disordered eating behavior, gateway drug use, hard drug use, sexual activity, and suicide' (Carroll et al., 2002: 1021). In another study, 34 of the 79 participants who had piercings or tattoos were found to have feelings of anger, depression and negativeness towards the body (Carroll and Anderson, 2002). Suicide index scores were almost twice as high, in this study, in females with tattoos as in those without, and risks of suicide were highest in those who had their body modifications at a young age.

A study of participants involved with the piercing website Body Modification Ezine revealed a high incidence of suicidal ideation and attempted suicide in this population of serious body modifiers (Hicinbothem et al., 2006). The study analysed 4700 responses. Of them 5 per cent described themselves as homosexual and 37.9 per cent as bisexual which does suggest a strong correlation with homosexuality in this group. The researchers reported higher rates of physical and sexual abuse and of being 'kicked out' of home among their respondents. Of the males, 43.9 per cent had never thought about suicide, 36.6 per cent had suicidal ideation and 19.5 per cent had attempted suicide. For the females, the rates were considerably higher with 25.9 per cent, 40.8 per cent and 33.3 per cent respectively. For the purposes of comparison, it should be noted that the rates of reported suicidal ideation in the past 12 months in two major US studies of suicidal behaviour were 2.8 and 3.3 per cent (Bender, 2005).

The practices that those involved in the Body Modification Ezine website engage in do not readily fit into the postmodern playfulness of the celebratory literature. The degree of injury I found described on the first three pages of personal advertisements on the BME website, containing 72 personals, appears to lack playfulness. If, as Victoria Pitts and other body modification theorists argue, cutting has healing powers for those in distress, the obsessive repetition and continuing severity of injury as a way of life, that are revealed here, suggest that it is not very effective (Pitts, 2003). A personal advertisement from a disabled, wheelchair-bound woman, 'bi, goth, single, submissive' describes the modifications she engages in as follows: 'Facial piercing, Navel piercing. Tongue piercing, Nipple piercing, Stretching piercings, Genital piercing, LOTS piercing, Other piercings, Tattoos, LOTS of tattoos, Scarification, 3D implants, Genital implants, Sculpting, Tongue splitting, Fashion corsetry, Genital stretching, Nipple stretching/enlargement' (Wheelywitch, accessed 2007). Though some of the personals do not reveal the modifications of the posters and require those seeking more information to enter the hardcore area of the site, some of those in the personals section reveal quite severe forms of injury such as croptache who is castrated, 'balls and sacks removed' and who seeks other men who have done the same 'eunuch/ nullo' (croptache, accessed 2007). Such practices are not easily reversed, even though the practitioners may change their minds.

Another personal advertisement for Ashley, 'F2M Trans' shows how the practices associated with transgenderism can be on a continuum of cutting practices. They show, too, how private self-mutilation can be mixed up with the public and commercial varieties. She states that her body modifications include 'extensive tattoo coverage, a number of piercings including advanced, internal piercings (self-administered), circumcision (self-administered), metoidioplasty (self-administered), split tongue (self-administered), bilateral mastectomy, changes to secondary sexual characteristics and muscle distribution through extended use of testosterone via intramuscular injection (self-administered)' (AshleyUK, accessed 2007). Metoidioplasty involves 'release of the suspensory ligament of the hypertrophied clitoris and placement of testicular prostheses in the centrally-approximated labia majora' to create a micropenis (Lawrence, n.d.). Ashley is also a professional cutter and piercer. A male transgender on the site who identifies as M2F Trans has body modifications which include various forms of genital torture, 'genital piercing' as well as 'Meatotomy, Urethral stretching, Urethral reroute' (meredithTG, accessed 2007). In his case too, modifications associated with transgenderism are but one expression of a serious regime of self-mutilation.

Two of the most extreme forms of body modification have been adopted by the medical profession as 'therapy' for 'identity disorders'. Sex reassignment surgery for 'gender identity disorder' predates the body modification movement's interest in castration and metoidioplasty. But the practice of limb amputation as therapy for amputee identity disorder (AID), now more usually called body identity integrity disorder (BIID), does seem to be associated with the recent Internet-driven surge of interest in this form of body modification (Elliott, 2000).

Medical self-mutilation by proxy

Surgeons have become active participants in the contemporary epidemic of self-mutilation. They act as proxies in the now mainstream and profitable practice of cosmetic surgery, mostly on women (Sullivan, 2002). It has now become routine for some of the same surgeons to perform sex reassignment surgery so that those who cut women's labia to make them more socially acceptable, and tighten their vaginas for their husbands' pleasure, also create labia and vaginas for men who are transitioning to become 'women' (Jeffreys, 2005). The venturing of surgeons into voluntary limb amputation is still controversial, but recent publications that I shall describe below, suggest that it is being normalised as a respectable 'therapy' for BIID.

In naming the desire for limb amputation AID or BIID, the psychiatrists seek to demonstrate its similarity to the desire for amputation of secondary sexual characteristics by those defined as suffering from gender identity disorder (GID). The process of normalisation of BIID, so that it could be accepted as a regular psychiatric disorder with a standard treatment, amputation, began only in the late 1990s (Furth and Smith, 2002). Some of the psychiatrists and surgeons who have been involved in the creation of an industry of sex reassignment surgery are now working together to get BIID recognised in the diagnostic bible of the psychiatric profession, the Diagnostic and Statistical Manual (DSM). If they achieve this then in the future they may legally cut off the limbs of those who say that they have always felt uncomfortable with their body shape. A Scottish surgeon has already cut legs off two healthy men (BBC, 2000). The Internet is enabling those experimenting with amputating parts of their bodies, such as fingers, and seeking to lose one or even all four limbs to grow in numbers and support each other's self-harming behaviour (Elliott, 2000).

The psychiatrist Michael First, editor of the DSM, is one of those working towards getting the term BIID accepted by practitioners. He has conducted research on aspirants to find out their motivations and characteristics which is useful for understanding its relationship to other forms of self-mutilation (First, 2004). First interviewed 52 people, 47 of them male. Nine had already achieved amputation of an arm or leg, either through their own efforts or with the help of surgeons. They had used shotguns, chainsaws, wood chippers and dry ice. Three had managed to get surgeons to amputate their limbs. The percentage of homosexuals in the group, 31 per cent, was high. Interestingly, five had amputated one or more fingers using methods such as a saw, a pruning shear and a hammer and chisel. Of these three who wanted a major limb amputation had 'amputated a finger to explore what having an amputation would feel like' (First, 2004: 4). This does suggest that amputation is the overriding interest, with some flexibility about the body parts that are selected.

The criteria for recognising the disorder that appear on the BIID website are modeled on those for transsexualism. Aspirants have to say that they have felt they had one leg too many, for instance, since an early age, and that they have 'pretended' to be disabled by using a wheelchair. The similarities between the two disorders are being openly discussed by psychiatrists in the field. One similarity is the fact that both interests of men appear to be sexually motivated and forms of masochism (Lawrence, 2006). In both cases the aspirants themselves proclaim that their disorder has nothing to do with sex, but is rather an issue of 'identity', which can only be resolved through surgical removal of healthy limbs or sexual characteristics, that is legs or penises. The reasons supplied by the aspirants in First's study complied with the requirements of the psychiatrists who have given the condition the diagnostic label, 'identity disorder', thus 61per cent gave as their primary motivation 'restoring true identity as an amputee'. Only 15 per cent gave sexual excitement as their primary reason, though 87 per cent admitted some sexual motivation behind their practice. The issue of the significance of sexual motivation resembles the very similar debate about transsexualism. Admission of a sexual motivation for a desire for amputation, whether for secondary sexual characteristics in transsexualism or for limbs in BIID, is seen as problematic by aspirants because it is not likely to sit well with medical insurance companies or with many of the psychiatrists and surgeons whose aid is sought. But significant practitioners and researchers on transsexualism have posited a sexual motive for that behaviour (Blanchard, 1989, 1991; Lawrence, 2006).

Both First (2004) and Lawrence (2006) point out other similarities between transsexualism and BIID. One parallel is the fact that a larger-than-expected number of First's interviewees had transgender interests (First, 2004). Eight of his 47 male interviewees reported being sexually aroused by cross-dressing, Ten reported 'feelings of wishing to be the opposite sex, or having the feeling of being in the body of the wrong sex' (First, 2004: 10). Lawrence points out that another similarity is that a high proportion of transgenders report interests in sadomasochism, which is the sexual motivation of such importance in BIID (Lawrence, 2006), pointing out that in one study of 12 MtFs almost all had SM fantasies. Both categories, Lawrence points out, speak of being trapped in the wrong body. Another similarity is a feeling of discomfort with an aspect of 'his or her anatomical identity . . . with an internal sense of the desired identity' (First, 2004: 8). Other similarities include early onset, 'successful treatment by surgery for some subjects, frequent mimicking of the desired identity' and 'for a significant subgroup of each, paraphilic sexual arousal by a fantasy of being the desired identity'.

Interestingly, women seem to suffer this condition rarely, as was the case with transsexualism until quite recently. First's interviewees included only four women among 52 and their approach to the disorder was different. Only one of the women reported any sexual arousal and three of the women wanted both legs amputated above the knee. Only four of the 47 men wanted this. One woman who wanted both legs amputated reported feeling 'that her legs did not feel part of her' but reported some decrease in intensity of desires which she attributed to 'doing body work . . . focusing on remaining connected when my legs are being touched' (First, 2004: 8). This form of disassociation is associated with childhood sexual abuse 'a sense of physical fragmentation or separation from part of one's body, such as an absence of feeling, a feeling of numbness or disconnection from one's emotions, a feeling of being dead' (Steinberg, quoted in Cassese, 2000: 130). A feminist perspective which looks at the differences between men and women is needed here.

Though voluntary limb amputation is in the process of normalisation, for many psychiatrists and surgeons it may still be seen as an inappropriate treatment for a mental condition. Sex reassignment surgery, on the other hand, has been normalised to such an extent that its inclusion here as a form of self-mutilation by proxy, especially alongside BIID, may seem more bizarre than the idea of surgically mutilating the body as therapy for a mental condition itself. The US medical ethicist Carl Elliott has used the phenomenon of BIID to throw the issue of sex reassignment surgery into question. He has stated that the idea that surgery is the correct therapy for mental conditions that arise at a particular historical moment and are in the process of being promulgated via the Internet is brutal and absurd (Elliott, 2000). He expresses the hope that in 50 years people will look back at this time in amazement that such barbaric remedies could have been accepted.

Transgender surgery

Transgenderism has only been an accepted disorder for which the treatment of choice is amputation, or other surgery, for a comparatively short time. As Joanne Meyerowitz's history of transgenderism points out, many US physicians contested the idea of surgery for the condition well into the 1950s and 1960s and some still do (Meyerowitz, 2002). Transgenderism is not usually included in the range of practices typical of body modification, perhaps because it is not usually seen as voluntary. The medical construction of the condition, to which aspirants have to conform, treats the desire for surgery as compulsive and undeniable and usually posits a whole or partial biological explanation in terms of the wrong 'gender' getting into an apparently healthy body (Gooren, 1999). Radical feminist theorists have criticised the concept of transgenderism on the grounds that 'gender' is a social construction of male dominance which, in both its male dominant and female subordinate forms, will not survive the downfall of this political system (Raymond, 1994; Hausman, 1995; Jeffreys, 2006). Thus seeking to carve the contemporary requirements of this social construction onto bodies is a cruel attempt to cut people up to fit into political requirements which should not be carried out by doctors or given the imprimatur of the state. The idea of GID has become so normalised that hormonal treatment is now being prescribed for children before puberty to modify their bodies and ensure that they do not develop the body shapes that they seek to avoid (Jeffreys, 2006).

The description and illustrations of MtF surgery presented in an issue of the *International Journal of Transgenderism*, the house magazine of the society of psychiatrists and surgeons specialising in this condition set up by the sexologist Harry Benjamin, suggest similarities with the way that body modification procedures, including castration, are demonstrated on the Internet for the sexual satisfaction of devotees (Perovic et al., 2005). The Body Modification Ezine website, for instance, carries bloody and graphic photos of brutal cutting practices such as suspension, which can be downloaded by aficionados for a price, just like any other pornography on the web. The journal article includes seven pages of hand-drawn pictures illustrating how a particular group of surgeons cut up the penis and then 11 pages of full-colour photos of the 'disassembled penis' which are extremely gruesome with bloody bits and pieces of the penis held up by medical instruments for appraisal. The authors explain that they invert the skin of the penis to form a vagina and insert this into a 'previously prepared cavity'. Then they form labia from 'the remaining penile and scrotal skin' (ibid.: 43). This public presentation of the mutilation of the penis is not obviously very different from the forms of disassembly of the penis engaged in by male body modifiers, particularly nullos and transgenders, on the Body Modification Ezine website, and may offer similar satisfactions to those involved. But it is presented under the mantle of science which offers more respectability.

This mutilating practice has been so normalised as a 'therapy' for the problem of psychological distress about 'gender' that the physical harms involved are seldom remarked upon. But problems, as the *Journal of Transgenderism* article explains, can occur. They include unsatisfactory levels of moisture, 'rectovaginal fistula due to intraoperative injury to the rectum', 'vaginal shrinking in two patients', 'stenosis of vaginal introitus', 'late stenosis of urethral meatus in one patient due to injury during sexual intercourse', 'urethral prolapse', and 'posterior vaginal wall rupture during intercourse' (ibid.: 57). Patients whose vaginas have been fashioned from sufficient penile skin need to place objects called 'stents' in the surgically constructed vagina at night to keep it open 'until sexual intercourse is regularly practiced' (ibid.: 64). Those who have 'insufficient penile skin' are advised to apply stents 'continuously day and night for one year in order to prevent contractures following secondary epithelializaiton or free penile skin grafts' (ibid.). The patients are advised to use their constructed vaginas for sexual intercourse as soon as possible 'even though bleeding may occur'. Pain is not mentioned. The problems presented by reassembly in the case of those who change their minds are not addressed (Batty, 2004; Australian Story, 2003).

Queer theorists who take a postmodern approach, generally derived from the work of Judith Butler (1990), are thoroughly involved in normalising the desire to 'transgender' and even the hormones and surgery themselves. They use language similar to that used to celebrate other forms of body modification. They argue that transgenderism is 'transgressive' because it throws traditional notions of gender into question (Bornstein, 1994; More and Whittle, 1999). They speak of choice and even social justice. The respected queer theorist Judith Butler (2004) employs both these arguments, arguing that access to sex reassignment surgery is a matter of social justice because 'Those who claim that transsexuality is, and should be, a matter of choice, an exercise of freedom, are surely right . . . a basic human freedom is being suppressed' (Butler, 2004: 88). She has not expressed an opinion on the necessity for voluntary limb amputation to be available in the same way. As with other practices of self-mutilation by proxy there is a startling absence of criticism of sex reassignment surgery from a feminist or radical social constructionist perspective.

Conclusion

This chapter has sought to contribute to a critical feminist literature on the practice of self-mutilation in both its private and commercial forms. Body modification is not just a marvellous opportunity for expression, resistance and transgression, which modern technologies have delivered to a daring and experimental audience. The fact that the practices are carried out as extensions of private self-mutilation on subordinated social groups such as women, lesbians and gay men, and the disabled should be a matter of concern. Public demonstration and performance of the destruction of human flesh in sadomasochist rituals involving wounding, bleeding and injury is not a reason for celebration. The exhibition of freaks in nineteenth- and early-twentieth-century circuses might well be seen as the unreasonable and distasteful exploitation of the vulnerable, but this consideration is not being extended in the present to performance artists who mutilate on stage, or gay men who get castrated on the Internet. Political questions need to be asked about this commercialised epidemic in which the pain and distress caused by subordination, abuse and stigma are carved onto healthy bodies by a range of perpetrators of body mutilation for profit or sexual satisfaction. The body modification movement, in which scarification parties can be seen as therapy for child rape and domestic violence, can be seen as a form of backlash against feminism and gay liberation in political times where there seems little hope of social transformation. The strategies of 1970s feminists were very different. They invented incest survivors' groups in which women could support each other in their rage against male dominance and recover their strength without subjecting their bodies to punishment. Promotion of self-mutilation is an obstacle to the creation of a future in which women, lesbians and gay men, the disabled and men distressed by their failure to measure up to masculinity can cease blaming their bodies and love them in their entirety without wounds.

3

Breast Augmentation Surgery: Carving the Flesh as Female

Taina Kinnunen

Female breasts carry an interesting symbolic and political history. Their status as a source and object of erotic pleasure has varied within and across cultures. The size and form of breasts have represented race, level of cultivation, social class and nationality. In Western countries, breasts were medicalised at the end of nineteenth century, when the first breast operations were carried out. Since then, breasts have been both reduced and enlarged. They have been supported by bras, and sometimes freed from bras (Gilman, 1999: 218–49; Haiken, 1997: 228–84; Yalom, 1998). I remember a time when push-up bras seemed ridiculous. Even visible bra straps seemed obscene. Breasts were hidden rather than accentuated. Nowadays, the fashion is quite the opposite: breasts should be 'femininely' and 'sexily' pushed out as much as possible.

This chapter examines what kind of lived experiences push women to undergo breast operations and what kind of cultural *morphology* of the sexual female body is revealed in them. The discussion is based on interviews and a survey of breast augmentation patients, and interviews with plastic surgeons and cosmetic surgery consultants in Finland.[1] In my use of the term 'morphology', I refer to discourses about gendered shapes and forms of bodies (Weiss, 1999: 72). Applying Arthur W. Frank's (1991) notion of the body as constituted by *corporeality, institutions* and *discourses*, I trace how cultural discourses are materialised in patients' bodies and modified by the practices of cosmetic surgery. The viewpoint here is subject based. Both discourses and institutions emerge from acting bodies, although bodies cannot escape understanding themselves through these parameters (ibid.).

The sexuality of the wounded body finds its special mode in cosmetic surgery, as will be seen from my research material. Although breast augmentation is one significant way to become a sexual female body, the operated body pretends to be natural, that is to say, woundless. The operation may damage sensual nerves in the breasts. The woman still gets erotic pleasure through the imaginary gaze aimed at her breasts. However, signs of the surgery should not be noticed. The scars are socially stigmatised; they paradoxically threaten the sexual connotations of the body that has just tried to attain sexual perfection.

I will show how medical-technological 'fixing' of the female body is naturalised in our culture. The gendered ideology of cosmetic surgery clearly illustrates this. Cosmetic surgery is an institution which (re)produces the cultural discourses, the 'truth' of the normal female body. As a socially authorised practice, it can, to a certain degree, be compared to circumcision and reinfibulation through which female bodies are in many cultures concretely carved as sexually desirable. Besides, the surgical female body also represents the overall aesthetisation, technologisation and individualisation of the Western body, which also concerns men. Breast augmentation is one of the voluntary extreme body modification techniques, like bodybuilding and modern primitivism (for example, Pitts, 2003) that are used to articulate the cultural grammar of gender and sexuality, albeit in different ways.

Shame and relief

In my research breast augmentation patients tell stories of psycho-social metamorphoses. Thirty-one-year-old schoolteacher Mari had already realised at high school that her appearance was not 'as it should be'. Her 'small' breasts 'handicapped all areas of [her] life' and 'had a big impact on [her] self-esteem, sense of womanhood and, most of all, [her] sexuality', she explains. No push-up bra could relieve her suffering. She could not even imagine herself going to a swimming pool or beach, or taking off her clothes voluntarily in front of her boyfriend. Two years ago Mari got silicone implants. The operation has left two ugly scars which have been corrected twice. Still, Mari has never regretted the operation.

Mirja, on the other hand, who is a 47-year-old psychologist, thinks that she had 'something fragile in [her] womanhood' in her youth. Now she has 'refused to grow into an asexual granny' and has been reborn as a woman. Besides breast augmentation, Mirja has also had upper eyelid surgery and lost a great deal of weight. She enjoys being looked at, and sexually she has changed from being passive to being active. Roughly the same kind of change has happened to Satu, a 37-year-old communication manager, who felt that there was 'something missing' from her body. The feeling was present all the time. After surgery, she burst into tears of joy when she tried new bras on in a store. For the first time in her life, she felt complete.

Over half of the women operated on had sometimes heard comments on the imperfection of their breasts. It had usually been only a single experience, during their youth. With only one exception, nobody had ever heard anything negative from their male partners, who had also typically objected to the operation at first (cf. Gagné and McGaughey, 2002: 825; Gimlin, 2000: 93–4). Nevertheless their suffering was so great that the women were ready to risk their health to get perfect breasts.[2] It was striking to hear the story of 19-year-old Heidi. She is an exceptionally beautiful and feminine young woman, like a living Barbie doll, with her long blond hair, neat make-up and fashionable clothes. She speaks and behaves well. Heidi's lips have been made 'full' by collagen injection. In addition, she is considering liposuction, cosmetic dental treatments and upper eyelid surgery, 'all kinds of little adjustments', as she says. She has also planned a nose job, but given up the idea for the present. Heidi says that at the age of 16 she had already decided to have an augmentation. She describes her suffering:

> H: I knew that I am not the only one with small breasts, and that there are certainly people with no breasts at all . . . Nobody ever told . . . it was just so deeply rooted within myself . . . I didn't want to go into the sauna with my best girl friends . . . and in front of a new boyfriend . . . for the first time without clothes . . . Really embarrassing – a really shameful feeling.
>
> TK: Did anything catastrophic ever happen when you took your shirt off?
>
> H: Nothing. Maybe it was just fear that something would happen – that the guy would say something, that somebody would walk away.

The possibility of body image disorder is often discussed in the context of extreme body modification practices. The psychological profile of breast augmentation patients has been studied with conflicting results (see Sarwer, 2002; Schofield et al., 2002). However, defining a healthy body image is complicated because of the fact that a body image is a morphological projection, a way to see and imagine one's own body through cultural discourses, although it is enacted and constructed by one's own, unique body (Weiss, 1999: 77, 86). It is also obvious that bodily techniques representing psychological disorders change across time. Take, for example, bodybuilding. Thirty years ago, it was connected with pathological narcissism. Today, it is often seen as a healthy way of keeping fit. The same is happening to cosmetic surgery. All women are encouraged to 'enhance their quality of life' through surgery, for example in cosmetic surgery's public rhetoric and in women's magazines (Brooks, 2004; Fraser, 2003), although these women might still be pathologised, especially when they complain about complications (cf. Kent, 2003; Jasanoff, 2002). Instead of tracking individual psychological (dis)orders it is important to resituate the concept of body image away from its psychoanalytical roots into cultural grounds and to ask why so many women today believe that their breasts are too small, especially in the light of the cult of slimness.

The surgery clearly strengthened women's sexual self-confidence as the shame was gradually dispelled (cf. Stofman et al., 2006). It not only changed their feelings about their bodies but also their ways of moving socially and spatially in the world. Kathy Davis (1995: 141) has also noticed this in her interviews and attaches her interpretation to the social context. She emphasises that women's decisions to have surgical operations must be understood as their way to 'try to alleviate pain and negotiate some space for themselves in the context of a gendered social order' (ibid.: 180). It is easy to agree with her. The space is controlled by male-dominated plastic surgery which gives licence to women's sexual enjoyment. In the context of cosmetic surgery, sexuality must be understood as being of a predominantly visual character and as such, an object of different gazes: the patient's own, real and imagined men's, other women's and the surgeon's (cf. Gagné and McGaughey, 2002: 818). The operation sometimes weakens the sense of touch in the breasts or destroys it totally. Even then, the woman feels mediated enjoyment by imagining her body through the man's gaze and touch (cf. Young, 1998: 126). Twenty-six-year-old student Saara says:

> S: I am much more relaxed in bed. I love it when X [husband] touches my breasts. Before, I would always say 'don't touch them, because they're so small'.
>
> TK: So the size really mattered . . . It could be assumed that touching always feels the same.
>
> S: But it doesn't. And when . . . X takes those breasts into his hands and when I see that there is something in them, it is really a different feeling for me.
>
> TK: So it makes you excited too
>
> S: Yeah. I feel more harmonious in every way.

Cosmetic surgery has been seen as a tragic example of internalising the male gaze. This 'false consciousness' leads women to believe that they do it for themselves and of their own choice (Bordo, 1993: 247, 296; Morgan, 1998; Wilson, 2002; see also Gagné and McGaughey, 2002: 815–16). The US psychologist and feminist activist Margo Maine (2000) talks about the culture that promotes 'a war against women's bodies' by wounding women psychologically: dismissing, disrespecting and disempowering. More and more women have internalised the enemy and are destroying themselves physically by 'fashion surgery' and other means (cf. Palm, 1996). The women quoted above clarify how the enemy works at the embodied level. They were ashamed of their inadequacy without recognising the origin of that feeling, and just wanted to get rid of the pain through surgery. This seems to match exactly what Michel Foucault (1973) meant by the modern 'intelligent' power aimed at bodies. It is a power of knowledge of 'normal' bodies, which individuals adopt as their fundamental experience. They start controlling their bodies to avoid being categorised as abnormal. The result of this is that there is a docile body that may be subjected, used, transformed and improved.

The abstract power of media representations

Media images are discursive condensations of gender and sexuality, and they powerfully set the models for body discipline. As part of the pornographisation of culture, the female body is excessively sexualised in the media. As can easily be observed from public representations of the female body, big breasts in an otherwise slim body are evidently a prerequisite of femininity and female sexuality (cf. Young, 1990; Davis, 1995: 9, 60). Media representations teach us what is normal and what is not. Susan Bordo (1999: 283) surmises that, today, boys unhooking their first bras are taught to expect to see two 'glorious globes standing at attention even when supine'. Bordo's characterisation of body representations is apt: 'Real breasts are the anomaly in visual culture today; it's rather a shock when a naked actress lies down and her breasts flop off to the side. It doesn't look *right* anymore' (ibid.).

It is not a coincidence that the first wave of breast augmentations was in the 1950s, when the Hollywood industry and *Playboy* magazine launched the new bosomy female ideal (Haiken, 1997: 235–43). Accordingly, the development of the techniques of cosmetic surgery promoted the ideal. Now the ideal is so established that the stereotypes of the ideal female appearance, beauty pageant winners, do not succeed in international competitions anymore as 'naturals'. The same figure recurs everywhere from Barbie dolls to video game heroines. Dissatisfaction with their bodies among girls and women is well known nowadays (for example, Bordo, 1993; Maine, 2000; Renshaw, 2003). They are socialised from the age of a couple of years old to adhere to the idea that the core of femininity is concern for one's appearance (see Schor, 2004: 44–5, 57). Little girls who have just started school are taught to accentuate their 'breasts' with bras designed for them.

The effects of media representations on women's body experiences are not something that can be analysed through interviews. Still, I wanted to discuss the subject with my interviewees. They typically admitted the power of media representations over their body images. Women also criticised the general sexualisation of the female body and the body ideal that is impossible to achieve without surgery and strict daily body control. Nevertheless realising this had not relieved their suffering. This proves the power of media representations to colonise thinking. We all know that pop singer Cher's appearance is fabricated but it has become an 'empty abstraction'; it is pursued anyway, as Bordo (1993: 104) says. Bodies like hers have actually become the standard of beauty. Still, rebellion is possible. Merja described her experiences of humiliation, how she learnt to consider herself 'invalid' as a teenager when her father read *Playboy* and her brother teased her about her breasts. Fifteen years after her operation she thinks: 'I could be pretty enough without this surgery.' She has considered removal of the implants and 'returning back to herself'.

> The surgeon claimed that my breasts would look totally natural. They really are not natural at all, except when I have clothes on. My breasts are not getting old along with me. At the age of 43, I have the breasts of a fifteen-year-old. Moreover, they are quite hard when I lie down.

On the one hand, surgeons emphasise that the patients seek the augmentation on the basis of their subjective needs. The success of breast augmentations is promoted by the fact that breast patients have always been thankful patients to the surgeons (Gilman, 1999: 208–9). This is still the case, as my interviews showed. In particular, the surgeons described women who have undergone silicone implant operations as 'almost 100 per cent satisfied patients', who 'motivate' them as doctors. On the other hand, they admit the connection between patients' needs, media representations and cosmetic surgery. Anyway, as doctors they see themselves as only *reacting* to cultural pressures, rather than creating and reproducing them. This reaction is fairly direct in surgery in the US, for example, because the surgeons ask patients to bring in pictures exemplifying the breasts they would like to have. These pictures are often taken from pornographic magazines (Gagné and McGaughey, 2002: 829). Finnish surgeons, on the other hand, (still) see this kind of practice as worrying. In any case, perhaps the media has colonised their thinking as well, and, correspondingly, cosmetic surgery actively reproduces a certain ideal of femininity in the media. The surgeon's words below show how breast augmentations are justified by referring to 'natural' facts and to the patient's own will. The latter is drawn into the discussion when I remark that not all men want women to have implants:

> S[urgeon]: Women who have really masculine breasts might have a very big problem . . . It is indeed a fact that men look at breasts. When these women are searching for a partner, they may find it very important to have . . . breasts . . .
>
> TK: At least, that is their idea . . .
>
> S: Their idea, yeah, and I think that some men also think . . . that if the woman is totally flat-chested . . . But people are different, sure, there might be some men who also like flat-chested women. That is possible too.
>
> TK: Or natural breasts. There was this public appeal . . .[3]
>
> S: That's right, but this is a very personal thing. I think that it is so wrong that someone from the outside criticises a woman for having an augmentation or reduction surgery . . . The case of augmentation surgery in particular – why the women who are so strongly opposed to it have become *so* involved in this issue [emphasis in interview].

Details of the perfect breast

The necessity of breast augmentation is only rarely denied by surgeons. A cup size of A or AA is practically seen as a self-evident indication of the operation. The augmentation is often done with 200–300 cc implants, aiming at C or D cups. Another unquestionable reason for the operation is the 'damage' caused by breastfeeding or ageing. The surgeons interviewed mentioned a 'problematic group' among the patients: women with 'normal' (B-cup) breasts, to whom they recommend giving up the idea of augmentation. On the other hand, the surgeons admit that porn models and strippers, for example, do get exceptionally large implants. 'They must have proper equipment – they make a living from it', as one surgeon clarified. Undoubtedly, 'as large implants as the thoracic cavity can bear', as another surgeon described very large implants, are sometimes given to other patients too. Every surgeon knows a colleague who does it, although all of them deny doing it themselves.

Twenty-four-year-old Jenni had the augmentation operation when she was only 17 years old, because her boyfriend put pressure on her. Jenni does not know exactly what kind of implants she has, but she thinks that their size is about 450 cc. Her boyfriend had told the surgeon to provide implants which were 'as big as possible'. The surgeon was one of my interviewees. Still, all interviewed surgeons insisted that they refuse to operate if they suspect that anyone other than the patient is the initiator of the request for surgery. All the surgeons also said that they have experience of this kind of 'troublesome' case.

Doctors and patients tell slightly differing stories about the usual negotiations in the consulting room. Patients seem to find them pretty straightforward. Agreement on the size of the implants had been reached easily, according to my interviewees, although in some cases the patient had first hoped for bigger implants than the doctor recommended. For the surgeon, the negotiation is more complex. It often ends up with the patient having to choose between two alternatives offered by the surgeon. At least in his/her mind, the surgeon often supports the smaller alternative for medical and esthetic reasons. Regarding the latter, the surgeons proportion the size of the breasts to the ideal Finnish or European anatomical scale, which differs from the US scale. As a rule, the implants used are 100 cc smaller than in the US. On the other hand, the surgeon must be able to anticipate the satisfaction of the patient. The surgeon therefore usually encourages the patient to choose the bigger alternative, because otherwise she will probably regret her choice later, as one surgeon explained. Besides, he thinks that 'women always want slightly bigger implants than they admit'.

Implants can be inserted either under or over the breast muscle, and there are different shapes of implants. According to a consultant who acts as an intermediary between patients and surgeons, patients do not always have realistic expectations concerning the advantages that can be achieved through implants. Sometimes the breasts 'hang down' so much that the augmentation would not 'lift' the breasts enough. Furthermore, 'triangular' breasts cannot be made 'round' solely by implants. In these cases, breast lift surgery is also recommended. The aim of the augmentation is always erect and round breasts, which, partly because of the surgery itself, have started to be considered as the *normal* shape of the breasts.

Stigmatising scars

An ex-boyfriend decided to leave Heidi after a relationship of a few months when he noticed the scars on her breasts in an intimate situation. He was upset: why had Heidi not told him that she had got silicone implants? What would his friends say when they found out that the attractiveness of his girlfriend is 'fake'? The boyfriend's reaction shocked Heidi. Now she is wondering if she needs to start feeling ashamed of her silicone implants. The scars revealing the augmentation sometimes truly cause a catastrophe in a woman's sexual life. The operated body is ultra sexy only as long as the scars are not noticed, and unfortunately, scars are usually the most common reason for dissatisfaction after the breast augmentation. Thus, the earlier bodily stigma, small breasts, may only change in mode of dissatisfaction (cf. Kent, 2003: 408). The woman wonders whether 'to display or not to display; to tell or not to tell; to let on or not to let on; to lie or not to lie; and in each case, to whom, how, when and where', as Erving Goffman (1968: 57) valorises the dilemma of how to manage and negotiate socially with the stigma symbol which brings about a 'spoiled' identity (see also Williams and Bendelow, 1998: 59–60). Some women start avoiding public places where they could be seen naked. For one woman the scars were so annoying that she decided to have tattoos to hide them. After that, the stigma moved to the tattoos instead, and she could not imagine appearing naked anywhere. For some interviewees, I was the only person outside the clinic to know about the augmentation.

The stigma of the scars stems from the meanings attached to the naked body in Western culture, where it is an object of extreme dual interests; this is in contrast to many other cultures. The body which is not decorated or 'clothed', for example, by colored or scarred tattoos has been admired as the most sexually exciting and, on the other hand, seen as a symbol of sin and destruction. The naked body is also seen esthetically, erotically and morally as sharply distinct from the clothed body (Dutton, 1995: 173–5; see also Lévi-Strauss, 1955: 235–6). In its mythic naked purity, the Western body is closed. It is not open to intrusions and it does not bleed. This is one of the conceptions that are consciously defied by the sub-cultural sphere called *modern primitivism*, which was born in California in the late '70s and has since spread to Europe as well. By wounding the skin and tissue with tattoos, piercing, cutting, scarring, branding and other extreme techniques, modern primitivists want to explore a non-Western bodily way of being. The techniques are adopted from indigenous cultures. The practices carry sexual meanings for their performers, but in a different sense from that of cosmetic surgery. The scars are manifestations of sexuality as such, and are interpreted as sexually appealing ornamentation. Scars may also symbolise pain and sadomasochistic sexual preferences connected with pain. Sometimes scars mark the individual's new 'own' body after traumatic experiences, such as sexual abuse (for example, Pitts, 2003).

The closedness of the Western body causes an interesting confusion in the context of cosmetic surgery. Scars reveal the 'dark reality' of their carrier, who is trying to deny her natural body (Gilman, 1998: 8). The cult of the authentic self is very strong in the individualised Western culture, which means a dilemma with the new medical body enhancement technology. Some people feel they can become themselves by using serotonin pills or having breast augmentation surgery, for example, while others feel that they lose themselves or are interpreted by others to do so in undergoing those practices. Every advance in body manipulation technology again raises the fundamental questions of 'what is the body?' or 'what is the self?' (Elliott, 2003).

Nostalgia for the untouched body has in any case given way to the techno-body ethos. In the spirit of cyberfantasy, the combination of organic and inorganic body parts feels natural for the majority of implant patients. Worries about the 'strange material' in the body have come to some women's minds, but they nevertheless feel the implants to be parts of their own new bodies. When asked how they imagine their breasts in 20 years, it seemed that for most it was almost impossible to think so far forward in the future. But in case of any problems, the implants would simply be removed or changed. Even a woman whose implants encapsulated (a scar tissue formed around the breast implants causing the breasts to harden) and were removed thinks:

> A human being is not untouchable; I have had many other kinds of operations too . . . This is not sacred, only the spirit is. But the body, this is only material. You can mold it as much as you want.

This attitude resembles performance artist Orlan's philosophy of her body as 'just an inert piece of meat, lying on the table' (see Davis, 2003b: 110). It also corresponds to the image of cosmetic surgery that is already reproduced in women's magazines, for example. Cosmetic surgery is represented as a 'civilised' high technology which lacks bloody vulgarity and whose risks are manageable. A woman choosing a surgical operation is actually represented as a pioneer of scientific and technological advancement, who bravely encounters the risks too (Brooks,

2004). According to the surgeons, patients often have unrealistic perceptions of the possibilities of designing living flesh. For example, they do not accept the fact that 'every time you cut, it will leave some kind of scar', as one surgeon emphasises. In the history of cosmetic surgery, scars have always caused anxiety among surgeons too. It is a built-in principle of the practice that the more visible scars there are, the more the operation has failed. Techniques to minimise, hide and mask scars have self-evidently been among the interests of technological development work of cosmetic surgery (Gilman, 1999: 313–4). Despite being a reminder of the unavoidability of any scars, surgeons themselves reproduce the conception of the technologically controllable body in the hands of the professional:

> Encapsulation depends on so many things – the skills of the surgeon, technique, facilities, asepsis, the chosen prosthesis, planning . . . and the patient herself. If it is done well and the circumstances are optimal, the probability of the encapsulation is much lower than when you just squash the implant in there.

Carving the flesh as female

Cosmetic surgery is set in the cultural context of white, Eurocentric patriarchy. It has become very popular also, for example, in some Asian countries such as Korea, Japan and China, and also in countries such as Brazil, Iran and Turkey. Still, *all* cosmetic surgery has been stated to be ethnically Eurocentric, because everywhere the technique is used to achieve the Western and white beauty ideal (Davis, 2003a; Kaw, 1998; Kim, 2003; Morgan, 1998). However, carving and wounding the body is not solely a Euro-American phenomenon by its origin. Initiation rites, for example, are known all around the world. They often include painful practices of wounding, cutting, scarification and piercing, many of them done to sexual organs, to gender the bodies (see Burton, 2001: 69–87). In other words, Western bodies are not more social or controlled than any other culture's bodies, as might perhaps be concluded at times from the constantly expanding discussion on the postmodern body-boom. The human body is always regulated by institutional and discursive practices, and social identity is inevitably marked on the body (for example, Blacking, 1977; Douglas, 1966; Sullivan, 2002: 3–6). Even the commercialisation of the human body, a feature which is so often emphasised in the context of modernity, has had many varieties in the course of human history (see Sharp, 2000). US professor of bioethics and philosophy Carl

Elliott (2003: 195) valuably reminds that it is not the standards of beauty themselves that subordinate, in particular, women, but the *contents* of the standards. Thus, it is important to critically discuss different cultural ways to gender bodies (cf. Grosz, 1994: 138–44).

This has been done in a few comparisons of breast augmentations and female circumcisions/reinfibulations by anthropologists. Tamar Diana Wilson (2002) equates breast augmentations with (even Pharaonic) circumcisions which are carried out in many parts of the Middle East and Africa and in immigrant societies from these areas. Both techniques are practiced by professionals, who literally carve the woman's body as 'female' and 'sexual' in order to please men. The practices are meant to ensure the man's sexual pleasure, not the woman's. Patriarchy serves as an ideological background for circumcisions, including the principle that a woman's virginity is a prerequisite for marriage. Breast augmentations, on the other hand, have become popular in neo-patriarchical capitalist societies. The female body is subordinated in these societies by phallocentric fetishisation and commodification, which smoothes out class differences between men. Women also start to appreciate themselves primarily as sexual objects, who have to 'win' the husband, in the absence of arranged marriages.

Laura Nader (1997) also sees breast augmentations and circumcisions as body mutilation techniques which belong to cultural rites of gendering the body. A Sudanese and a US woman, for example, both experience the body modified with these techniques natural. The only difference between the techniques is that circumcisions are carried out by *social* force, whereas *cultural* force is behind breast augmentations. With this slightly simplified comparison Nader aptly clarifies the nature of cultural forces in the mediated post-Fordist economy. Individuals get tips, especially from the media, as to how they should control their bodies.

Circumcision and breast augmentation represent cultural morphologies of sexual differences. They are the 'ways in which the shapes and surfaces of the particular anatomical bodies are marked and mapped within cultural system of meanings, which include, of course, specific cultural cognizances of biology', as Norwegian anthropologists Vigidis Broch-Due and Ingrid Rudie (1993: 33) define the concept of morphology. Non-gendered or androgyne bodies are cut into the female shape by these techniques. In Somali culture, for example, the female genital organs are purified of 'male' features by infibulation, to accentuate the difference between female and male genital organs. The flattened, smoothed and tied vulva is the opposite of the protruding, hard and open penis, and this gendered symbolisation cuts across the whole cultural system of meanings

(Talle, 1993). Correspondingly, small breasts, representing a manly body, are reshaped as female in the Western culture. Breasts have an essential role in performing normative womanhood and female sexuality. In fact, there are also forms of genital surgery in societies where cosmetic surgery is practiced, but that has not been discussed by anthropologists. Hymen reconstruction, tightening of the vagina, labia reductions, fat injections and liposuction on the labia and pubic elevation are examples of female sexual enhancement surgery, which is a fast-growing trend in cosmetic surgery. The trend's connection with the pornography industry and the pornographisation of the culture is obvious (for example, Kobrin, 2004). Genital surgery is one way to fulfil aesthetic criteria of the ideal femininity and its aim is to enhance primarily male pleasure.

In any case, breast augmentation or genital surgery cannot straightforwardly be equated with circumcisions because of their different cultural contexts. I still see a big difference between concrete social force and abstract tip-power. The real possibility to refuse to undergo the surgery must be taken seriously. Choosing cosmetic surgery *is* partly genuinely one's own choice, although it is *also* a reflection of power relations, including submissive discourses. Postmodern 'body projects' (Shilling, 1993), including gender initiations, are individual choices from the many possibilities in our society (cf. Featherstone, 2000; Burton, 2001: 70). One can choose to have one's breasts augmented or one's nipples pierced, or neither. Modern primitivists, for example, mark genital organs, and other parts of the body, by piercing, implants and scarification. Castration, splitting the head of the penis and urethral rerouting are also part of the techniques performed (Jeffreys, 2000: 418; Pitts, 2003: 168, 172–3). In contrast to non-Western cultures, these techniques represent individualism and rebellion against the dominating culture to their practitioners. Instead of fixed social identities, including gender, modern primitivism aims at dissolving the conventional gender dichotomy and Western beauty ideals, and at encouraging its adherents towards queer identity (Braunberger, 2000; Pitts, 2003; Sweetman, 2000). Certainly, modern primitivism can be interpreted from different power perspective. Sheila Jeffreys (2000), for example, criticises the blindness to seeing commercial Western body modification modes, such as cosmetic surgery *and* modern primitivism, as harmful cultural practices (as circumcisions) adopted by subordinated groups.

For me, the 'victim of sexist culture' interpretation is only one side of the coin. A breast augmentation can also be seen as a conscious act by which at least some women add to their beauty capital for its own sake, beyond immediate heterosexist power relations (cf. Blum, 2003: 17–20;

Holliday and Sanchez Taylor, 2006). In the aesthetisised culture, sexuality is a detail within good looks. Cosmetic surgery is one sign of the materialised female body in our culture (cf. Negrin, 2000) and for some, this arms race represents a positive freedom to construct identity and even to object to the power structures between the genders (for example, Scott, 2005). Although, for example, Heidi's suffering due to her small breasts is real, it is obvious that she wants more than just to be normal:

> It is very important for me what others think about me . . . When a day goes by and nobody has looked at me on the street, it can feel like a real tragedy . . . Yeah, I want people to think that I am good-looking. I want it to be the first thing that comes to their mind when they see me. Not just pretty cute but *really* cute [emphasis in interview].

The gender of sexual enhancement surgery

The male body is indisputably also aesthetisised and sexualised in the mediated consumer culture and subordinated to ever-growing pressures concerning appearance (for example, Bordo, 1999; Dutton, 1995; Kinnunen and Wickman, 2006). Men spend their time in gyms in order to achieve at least the minimum criteria of the male body. Muscles are fetishised representations of the male gender in our culture (Dutton, 1995). As in Somali culture, for example, the male body is understood as the opposite of the female body: it is hard, big and strong, unlike the soft, small and weak female body (Connell, 1987). Thus, the morphology of the male body is constructed in parallel with the determination of the female body. Muscularity also represents all the ideal features of hegemonic masculinity: hard work, competence, self-control and power (Jefferson, 1998). Bodybuilding is a form of growing into a man which consists of autonomous, serious and hard work in the gym. Extreme muscularity is achieved by no more tender techniques than ideal female body. Serious body building is about wounding and tearing the muscle issue by hard training, controlled diet and anabolic steroids, among other pharmacological substances. The pain in the muscles while training represents the 'clean' technique and is thus an objective to be sought. Bodybuilders constantly vary their training methods to 'attack', 'shock' and 'blow up' the muscles to ensure their maximum growth (Kinnunen, 2004; Klein, 1993).

Certain enhancement technologies for the male bodies, like potency medicine, menopause hormones and anabolic steroids, have constantly growing markets (for example, Pope et al., 2000; Loe, 2006; Szymczak and Conrad, 2006). The number of men undergoing cosmetic surgery is also growing fast, comprising about 10 percent of all patients in many countries. It has therefore been proposed that the traditional gendered order of cosmetic surgery is gradually dissolving (Gilman, 1999: 32–3; Holliday and Cairnie, 2007). Virginia L. Blum (2003: 34) states that cosmetic surgery is about *any* body as an object of technological improvement.

According to my research, this is not reality yet. The gendered nature of cosmetic surgery, especially sexual enhancement operations, becomes clear when considering men's operations. Penis enlargement and silicone implants imitating developed muscles can be considered to represent the forms of men's sexual enhancement surgery in our culture (cf. for example, Dutton, 1995; Klein, 1993; Gerschick, 2005). It is possible to surgically increase the length and girth of the penis, and silicone implants can be inserted in the calves, biceps, triceps, bottom or chest, for example. Both of these types of operations are practised particularly in the USA and in other meccas of cosmetic surgery, like Brazil (cf. Gilman, 1999: 214). When I was doing my fieldwork with devoted bodybuilders in California in 1997, some interviewees made guesses at which top world-class bodybuilders might have 'paid' calves or biceps. Some clinics were advertising the operations as a 'finishing touch' to an otherwise perfect body. It seems to remain, nevertheless, a marginal practice, whereas all female competitive bodybuilders and fitness athletes, and many non-competitive lifestyle bodybuilders, reconstruct their femininity with breast implants.

I asked the surgeons interviewed how they treat male patients asking for silicone implants. Most of them found my question strange and amusing, even indiscreet. I was surprised, perhaps partly because of my experience in California and, secondly, because technically the surgery does not differ from female breast augmentation, as I learnt. Nonetheless surgeons' attitudes were definitely negative, and the opposite of their attitude to women's implant surgery:

> If there is an A or AA cup or even smaller breast, it can be repaired easily and, as far as we know now, also without risks . . . But then, there was one guy who came and said that his bottom was too flat, he wanted little implants. I am not going to do that. Of course, it depends on my skills as well.

A female consultant used men's implants as an example of 'stupid ideas' that patients may have. For men, silicone implants may cause health problems, which 'is not nice'. Previously, the same person had assured me that silicone is safe for women. She said that implants in a male body are problematic because they are in areas which move all the time. One surgeon, on the other hand, said that bottom implants are no more dangerous than breast implants. Still, he had also refused to carry out such operations. When I asked if I, as a woman, could get implants in my calves instead of my breasts, the answer was 'definitely no'. The reason was that surgeons have to 'apply sane principles' and 'listen to their conscience', and 'refuse to consent to stupid and dangerous' operations. So, I learnt that there is a strictly defined right place in the human body for silicone implants: the female chest.

The attitude towards penis operations is also one of reluctance, although these operations are carried out to some extent in Finland and Estonia, amongst other countries. One surgeon thought that lengthening the penis does not carry significant risks, unlike increasing its girth. Anyway, the reason for the operation is always 'between the ears': men with this kind of problem should turn to a psychiatrist rather than a plastic surgeon (cf. Davis, 2003c). In general, surgeons determined penile enlargements as senseless, because of the risk of damaging the tactile nerves and erection. Besides, such surgery risks the reputation of the whole practice. One surgeon explained why he once refused to give a lecture on penile operations in a sex fair:

> I don't want to give an impression that this has something to do with sadomasochism or exhibitionism or something perverse . . . This is exactly the kind of thing that feeds the myth that this is about something mysterious and weird, not traditional medicine, too sexual . . . Whereas, for example, a young woman comes and shows me that her minor labia . . . extends asymmetrically an inch out from her genitals. With pre-medication, local anesthesia and a laser I can cut the extra area off beautifully, into a half-moon shape, sew it . . . Wash it and apply cream, and after a week she is satisfied.

Breast operations have, earlier, awkwardly sexualised cosmetic surgery, casting doubts on its medical nature. Surgeons have tried to alleviate this by arguing the necessity of such operations for women's gender identity and self-esteem. They have succeeded. Female sexual enhancement operations do not pose a threat to the reputation of the whole institution of cosmetic surgery. The above-cited surgeon in fact emphasised how unproblematic the operations are by showing me tens of before and after pictures. I learned how 'under-developed', 'almost masculine', 'quite cute little' or 'overly large' breasts can be lifted, augmented, reduced and reconstructed as 'quite tolerably beautiful' breasts. Through female sexual enhancement surgery the surgeons willingly follow the cultural beauty ideals despite the medical risks. One surgeon valorised the ideological core of the practice:

> There was a congress once, and one speaker started by showing *Playboy* magazines. First, there were North American magazines with erect breasts in all of them. Then there came South American magazines and they all had bottoms.

In other words, the sexual enhancement surgery reflects and produces cultural morphology of gender and sexuality at an extremely carnal level. This was most concretely illustrated by one surgeon, who performs various intimate surgeries all around the world. His ideological principle is 'when in Rome do as the Romans do'. In Finland and other Western countries, he augments breasts, tightens vaginas and cuts labia. For men, he performs penile enlargements, as the only one of the interviewees. In Islamic countries, on the other hand, he reconstructs hymens. Regarding the latter, he talks about social risks rather than medical risks. If the operation is discovered, the patient's and the doctor's lives are both in danger.

Conclusion

I have here discussed the lived, discursive and socially relational nature of the sexual female body that is created through breast augmentation. Following Arthur Frank's (1991) notion of the 'three-dimensional' body, I have analysed how cosmetic surgery is an institutional practice where patients' lived experiences of abnormality and cultural discourses of ideal femininity, represented especially by the visual media, are embodied. The popularity of breast augmentations and effects of the operation are illustrative examples of how the abstract cultural control over bodies works. Women learn to feel shame for their small breasts and voluntarily choose having a surgical operation. The aesthetic correction of the breasts helps women to accept themselves better and enjoy their sex life more, although the surgery sometimes weakens the tactile sense of the breasts. This indicates the aesthetisation of the body and shows how corporeal experiences and discourses of the body are inseparable; cultural conceptions of ideal femininity become a part of women's deep bodily experiences.

Breast augmentation is one of those technologies through which women are carved gendered bodies in our culture. In spite of its moral dilemmas in the context of feminist endeavours and Western conceptions of the natural body, cosmetic surgery is gradually becoming everyday beauty technology. Sexual enhancement of the female body achieved surgically is seen as natural both by the patients and the surgeons, as has been shown here. In this regard, I have equated it with circumcisions that are done in many non-Western cultures to carve the body as female. Still, interestingly, in Western cultures individual women can choose between breast augmentation and modern primitivist techniques, such as piercing and tattooing. Male patients also seek surgical operations to accentuate the 'male' features of their bodies, but at least in Finland, those surgeries remain uncommon partly due to the surgeons' attitudes. Instead, I have suggested that bodybuilding is the parallel technique to bodily grow into a man in our culture. An interesting difference between the gendered body modification techniques is that women are bodily objects of (male-dominated) institutional practice, while men are bodily subjects constructing themselves.

Women's personal views and socially shared morphology of the female body are the basis from which the surgeon and the patient negotiate the aims of the augmentation. Anyway, as I have pointed out, cosmetic surgery is an institution which not only reflects the patient's or culture's expectations but actively determines the criteria for the normal and feminine body. The plastic surgeon works in accordance with the legitimised principles of the field and his (or her) own clinical experience when deciding who he (she) will operate on and how. Further, the surgeon follows his (her) subjective conceptions when deciding which operations are correct to perform.

Notes

I warmly thank Anne Puuronen, Hanna Snellman, Tiina Mahlamäki and Jan Wickman for their discussions of my research. I would also like to thank Barbro Blehr, Ulla Brück and Karin Högström for their valuable comments on an earlier version of this chapter presented in the Department of Ethnology, University of Stockholm, Spring 2007.

1. The material was gathered between October 2003 and September 2004 as a single group within the larger material, which consists of patients who have undergone different types of cosmetic surgery operations. Interviewees were selected through cosmetic surgery clinics and a newspaper announcement. Altogether, 22 breast augmentation patients participated in the research either through an interview and/or through the survey. Over one-third of

the operations had been undergone in Estonia and the rest in Finland. Eleven of the interviewed surgeons and two consultants were Finnish, and one surgeon was Estonian. All interviews were semi-structured and lasted 1.5–2 hours.

2. One-third of augmentation patients suffer from some kind of complication after surgery, and one in five is obliged to have a corrective operation. The most common complication is encapsulation of the implants, in other words, the growth of scar tissue around the implant under the skin. Others include asymmetry of the breasts, skin damage, infection and hematoma (Kulmala et al., 2004).
3. Some years ago, many well-known Finnish men signed a public appeal for 'natural' breasts against breast augmentations.

4

Physical Bruises, Emotional Scars and 'Love-Bites': Women's Experiences of Men's Violence

Michelle Jones and Jeff Hearn

Marks on human bodies can have many identifiable social and public meanings (Lingis, 1984: 22). Various forms of 'body writing' and techniques of social inscription are practised in many cultural contexts, including violent ones. This chapter explores the body of the female victim of violence from men known to them as partners or ex-partners. It analyses the personal and social meanings of physical marks, such as bruises and love bites, as well as the ways in which emotional scars can manifest themselves in and on the physical body. Men's violence to known women remains an urgent social question; women form the vast majority of victims of men's violence (Taft et al., 2001; Kimmel, 2002). Men continue to perpetrate most interpersonal violence in intimate relationships, especially planned, repeated, heavy, physically damaging, non-defensive, premeditated, non-retaliatory and sexual forms of violence, along with most economic, collective, institutional, organised and military violence, which themselves are usually also interpersonal (Hearn and McKie, 2008).

Bryan Turner (1996: 233) argues that the study of the control of bodies is primarily the control of female bodies; thus a sociology of the body is also a study of patriarchy. It is against this backdrop that we focus on the bodily inscriptions found on the surface of the female body as the victim or target of the violences within violent heterosexual domestic relationships.

Elizabeth Grosz argues that 'bodily markings can be read as symptoms, signs, clues to unraveling a psychical set of meanings' (Grosz, 1994: 139), thus also carrying 'depth' or social meaning. She explains 'cicatrizations and scarifications mark the body as a public, collective, social category, in modes of inclusion or membership; they form maps of social needs, requirements, and excesses' (Grosz, 1994: 140). Such markings 'bind all subjects, often in quite different ways according to sex, class, race, cultural and age codifications, to social positions and relations' (Grosz, 1994: 141). These processes involve both physical harm and more than physical harm, for it is both the inside and outside of women's bodies and lives that are damaged, swollen and bruised.

In violent domestic relationships women's bodies are battered, bitten, bruised; hair is pulled; clothes are torn; bodies are hit, pushed, shoved, punched, kicked, pinched, strangled, headbutted; and sex or sex acts are forced or coerced (Jones, 2004). For men, bruises, scars and 'love-bites' may conjure up heroic images of sporting battle (Messner, 1990) or sexual desire (Alapack, 2007); for women, they are more likely to victimisation or signify sexual promiscuity (Alapack, 2007; Alapack et al., 2005; Tea, 2002). Bruises, physical and emotional scars and 'love-bites' on women's bodies position them either as promiscuous/victimised, or actively resistant, including resistant of these constructions. The existence of markings on women's bodies resulting from men's violence has specific social and cultural implications, including how women experience the 'traces' of violence, abuse and wounding.

The organisation of this chapter borrows from Grosz's (1994) concepts of the 'Outside-in' and the 'Inside-out'. In her book *Volatile Bodies*, Grosz disrupts the binary opposites of mind (inside)/body (outside) and of mental/physical that compose subjectivity. She argues for a reconfiguration of the body whereby both the inside and outside are valued – 'two surfaces which cannot be collapsed into one and which do not always harmoniously blend with and support each other; a model where the join, the interaction between the two surfaces, is always a question of power.' (Grosz, 1994: 189). The outside-in concerns social inscriptions on the surface of the body and how they generate a psychical interiority or depth. The outside-in is considered here in terms of the obvious case of physical bruising from physical force on the surface of the body and the psycho-social impact on the woman of that bruising.

The inside-out refers to how psychical interiors have played themselves out upon the surface of the body, its exteriority. The inside-out refers here primarily to the experience of non-physical violences, such as verbal and emotional abuse, and being emotionally scarred. In these, while there are no specific physical marks or injuries on the outside of the body, they are usually perceived or experienced, in Western cultures at least, as existing inside the body. This is also one case for consideration of psychosomatic illness where the female victim of violence considers how her partners' verbal and psychological abuse has impacted and played itself out upon the surface of her body.

The case of 'love-bites' follows, resulting from sometimes ambiguous physical/sexual force from the lips, usually of another person. These markings on the skin generate various internal meanings, made more complex by the intersections of (previous) sexual relations and violence. Such internal meanings arguably act back subsequently on the body and the skin, in terms of the relations of sexuality (including the absence of sexual relations) and violence (remembered, actual or potential). As such, the chapter examines the surface of the woman's body, seeking meanings from within, and how this might manifest itself on the outside of the woman's body, along with their complex interrelations. But first, some remarks are necessary on how the primary data on these embodied matters were gathered.

Gathering the data

The methodological approach adopted here is multi-paradigmatic, combining feminist, post structuralist and other interpretive approaches (Reinharz, 1992; Neuman, 1997). This involved a depth of understanding about women's experience of men's violence, through commitment to the influence of language on the construction of people's experience (Gavey, 1989), the use of interpretation to produce meaning (Neuman, 1997), the significance of context to experience (Allen and Baber, 1992) and the value of qualitative methods (Patton, 1980).

The interviews upon which this chapter is primarily based were conducted by Michelle Jones for an evaluation research project on men's programme groups for perpetrators of 'domestic violence'.[1] Ethics approvals for the men's group evaluation also included the use of the data for a doctoral research project (Jones, 2004) and associated publications. This gave access to men's accounts of their experience of being perpetrators of violence (cf. Hearn, 1998), and also their women partners' accounts of their experiences, as the targets of that violence (cf. Hanmer, 1996). All 11 men's groups that were run in Metropolitan Adelaide, Australia, in 1996 on the 'perpetrator responsibility' model (rather than, for example, an anger management model) agreed to be involved in the research. Nine of these were being run through the community health sector at no cost to participants; two were operated through the advice and counseling organisation, Relationships Australia, with a fee for attendance. All group leaders strongly encouraged men to participate in the evaluation research; ultimately, however, the men self-selected to be interviewed. At the first meeting of the men's groups, men were asked to provide their (ex-) partner's contact details. Subsequently, each woman was approached separately to invite her to be involved in the research, and informed that this was voluntary, confidential and independent of their partners' involvement.

The men (perpetrators) and women (victims-survivors) were asked on three separate occasions to complete both a questionnaire and a face-to-face interview. Sixty-six men[2] and 42 women[3] participated in this way. All the men were in attendance at the first night of one of the men's groups. They were interviewed in the first two weeks of the men's groups, the two weeks following their completion of the 12-week men's group and 18 months after the end of the group. Interviews were semi-structured, and between 15 minutes and two hours. In all, 259 interviews were conducted between April 1996 and May 1998. As often in longitudinal studies of sensitive topics, there was substantial dropout rate from one interview to the next.

Quotations have been selected from these interviews to best represent general features identified within the greater proportion of the material. Wherever possible, the interviewees' exact words have been used; in some places additional words have been added in square brackets for clarification or to maintain confidentiality. This primary data is supplemented and contextualised by research data from other relevant studies (for example, Hearn, 1998).[4]

Outside-in: Experiences and meanings of physical bruises

Physical violence results in various direct forms of damage, including open wounds and bruising. Bruises speak publicly of the violence without words. They are visible marks on the surface of the skin, signs with clear social meanings and implications; they result from injury, damage or wounding; they can be self-inflicted, the result of an accident or intentionally inflicted. Bruises are defined as a 'traumatic injury of the soft tissues which results in breakage of the local capillaries and leakage of red blood cells. In the skin it can be seen as a reddish-purple discoloration that does not blanch when pressed upon' (MedicineNet.com, 1996). Bruises are also coloured; they are red, black, blue, purple, green and yellow.

There is a burgeoning forensic medical knowledge about bruising (for example, Randeberg et al., 2007). This allows medical practitioners to determine how long ago the injury occurred (analysis of colour of bruising), make suppositions about what happened (that the alleged crime is consistent with the injury) and make judgements on the severity of the injury (Ohshima, 2000; Schwartz and Ricci, 1996). Forensic medical examiners when examining victims of rape engage in a process of mapping the surface of the woman's body. All marks, bruises, scars and injuries are recorded as evidence. A bodily history of damage is documented and used as evidence in legal proceedings if needed. The woman's body is considered as the text upon which the bruises and injuries are written. This is even though interpretations of this text are likely to vary according to different professional, occupational and other discourses.

Bruises can be read in different ways, and can also invoke different forms of self-surveillance. Some are kept hidden under the cover of clothes, which provide protection from a relative's, acquaintance's or stranger's eyes. The deliberate wearing of particular clothes to cover bodily marks is a means of self-surveillance. Some bruises, for example, those that indicate the arms have been held firmly by finger print markings, may be met with social silence when made public, even though they indicate the direct use of force against the body.

Women with obvious bruises such as a black eye are less likely to go out in public. Both the men and the women concerned may have their own somewhat different reasons for this restriction. Rosa felt it necessary to change her behaviours and remain in the home, away from the public gaze following a violent attack from her partner. She recalls:

> [H]e head-butted me in the passage-way and broke my nose and I went to the ground. . . . I couldn't go to work, not with my nose out of shape. I looked a bit of a wreck. So I rang work and I said, 'I can't come in to work'.

Rosa was ashamed and embarrassed; she was not wanting to be confronted, questioned or scrutinised by co-workers. She did not want to place herself in the position of having to explain how it happened or having to lie about what had happened. She was enacting self-surveillance and limiting her behaviours to protect her partner.

One of the women interviewed, Jan, recalled that she refused to drop her children off at school when she had a black eye, preferring to stay at home out of the public gaze. Foucault (1991: 212) states: 'disciplinary procedures, [are] not [only] in the form of enclosed institutions, but as centres of observation disseminated throughout society'. In her case, Jan felt that the 'centres of observation' had extended to the schoolteachers and other parents, required to report suspected child abuse but not suspected domestic violence against women.[5]

For some women the bruises, strangulation marks or black eyes were the warning sign they needed to do something about ending the man's violence, and more specifically ending the relationship. Jessica said, 'the arguments got too much, the pushing and shoving got too much. I suppose it was the black eye I think that finally did it,' and Emma recollected: 'I had strangulation marks. That was the last thing he did.' For both of these women the bruising was the symbol that the violence had gone too far and that the endpoint in their respective domestic relationships was near.

Many women also reported the legitimacy that having bruises provided them – legitimacy that the violence existed and was real. Some women felt the need to show their husbands or partners the extent of their bruising, appealing for it to stop. So the men, who on occasions denied their violence, could see the results and extent of their treatment. In her first interview Olivia stated:

> He was just carrying it on and I told him to stop and he hit me and I said, 'You're hurting me'. I was crying and he was going, 'Don't be pathetic, I'm not hurting you'. Every time he used to hurt me beforehand I used to have bruises on my arms and he used to say, 'I didn't do that', you know. He just hit me and I just laid there and I curled up like a baby and I was crying – I couldn't believe it. I could feel my face was really throbbing. I'll never forgive him for that. And I went and looked in the mirror. [upset] I couldn't believe he could do it, you know. So I went in to him and I said, 'Look what you've done' and he looked at me and he just cried. He didn't think he was hurting me and he just come [came] in and said, 'That's it, it's finished' and he cried and he said he'd never hit me again, which he never has. Oh, he's hit me back but never to the extent that he did then. But I fear him.'

Olivia's action of showing him her bruises resulted in shame, guilt and a promise that he would not repeat the behaviour. There was recognition from him that his violence on this occasion had gone too far; sadly the promise to never hit again was not realised, but she reported that he had not hit to the same extent as in this incident. In her third and final interview with me Olivia described how the bruising gave her the legitimacy to seek help outside of the relationship and seek a Restraining Order.[6] 'Bruises come up on my arms. He denied he did that. They came up in about an hour after he held me and that. So I put a restraining order on him.'

In a UK study of men who had used violence against known women, one man reported how he had damaged the face of the woman and so, inconveniently for him, as he saw it, he decided that she had to stay in the whole of the next week:

> [T]hese two massive black eyes and a broken nose. I couldn't believe it. I had two weeks off work. Anybody come to the door, I had to go to the door, I wouldn't let anybody in. Cos I felt ashamed of what I'd done. She wouldn't even go cash us child benefit. I had to go. I had to lock her in the house, take the keys with me. Lock her in the house in case somebody came.

From his point of view he had gone 'too far' in his violence, or had been too careless in its direction. In particular, this might have brought him into contact and difficulty with agencies and others outside the home, with further unwanted implications for him (Hearn, 1998: 211). In this sense, violence may also be used by men so that the woman is not visibly damaged more than is deemed necessary by the man.

The mark on Cheryl's face also had social consequences for her and her partner. It forced her to confide in her close male friend about her husband, Doug's violence. She was asked about the origin of the mark and then described his reaction: 'He said, "I don't know if I'm going to be able to work with him knowing that he's done that . . . To see that mark on your face". He said, "I'm going to kill him".' This comment suggests that now the friend knows about Doug's violence that he has questioned his ability to work and socialise with him. Accordingly, the presence of the bruises changed the social interactions and social relationships of the couple.

For Foucault the body is the field upon which the play of powers, knowledges and resistances is worked out. In this instance, the woman's body is the site for the interplay of women's knowledge about themselves and medico-legal knowledge of the woman's body. Having bruises legitimated Chloe's claim for medical assistance:

> When he actually threw me that night at the wall and [the kids] were just screaming, I just felt, 'I can't live like this any longer. It can't be. I need to take a hold and do something', and I rang a doctor because I was pretty badly bruised and I had a crook thigh and I think she said, 'You need to take a stand now. Even if you don't ever do anything, you need to go and find out where you stand just so you know'.

This conversation with the doctor empowered and mobilised Chloe to seek information from social security about the implications of leaving her husband and then subsequently information about men's groups. For other women such as Francine the shock and severity of the violence immobilised her, stopping her from seeking any medical attention. She reported:

> He grabbed a chair from the kitchen table and he went for me with the chair, with the four legs of the chair facing me. I had my hands over my head protecting me, but he got me in the head and I had huge bruises, and on the fingers and my knuckles, and I had big bruises on my arms and my leg and on my hip. . . . I should have gone to the doctor because I had a huge belt just at the back of my head, nearly to the centre but not quite, and that worried me because I was feeling dizzy and light-headed and hoping that I wasn't going to have a bleed, because . . . You know, getting injuries right on the brain stem at the back there I know can be dangerous and I was worried. But I was numb – I['d] become paralysed.

While Francine had become 'numb and paralysed', Rosa also 'found it hard to move'. Notions of immobilisation were part of both their injury narratives, enabling the women to describe the extent of their physical injuries and inability to seek help.

Physical markings such as bruises can inscribe the subject position of 'victim' of violence on women's bodies. Her bruises function as reminders of his violence for her/him and the children. They limit women's (and men's) public interactions such as social and work commitments. Bruises also provide evidence that the physical violence occurred. Bruises present on the surface of the body result in both medical and self-surveillance. Following severe physical abuse, women may attend the emergency department or their general practitioner to seek medical assistance. In these cases, the doctor has access to the woman's body which s/he can survey for bruises or injury. Doctors rely on the woman to reveal details about how the injuries occurred. A woman may or may not disclose the origins of her injuries. This ability of women to refuse disclosure can be understood as a form of resistance to the doctor who may invoke victim status or an intervention that she does not want. Bruises and injury markings on the body define the woman as a victim for the medical profession.

Within the institution of the violent domestic relationship the woman's body is the text upon which her male partner's fists, feet, knees, head or other parts of the body are the writing tools inscribing a language of violence upon her, and so rewriting that bodily text. Bruises on the surface of the woman's body resulting from male partner violence have several meanings and implications. They also provide visible reminders of the physical violence, enact self-surveillance, limit social interactions, act symbolically to encourage an end to the relationship, either mobilise women to seek help or immobilise them and their help-seeking behaviours and can inscribe the subject position of victim. The next section examines the emotional scars on the inside of women's bodies and the externalisation of these non-physical violences on the outside of women's bodies.

Inside-out: Experiences and meanings of emotional scars

The women's experiences described above suggest that bruises provide evidence of the severity of the injury and legitimacy that the violence occurred. With a bruise consent is questioned and force is implied. The bruise may become a prized possession that provides authenticity to the victim. In contrast, Jackie describes her feelings of emotional battery and the belief that she lacks the ability to claim victim status as she does not have the legitimacy of bruises:

> So you see it's very subtle and that's what I hate about this. I think if there was something really open – if I was bruised, for example – then I could say, 'Look, this is what's happening', but the only guide I've got is my feelings . . . I haven't got any bruises but I'm sure inside I feel just the same because I just feel so haggard inside.

Jackie indicates that the presence of bruises allows the representation of emotional hurt but in the absence of bruises she feels unable to legitimately claim 'victim' status. The public marking of bruises on the surface of women's bodies allow victim-status to be claimed if this is desired. Women, like Jackie, who do not have bruises, may query their own ability to experience or demonstrate victimisation.

A scar can manifest as either corporeal or emotional or both. It can be both a mark on the skin after a wound, a burn or a sore that has healed over and the lasting effect of personal misfortune or unpleasant experience on somebody's mind. Physical scars provide a permanent reminder or memory of an event. While, perhaps surprisingly, none of the women interviewed spoke of physical scars (as opposed to bruises) marking their body, nearly all spoke of some form of emotional scars from being wounded. This domestic wounding took many forms, not only physical violence but emotional, verbal, social and sexual. Physical scars are a visible reminder that damage has occurred; they appear on the outside or surface of the body, yet carry depth. They symbolise a point of penetration into the underlying fleshy depths of the body. In comparison emotional scars are hidden inside the body, not visible to the naked eye. A unifying feature or similarity between physical and emotional scars is the permanence of the injury or damage on or below the surface of the skin respectively.

Richard's verbal abuse has emotionally scarred Helen. In the following quotation she describes the effects of his verbal abuse:

> He gets angry because I can't say I love him. I can't because I can't love someone who's like this – up high and then, you know, like low, low, low. I can't turn it on and off like he can. He gets angry because he says, 'I love you, I love you', and then I can't, and he says, 'You haven't said "I love you" for six months' – or twelve months or whatever it is 'and it hurts'. I said, 'Well I'm sorry. I care about you a lot but I'm not going to say something I don't feel, because I can't turn round and say "I love you" after you've abused me and called me "bitch" in front of the children' – or other names. I said, 'I hate you, Richard, when you're like that – I really hate you.'

Helen is unable to say 'I love you' to Richard as she has been hurt and wounded by his verbal abuse and violences. His behaviour has meant that she has questioned her love for him. She has not questioned her commitment to the family.

Many of the women talked about the difficulty they had having sex with their partner following abuse and violences. This contrasts with the reluctance of men in a UK study who had used violence to known women to talk about the relation of their violence to sex and sexuality (Hearn, 1998: ch. 8). For the women interviewed for the present study, the memories of his abuse and violence permeated all aspects of their relationship, including the sexual. Cheryl talked about being torn between the two dimensions of her husband, especially during intimacy and sex with Doug. She found it difficult or impossible to be intimate and enjoy sensuous touch with him when memories of 'his painful touch' were also real to her:

> Cheryl: It's something I've had a hard time explaining to Doug. The sexual side is very hard for me with Doug because sometimes it's almost like the hurt, the pain. It's like I remember what he's done and I think, 'I can't', and I'm just not in the mood for it.

Michelle: The intimacy?

Cheryl: Yes, [pause] 'If you hurt me that many times Doug and you've touched me in anger that many times, how can you want to be intimate with me, and I don't want it from you just yet. I want to be able to say to you, 'No', without feeling frightened that I'm going to get hurt'. He hasn't been able to accept that.

The dissonance, articulated here by Cheryl, emerges from seeing Doug, who is both her husband and a perpetrator, as a fragmented subject containing both 'normal' and violent qualities. This echoes some men's own accounts of separating a past violent self and present non-violent self (Hearn, 1998: 106–7).

Liz Eckermann (1997) describes modernist sociological theory as engaging in a universal search for the integration of an individual's beliefs, attitudes, values and actions. Foucault argues against the search for 'internal consistency' proposing instead fragmented subject positions. He argues for a decentred approach to individual identity and social formations. Eckermann states that to agree with Foucault means that 'any given individual, and any particular society, can contain multiple, shifting and often self-contradictory identities' (Eckermann, 1997: 153).

While physical damage on the outside of the body, such as injuries and bruises, provide emotional scars on the psyche or inside of the body, so psychical injuries can manifest themselves in physical conditions on the outside of the body, that is psychosomatic complaints. In examining skin ailments, Jay Prosser (2001: 54) states: 'Psychic disturbance can inscribe on the skin traumatic memories according to the hysterical symptomisations of the unconscious.' In this view the unconscious has the capacity to inscribe its injuries upon the body. In the interviews Kate reflected on her experience of the corporeal manifestations of Sam's non-physical violence. Sam did not abuse Kate physically; his abuses were verbal, emotional and social. Sam and Kate would battle about many things, including the parenting of her children from a previous relationship. Kate was interviewed three times over a two-year period. Several attempts were made to meet with Kate who had extended periods of absence from work and had been in and out of a private psychiatric institution. When she was met on the second occasion she used a walker to assist her to move around. At this second meeting Kate explained her illnesses:

I ended up back in hospital – oh actually I was in hospital after [my daughter] left [home] for some time – because I developed what they

> call panic disorder as a result of extreme and prolonged stress. I also had arthritis, that's psoriatic arthritis, and fibromyalgia which both pop their ugly heads up when I'm under a lot of stress, so I'm also dealing with that at the moment as well. Yes, so I've got Domiciliary Care come out and give me some walking aids and stuff like that. I'm out of hospital but I rang my doctor today because I had a panic attack last night, quite a severe one, and I have troubles myself with suicidal thoughts even though it's not like me normally to be like that.

At this interview Kate discusses her series of illnesses – physical and mental ailments – she concludes that these thoughts and behaviours are not 'normal' or usual for her. At the third and final meeting Kate and Sam had broken-up and she was hesitant to meet. Kate had changed physically, besides her new haircut and colour, she had walked to answer the door to offer her greetings. During her final interview Kate accounts for the dramatic physical changes:

> I made up my mind at that moment [once the relationship was over] that I was going to move forward even if it was just a millimeter every day. And I started walking every day. Walked up to the top of the hill . . . There's a 'No Standing' sign [up] there. It should have a dent in there because every time I got there I used to belt that and go, 'That's for you Sam', because he told me I was useless and everything else and when I left him I couldn't walk, and I walked up that hill– I made myself walk up that hill – I hit that 'No Standing' sign and thought to myself, 'I'm going to walk'. I got rid of my walker, I got rid of everything. I stopped having headaches. Then I thought, 'I'll get a job'. Contacted my old bosses. They said, 'Never mind the reference. Will you come back and work for us?' and so I've been working ever since. . . . When I stopped getting the migraines. Sort of down the track and I thought, 'I haven't had a migraine for two months. Fancy that. It just happens to be the same amount of time I haven't been with Sam. I can walk now. Fancy that'. . . . there isn't anyone holding me back any more.

Kate identifies the corporeal and psychological healing that occurred after leaving the emotionally abusive relationship. Upon reflection and with hindsight Kate locates the source of her bodily and psychical ills as the manifestations of Sam's abuse. For Kate, the emotional wounding and scars manifest themselves as physical ailments. She believes that her mental and physical dysfunctioning would not have existed without his verbal abuse and violences. The most striking evidence of this is how Kate describes the timing of her newfound health, her bodily and emotional wellness, with the ending of the violent relationship.

Emotional scars exist and persist within women's bodies after the experience of men's violence. Emotional scars are not visible and so do not have the medical and legal legitimacy like physical scars and bruises on the outside of the body. Women describe them as being just as debilitating, if not more so, partly because the woman herself questions her legitimacy to claim victim status as there is no physical evidence of the damage or injury. Following the end of the relationship Kate interpreted her experience of a series of mental and physical ailments as being the result of living in a violent relationship. Kate was the target of Sam's repeated verbal, emotional and social violences. She appeared to absorb these violences internally, and they manifested themselves as physical ailments, including psoriatic arthritis and fibromyalgia.

Experiences and meanings of 'love-bites': A complex case of sex and violence

In talking about violence and the meanings that his violence has for them, some women spoke of 'love-bites', 'love bruises' or 'hickeys'. This was even though the women and men in this study were not specifically asked about love bites. The comments received about love bites were volunteered by women in the context of a broader discussion about women's experience of men's violence. None of the men interviewed offered a discussion on bestowing or receiving a hickey as part of his violence. This suggests that the men were not aware that women consider their hickey-bestowing behaviours as acts of violence. Compared with both physical bruises and emotional scars, 'love-bites' are arguably a more complex case. The experience of the love bite, whether it is defined (or redefined) as sexual or not, can be understood as existing at the intersections of outside-in and inside-out. It problematises that possible binary; its meanings may shift back and forth, from force upon the skin to force within the body, from sexual to violent, from internal memory to external sign.

Though love bites or hickeys can be found all over the body, their presence is only known to the public when visible outside of clothing, for example, on the neck of a woman signifying sexual activity, or even promiscuity. The meaning of a 'love-bite' is context-bound, often ambiguous; in the absence of another context, consent is usually assumed and pleasure implied. The love bite alone does not necessarily signify a violent relationship nor does it represent victim status. Without other signs of violence a 'love-bite' is, or at least can be, considered erotic. Love bites or hickeys can also suggest to some viewers sexual 'easiness' or kissing that has 'gone too far' (Alapack, 2007; Alapack et al., 2005; Tea, 2002). There can be both pride and/or embarrassment in the mark depending upon the audience – it can be shown off and worn as a 'badge', or ashamedly disguised.

The Norwegian and Danish psychologists Alapack et al. (2005) asked 52 adolescent students to describe one of several bodily experiences (including 'first kiss', 'most severe bout of jealousy', 'blushing in gendered encounter', 'moment of being caressed or pawed' or 'receiving or bestowing a hickey'). Eleven described the experience of receiving or bestowing a hickey, with a variety of meanings for the women and men interviewed. At the time of being interviewed the interviewees did not report being in a violent intimate relationship. Descriptions of hickeys in non-violent relationships involved awakening sexual desire, pleasure and new sexual thoughts. More private locations where no one else would see the hickey, such as on a male's inner thigh, were reported in some cases. One interviewee reported how the couple had hidden hickeys secretly located: 'near our genitals . . . in the afterglow of our first love-making . . . as tokens of our commitment . . . like fleshy engagement rings' (Alapack et al., 2005: 57).

In the interviews in the present study, whether as perpetrator or victim, the location of the hickey was found to be very significant and most usually public, as signs of possession or branding. From the interviews, Jodie commented about her unwanted hickey: 'he was carrying on before I was going out and forced a love bite on my neck, which made me more disgusted in him.' For her, it was significant that the non-consensual and 'forced' publicly located love bite came before she was going out. She was embarrassed and forced to wear the hickey as a body accessory in public; she had the ability to choose her clothes but not the hickey. The hickey served as a reminder of her disgust in him. In this case the use of the hickey may have been intended to prevent Jodie from going out socialising, itself a form of social control or social violence (Hanmer, 1996). So, while it would be difficult to argue that all love bites are violence, when they are delivered with violence or in violent contexts this is a more viable interpretation.

In a violent relationship love bites may be used as a means of control and (sexual) possession rather than for specifically erotic purposes. Sally discussed her partner's use of love bites on her neck as a method of control. He had given her hickeys on her neck the night before she started a new course at college. In this instance, the presence of recent hickeys on Sally's neck would provide a symbol, indicating to other men and women that Sally was not available sexually, and that she was already in a relationship. They were not married and had not exchanged rings, the usual sign of being unavailable sexually. In this instance the hickey's presence can be interpreted as signifying ownership or possession.

Within a relationship the hickey can also present itself as evidence of an affair. Chloe states:

> Things had been going so well and now this. It was really funny because like two days prior to that he had a mark on his neck and he was saying how something on the submarine had hit him and I thought, 'Oh strange place to hit you, on the neck', so I just started putting two and two together.

For Chloe, there were a series of suspicious events that lead to a confrontation with her husband about him having an affair. Even following this she could not be absolutely sure he was not having an affair because of the claims he made about the origins of the mark on his neck (that she assumed to be a hickey). She comments:

> [B]ut still to this day I don't really know if I know the truth about that because there was a mark on his neck and I don't know if that really scared him, because of this evidence, or whether it was something that knocked him at work and someone was trying to have a go at him.

While Chloe's interpretation of the mark on her husband's neck as a love bite provided her some visible evidence of an affair, his denial meant that she needed more information as the mark could plausibly be explained in other ways.

In the context of violent relationships love bites point to the complex intertwining of both sex, violence and marks and traces on the body, and also the Outside-in and the Inside-out. Love bites are also likely to have quite different meanings, for the men and women concerned, and depending on which party has the love bite, as well as where it is on the body. In particular, key questions are the relations of the love bite to violence (before, during, after), who gave it, when, and under what sexual, violent, sexually violent or other conditions. In such situations love bites may be better thought of as marks of sexual possession comparable to other forms of rape and sexual assault within marriage, dating and similar intimate relations, where sexual relations are usually presumed by others. Moreover, their very ambiguity, both as love bites themselves and in terms of the specific or assumed etiology adds another layer of embodied power and oppression. The very term, combining 'love' and 'bites', speaks of these ambiguities and thus the furthering of violence and wounding: the violencisation of sexuality in action (Hearn, 1998: 158).

Conclusion

Grosz's model of Inside-out and Outside-in is a powerful way of analysing the woman's body as target of men's violence in domestic and related contexts. It points to the examination of both physical and non-physical forms and effects of violence as they play themselves upon the inside and outside of women's bodies in the context of the violent relationship.

Marks of violence such as bruises on the outside or surface of the woman's body are when visible likely to be read as resulting from violence. Non-physical violences such as emotional scars do not always mark the external body skin in any clear and direct way but *appear* to mark or leave their mark on the interior life, the inside of the body, the 'soul'; they are not easily visible and require decoding. While love bites are markings on the outside of the body that are often visible, they also require specific contextual decoding, in relation to the complex intersections of sex and violence.

The bruise on the surface of the women's skin transgresses the privacy of the domicile and makes public the violence that is usually hidden and private. Bruises on the surface of the woman's body have the capacity to signify the woman as victim of domestic violence. They can result in public inquiry or forced confession about the violence. The bruises can lead to self-surveillance – changing behaviours to cover-up or protect themselves and the male perpetrator from the public gaze. The bruises and scars of 'domestic violence' located on the woman's body inscribe the subject position of 'victim'. This contrasts with male bruises which are often read as the heroic, victorious marks of sporting battle or injury. Grosz (1994) argues that these types of inscriptions are capable of re-inscription and transformation, and are capable of being lived and represented in quite different terms that may grant the woman the capacity for independence and autonomy.

An interesting example of this is the use of the concept of 'survivor' (as opposed to 'victim') within feminist literature and among health and welfare practitioners (Kelly et al., 1996; Dunn, 2005). Charmaine Power (1998), the Australian nurse and academic, deconstructs the victim/survivor binary, identifying the notion of 'strong woman' as an alternative identity for women who experience men's violences. At an individual level the medical profession seeks signs such as bruises on the woman's body, which come to symbolise and mark her as a victim of domestic violence. Depending on the degree of injury, the woman can choose to make these signs public and seek medical intervention, risking the label of victim, or she can redefine herself as a 'survivor' or 'strong woman'.

Without the bruises on the surface of their skin, some women feel unable to legitimately claim they are in a violent relationship. In their view the emotional hurt, pain, scars and wounding are not enough to seek support or appeal for help through medico-legal interventions. One woman, Kate, reported the presence of bodily physical and mental symptoms, which, she suggested, were psychosomatic outcomes resulting from her partner's non-physical abuses. Hence non-physical violence such as verbal, emotional and social abuses and woundings may have somatic consequences. Damage or injury on the surface of the skin, such as bruises, has a different effect to those which are not as visible – such as Kate's inability to walk. In the first case a clear message about violence (of some sort) is being transmitted; in the second case the message is at a different level, and is open to diverse interpretations.

Of key interest, in this context, is the interplay between the degree of visibility of markings (in view, under clothing, at the edge of view), the physical and other damage from violence of various kinds, and the meanings, sometimes ambiguous meanings, of some markings, most especially of love bites. Meanings may shift from force upon the skin to force within the body, from sexual to violent, from internal memory to external sign. Bestowing a love bite on the surface of the body in a publicly visible location can be manipulative, branding the woman as taken or sexually unavailable. Importantly, love bites do not stand alone, out of context, as a symbol of violence within the relationship. The relationship context surrounding the nature of the mark is needed – that is, the non-consensual, forced and wounding context. Without the relationship context, the love bite is likely to remain the branding of being sexually unavailable, and even potentially erotic. What might be construed and experienced with pride in some sexual, loving and caring contexts might be a source of further pain and shame in another. In such potential ambiguity lies their experiential power. What can be a sign of love, devotion and commitment can transform to a sign of possession, ownership and violence, and thus be all the more wounding. Love bites stand, in some senses, at the intersections of outside-in and inside-out, and thus can be said to problematise further what are already problematised binaries.

Notes

1. The National Health and Medical Research Council (NH&MRC) of Australia funded this project, and Margie Ripper, University of Adelaide, was the chief investigator.
2. At second interview 54 men and at third interview 39 men.
3. At second interview 31 women and at third interview there were 27 women.
4. That study, conducted 1991–3 in the UK, involved interviews with 75 men on their violence to known women, of whom 60 were included in the main analysis, together with 130 follow-up research contacts with agency staff who had dealt with the men.
5. In South Australia schoolteachers are required to report incidences of suspected child abuse or neglect, through mandatory reporting legislation; this role does not, however, extend to the reporting of suspected domestic violence against adult women.
6. A Restraining Order is a legal remedy that may be sought in South Australia and elsewhere.

5

Harming or Healing? The Meanings of Wounding among Sadomasochists Who Also Self-Injure

Ani Ritchie

This chapter draws on the representation of self-injury[1] and sadomasochism (SM)[2] in the film *Secretary* (Shainberg, 2002) as a starting point from which to explore the narratives of women who, like the central character 'Lee' in *Secretary*, have engaged in both self-injury and SM (either historically or currently). I focus specifically on participants' relationship to wounding in those contexts, particularly the aesthetics of breaking the skin. The chapter begins by outlining academic approaches to self-injury and SM, and then describes the narrative of self-injury and SM offered in *Secretary*. Having thus contextualised the empirical work, the analysis focuses on the conflicting narratives of self-injury and SM that emerged in the research. Participants engaged either with a discourse of self-injury and SM as completely separate, or one which positioned them as similar with SM being a more 'healing' way of exploring emotions associated with self-injury. Finally, the chapter addresses the aesthetics of wounding and scarring, where participants drew on similarly conflicting discourses of harming and healing.

The epistemological position adopted here is social constructivist feminism (Percy, 1998), meaning that I am interested in the impact of 'cultural formations' (Sisson, 2005) on gender and on narratives of identity and sexual storytelling (Plummer, 1995). The social constructivist position argues that 'we actively and purposefully construct and interpret our own realities from the meanings that are available to us' (Taylor and Ussher, 2001: 295). Accessing narratives of that construction or interpretation of participants' 'own realities' enables researchers to explore the discourses available (for example, which are dominant in a given culture or subculture), and the ways in which individuals negotiate their own practices in relation to those discourses. The narratives presented here are drawn from focus groups (FG) and online interviews (Int.)

designed to explore constructions of self-injurious and SM behaviours. FG have been particularly advocated in research on sexuality (Frith, 2000) and on 'sensitive topics' (Farquhar with Das, 1999) and have been central to my previous work on SM (Ritchie and Barker, 2005). Frith warns that participants in FG can 'censure the views of their peers' (2000: 286), although she stresses that points of conflict can be useful for researchers to examine. In this research, follow-up online interviews enabled deeper exploration of points of conflict in the FG, particularly where group consensus might have inhibited participants' talk.

The participant focus in this work is bisexual women who historically have or currently self-injure *and* who historically have or currently engage in SM. Additionally all the participants had watched *Secretary* prior to the research process (although not as part of it). Fourteen participants took part in one of the two FG and/or an online interview. Consistent with previous research (and despite trying to attract a more diverse group), participants were predominantly white British women and 'also tended to be "middle-class", educated and belonged to professional occupational groups' (Taylor and Ussher, 2001: 296). They ranged in age from 21 to 43, with an average (mean) age of 28. Half the participants (anonymised here as Anne, Corrine, Eliza, Emma, Gemma, Jemima and Maddie) currently engaged in self-injury of some description. The rest (Amelia, Julia, June, Kath, Lin, Sarah and Tia) did not, with the length of time since their last experience of self-injury ranging from two to ten years. Participants described a range of self-injurious practices, including wrist and head banging, cutting, burning and bruising. All the participants were currently engaged in SM activities of some description and most had experience of both dominant (top) and submissive (bottom) roles. SM activities described included spanking, beating, burning, cutting and play piercing (temporary piercing of skin usually using hypodermic needles).

Approaches to self-injury and SM

SM has been central to feminist debates and in the 'sex wars' of the 1980s, divided feminism(s) into orthodox lesbian feminism and radical pro-sex feminism (Healey, 1996). Pro-sex feminists such as Rubin argued that the stance adopted by lesbian feminists who positioned SM as 'inherently anti-feminist' (Rubin, 1984: 302) was misinformed. Writers from this orthodox feminist perspective argued that SM was 'firmly rooted in patriarchal sexual ideology' (Linden et al., 1982: 5). For Russell, '[S]adomasochism results in part from the internalization of heterosexual dominant-submissive role playing and for lesbians, involves an additional 'internalization of a homophobic heterosexual view of lesbians' (1982: 176). These claims have been challenged by empirical work with lesbian, bisexual and heterosexual sadomasochists however, where some women explicitly link their SM practices to feminist ideals and a critique of gendered power (Taylor and Ussher, 2001; Ritchie and Barker, 2005).

Self-injury is (unlike SM) much more common in women than men (Babiker and Arnold, 1997) and additionally occurs with greater frequency in sexual minority groups (Davies and Neal, 1996), yet has attracted considerably less feminist attention. Research tends to focus on clinical populations, as has also been the case with empirical research on SM (Taylor and Ussher, 2001). Of particular note here is the extent to which research on both practices are therefore biased towards participants of white and middle-class backgrounds. Babiker and Arnold point to evidence suggesting that non-white and working-class people are less likely to seek and/or be offered psycho-therapeutic support (1997: 47–9) and would therefore be under-represented in the clinical populations from which research participants have historically been drawn. Most work focuses on 'treatment' (Walsh and Rosen, 1988) for self-injury; few authors have attempted to explore what Levenkron (1999: 104) calls 'the benefits of self-wounding' might be. Writing on the 'language of injury', Babiker and Arnold (1997) draw attention to the role of self-injury in communicating emotional distress. Walsh and Rosen highlight the role of self-cutting as a 'highly visible' marker of distress (1988: 32), while Miller offers an understanding of self-injury based on 'hidden pain, visible hurting' (2005: 7).

A central theme in much of the academic and psychological and self-help literature on self-injury is an assumed link to childhood abuse, and similar discourses operate in discussions of SM (see Linden et al., 1982). Strong (2000) claims '[O]ne of the most disturbing aspects of cutting is the strong link it appears to have to childhood sexual abuse' (2000: xviii). Strong draws a direct parallel between self-injury and SM in her book, *A Bright Red Scream*, in which she describes the narrative of 'Rita' who does not self-injure (indeed one might question the inclusion of her story in the text which is on self-mutilation), 'denies any abuse' and enjoys consensual piercing and blood play as 'good clean fun', but is pathologised by Strong for 'eventually' disclosing 'some darker issues that may shed light on her bodily preoccupation' (2000: 144–5). Miller supports this position in her description of women who engage in SM as 'attempting to master the childhood trauma by repeating it over and over [. . .] parallel to the experience she creates for herself when she engages in her self-harmful behaviours' (2005: 136). Implicit in these ideas and explicit in more recent writing by Jeffreys is the idea that SM might be a form of 'self-harming by proxy' (Jeffreys, 2000) for women.

Surprisingly little research has explored the discursive construction of boundaries between self-injury and SM by women who have experienced both, or who understand 'what it means' (Hart, 1998: 3) to engage in such practices, despite the parallels drawn in both sets of literature described here. Jeffreys (1986, 2000) claims internalised self-hatred feeds both behaviours (presumably Russell, 1982, would agree); Strong (2000) and Miller (2005) insist that both are attempts to re-enact childhood trauma. In contrast, Taylor and Ussher's participants are clear to draw boundaries between consensual SM and pathological SM where practitioners may go 'beyond the limits' and also self-injure (2001: 309). Here I explore the narratives of a group of women who (like Lee in *Secretary*) appear to have some links between their self-injury and SM practices, but who construct and police boundaries between them, relying on different meanings associated with wounding.

Cultural constructions of self-injury and SM

Recently authors have begun to explore the increased cultural visibility (Sisson, 2005) and 'mainstreaming' (Weiss, 2006) of SM in popular culture. This increased visibility adds to discursive constructions and meanings that are available to be drawn on or refuted in constructivist accounts of SM and self-injury. However the image of SM offered in these representations continues to draw boundaries between acceptable and unacceptable behaviours. Weiss claims that representations of SM such as that in *Secretary*

> Allow the mainstream audience to flirt with danger and excitement, but ultimately reinforce boundaries between protected and privileged normal sexuality, and policed and pathological not normal sexuality. (2006: 105)

This is supported in the participants' readings of the text (to be discussed shortly), where the representation was felt to construct certain kinds of SM (notably spanking) as acceptable but others as not, as well as succumbing to a heteronormative narrative resolution. Specific to the focus of this chapter, in *Secretary*, a narrative of self-injury being replaced by SM links the two practices in a way that draws on discourses of both pathology and 'healing'. Barker et al. (2007) suggest that in the film

> BDSM is fairly explicitly presented as a healthy method of achieving whatever the self-injury achieved, whilst self-injury is something that Lee has to stop completely in order to achieve her 'happily ever after'. (2007: 204)

Before I explore participants' responses to these narratives of pathology and healing, a more detailed introduction to the film is required.

Secretary opens with the central protagonist Lee Holloway (Maggie Gyllenhaal) shackled to a spreader bar. As she enters the office of E. Edward Grey (James Spader) and closes the door behind her, the film jumps back in time to 'six months earlier' (indicated by text to that effect). Here Lee's narrative begins with her discharge from a psychiatric institution. This sets up the discourse of pathology, which as Weiss argues 'allows the viewer to understand Lee as a person who is defined by a pathological sexuality' (2006: 117). Lee returns home as her sister is getting married, demonstrating the heteronormative relationship pattern that she will later be expected to assume. The family home is chaotic and abusive and Lee responds to this by retreating to her room to self-injure. Her method is ritualised and involves a carefully laid out 'kit' of implements for cutting, and she later self-injures by burning her thigh with a boiling kettle. Shortly after this, Lee starts working for Edward, whose characterisation also draws on narratives of pathology (he is obsessive and uses exercise as a form of self-control and punishment). Lee and Edward's working relationship becomes increasingly bizarre (for example, Edward has Lee searching through rubbish bins for files). He then notices wounding from her self-injury, and shortly afterwards interrupts her in the act at her desk. He calls her into his office to ask her why she cuts herself and when she has no answer, he offers one:

> Is it that sometimes the pain inside has to come to the surface, and when you see evidence of the pain inside, you finally know you're really here? Then when you watch the wound heal it's comforting, isn't it?

Edward then tells her that she is 'not going to do that again', and sends her home early, instructing her to walk 'in the fresh air' during which she muses (in a voice over) 'I was feeling something growing in Mr. Grey, an intimate tendril creeping from one of his darker areas, nursed on the feeling that he had discovered something about me'. The next day Lee leaves her self-injury kit at home, but makes a deliberate typing mistake. With no warning (or negotiation!) Edward bends Lee over the desk and has her read aloud from the mistyped letter as he spanks her. The SM continues, and seems to replace Lee's self-injury as well as increasing her self-confidence. Edward then abruptly ends the relationship, and in the climax of the film, Lee wins him back by abandoning her intended fiancé (Peter) and proving her submission to Edward by sitting at his desk for three days in her wedding dress. Weiss writes, 'the film's happy ending redeemed BDSM by refolding it back into normative constructions of sexuality' (2006: 115). The 'perils of this visibility' for SM (Weiss, 2006: 124) are that SM becomes viewed (for Weiss's non-SM participants) through either 'normalising' or 'pathologising' strategies (ibid.). In the following sections I explore the narratives of women who engage with *Secretary* not at the level of 'distanced consumption' (p. 105), as Weiss's participants do, where SM is viewed from 'detached, privileged, and normative' positions (ibid.), but as way of reflecting on and reconstructing their own connected, disadvantaged and non-normative experiences. *Secretary* is consequently used here as a way into participants' own narratives of self-injury and SM in the context of more dominant, discursive constructions.

Reading *Secretary*

Participant responses to *Secretary* focused on Lee's move from self-injury to SM, setting the foundations for later discussion about their own constructions of such behaviours. Participants expressed frustration at the film because 'it's the only thing we have! So it has to be right and it's not' (June, FG2). Jemima felt that since 'it's one of the few SM representations in the cinema, in Hollywood cinema then, um, you know, I wish it could have been a bit clearer that you know, it's not so borderline un-consensual as that' (FG2). Jemima also expressed disappointment that the film is 'one of the first Hollywood portrayals of SM and self-harm and [. . .] it links them' (FG2). This was echoed in Corrine's comment: 'I felt uncomfortable with the way that Lee and Edward's relationship could be considered an extension of Lee's self-harming' (Int.). Linking to discussions about consent, participants were particularly concerned about the narrative of Lee ceasing to self-injure because Edward tells her to. Jemima felt that this was 'well over the line' and June agreed that this was 'a bit like the SM version of blackmail, you know, if you love me you wouldn't do this'. In an interview after the FG however, Kath argued, 'while I can see why people objected to this as a narrative, it made sense to me on the level of personal experience' (Int.).

Corrine also drew on personal experience in her reading: 'I think the representation of self-injury is very realistic. The scene where she cuts herself in her room and quietly fixes herself up is very reminiscent of my own experiences' (Int.). Participants were less sure about the representation of Lee's response to her self-injurious activity, discussing the extent to which Lee looked 'almost like it's not painful at all, it's just this like, this look of pure bliss she's got on her face' (Eliza, FG2). June felt this 'idea of getting pleasure as the sort one might experience as a masochist out of it is not, that's certainly not my experience of it' (FG2). Similar debates played out in the first FG, where participants constructed different experiences of pain or hurting in relation to self-injury and SM cutting. Levenkron writing on self-injury claims: 'Our first task, then, is to interpret the act of self-mutilation. Is it a love of pain? Does the cutter *enjoy* pain? Is this like masochism, where the pain alone is the end in and of itself?' (1999: 26). Participants reading of Lee's expression as 'pure bliss' position her as pathologically masochistic, something participants were keen to distance themselves from. Emma (describing the difference between self-cutting and SM cutting) said 'when I cut it's not about hurting and it often doesn't hurt very much' (FG1). For Truscott (1991), an essential part of SM is the reframing (reinterpreting) of pain into 'sensations of changing, sometimes increasing intensity rather than considering it something to be avoided as we do under ordinary circumstances (1991: 24). This boundary setting seems to function to mark participants' construction of pain as 'different' from that of Lee and therefore challenge the pathologising discourse of masochism. Similar boundary setting was found in my previous work on SM where women made distinctions between fantasy and reality in order to construct SM activities as distinct from sexual violence, although importantly, as here, participants recognised the tensions in those discourses (Ritchie and Barker, 2005).

Participants also focused on the way Lee seems to replace self-injury with SM. Corrine wrote, '[A]lthough I was initially concerned that the SM element of the film could be constructed as an extension of self-injury/ self-harm, I don't believe this to be the case.' She went on to explain that she viewed Lee's self-injury as 'a coping mechanism' and that 'throughout the course of the film she becomes empowered through her SM relationship' (Int.). Kath agreed that 'I think she does it [self-injury] because she's not happy and then she becomes happy. [. . .] She stops partly because he asks her to and partly because she doesn't want to do it anymore' (FG2). In the FG Eliza had mentioned the overlapping of her SM and self-injury cutting (contrasting with Lee's narrative) and in her interview I asked her more about that. She wrote, 'Being a top that cuts may seem like a contradiction; I do often wonder how common it is' (Int.), but was otherwise keen to separate her self-injury and SM, writing 'Maybe there's some psychological reason – I don't really want to know'. This tension about the potential link between self-injury and SM was key to the conflicting narratives of participants' own experiences.

Conflicting narratives of harming and healing

In explorations of their own self-injury and SM, participants generally adopted one of the following two positions: that the experiences and/or emotions associated with SM and self-injury are 'completely completely separate things' (Julia, FG1) or that the experiences and/or emotions associated with self-injury might be explored through SM, drawing on a discourse of 'SM as therapy' (Lin, FG1). Participants were not necessarily consistent in these positions, highlighted in discussions about the potential for 'self-injury by proxy', which was used to underscore the boundaries between self-injury and SM. Further explanation of this was requested.

Participants who drew on the discourse that self-injury and SM were separate maintained that the emotions associated with self-injury were 'diametrically opposite' (Emma, FG1) from those associated with SM. Several participants such as Julia 'can't even imagine the two of them connecting in any way' (FG1). In the following extract Gemma explains her oppositional experiences of self-injury and SM:

> SM is massively positive and wonderful and self-harm is just absolutely everything that is horrible, experience of you know, mental anguish and being unable to express stuff and get it out, they're total opposites.
> (Gemma, FG1)

These types of statements position SM as 'massively positive' and often drew on a discourse of sexual pleasure, as June does here: 'SM is for fun and you know, it's sexual, and well, okay, for me it's sexual, it's a pleasurable thing' (FG2). In contrast self-injury is 'not the slightest bit fun' (June, FG2), but 'horrible' (Anne, Int.). Participants also marked self-injury as distinct from SM because it happened in private: 'it's like my dirty little secret and I keep it to myself' (Corrine, Int.), in contrast to SM which was about enjoying 'the dynamics with someone else' (Anne, Int.) or the 'positive synergy going on' (June, FG2).

The key distinction drawn in this narrative was of 'headspace' (Gemma, FG1), or as Kath said: 'the major and obvious difference is the mood you are in' (FG2). The different emotional/psychological positioning of self-injury and SM allowed participants to maintain separateness even where the physical wounding of both activities were similar:

> Another reason to keep them separate is because I SH [self-harm] as a coping mechanism and SM is something I enjoy. Sure, some of the physical sensations may be the same, but my mental reactions are different.
>
> (Corrine, Int.)

For Corrine, the experiences of self-injury and SM needed to be kept separate partly because of her (and other participants') concerns about using SM as 'self-harm by proxy'. Other participants echoed similar concerns and were worried about the ethics of bottoming (subbing) when they wanted to self-injure. In the first FG Gemma said that for her, self-injury and SM were 'utterly utterly different [. . .] completely different headspaces' and countered the idea that SM might be a 'better' way of expressing the feelings she associated with self-injury, to which Emma responded:

> If you're in that state where you're actually, coming to self-harm, coz I do, I mean if you're in that particular frame of mind getting someone to hurt you is just, is using them in a way that really you shouldn't.

Jeffreys claims that SM (as well as cosmetic surgery and piercing practices) is self-injury by proxy in which

> [A]lthough the cutting in these contexts is carried out under the aegis of medicine or beauty, or even sexual liberation, it often replicates quite precisely the techniques used by solitary self-mutilators. Self-mutilation by proxy is linked to self-mutilation in private.
>
> (2000: 414)

However, when asked about the relationship between their SM and self-injury all but two participants (Emma and Tia) in this study drew clear boundaries around SM not replicating their self-injurious behaviours, particularly in terms of 'techniques', also in terms of the site of wounding on the body. An important aspect of maintaining differences between self-injury and SM was participants marking self-injury as taking place on specific parts of the body, particularly where the act was the same, for example June self-injured by cutting her arms but preferred SM cutting to be on more 'sexually charged' parts of her body (FG2). Jemima had talked about doing cutting as part of SM with her partners but was clear she wouldn't want someone to use the same type of implement (a razor blade) that she used for self-injuring, because 'that would be too, too mixed up'. (FG2). Participants also drew boundaries between other SM activities that were similar to their self-injurious behaviour. Amelia had primarily used burning as her form of self-injury, and felt that being burnt in an SM scene would be 'too close', and that she needed 'limits around it not feeling like what I used to do' (FG1). The two participants who had described engaging in SM that replicated their self-injury in these terms both expressed tension about that replication. Emma self-injured by cutting her arm and had recently been consensually cut in the same place during an SM scene which afterwards she felt uncomfortable about. Some of these tensions around maintaining differences also appeared in the contrasting narrative of SM as potentially therapeutic, as will now be explored.

Recent work has highlighted a new discourse of SM as potentially therapeutic (Barker et al., 2007), and participants in this research drew (tentatively) on this in their discussions. Just as the notion of 'head-space' was central to maintaining very separate constructions of self-injury and SM, it played an important role in participants' narratives of therapeutic or 'healing' SM. Some participants felt that SM could be used to explore similar emotions to those involved in self-injury. Tia said, 'they are linked for me because a lot of the spaces I've explored submissively have been about that kind of place I can go with self-harm [. . .] so it's sort of, a bit similar.' Anne wrote that both self-injury and SM 'can be about physical pain and it distracting from emotions, the clearing out of my head' (Int.). Corrine (who was clear about wanting to maintain boundaries between self-injury and SM) wrote:

> However, the processes involved in both are a kind of escapism. It shuts out the outside world, leaving me to concentrate on what I'm feeling (or, if I'm topping, someone, what they might be feeling).
>
> (Corrine, Int.)

June felt that SM could be therapeutic because of this element of 'escapism', and had used 'quite heavy D/s' (dominant/submissive play) as a way of getting out of shitty feeling headspace' (FG2). In a later interview she explained:

> It feels like the same sort of outcome, but from a different angle – in some sense, SI [self-injury] is about increasing control, or exerting control on yourself, and that's what quiets the panic/upset. Whereas heavy submission is about giving up control. [. . .] But in both cases there's a refocusing of your mind on something other than the stress/upset/panic/etc.

In contrast to the concern voiced by some participants about the potential for self-injury by proxy coming from negative headspaces, June felt that SM could be therapeutic in '[T]imes when there's just too much noise going on in my head and I want to cut [SI] and I've been able to do that [SM] instead' (FG2). Lin was cautiously positive about this potential for SM, saying

> if somebody came to me and said 'I cut myself and I find it therapeutic and I'd like to experiment with it in a scene', I would certainly consider it, you know, but then it's part of the SM as therapy thing for me.
>
> (Lin, FG1)

Weille's (2002) participants drew on a similar 'therapeutic' discourse in their themes of 'repetition' and 'repair' in their SM practices. In this work only one participant, Tia (who primarily engaged in face slapping as self-injury), had actually experimented with replicating that in SM scenes where she felt 'that could be done in a positive way' (FG1). She described scenes that were about

> letting someone feel really crappy about themselves and get out that kind of low self-esteem and then the aftercare bit of really negating those, letting them get out those voices and then kind of countering those voices.
>
> (Tia, FG1)

Both Julia and Emma agreed with Tia to an extent with the idea of the 'catharsis of getting it out' (Julia) and then 'afterwards to be looked after' (Emma) (all, FG1). Although Jemima (FG2) was wary of linking self-injury and SM, she echoed the idea of aftercare being centrally important to her, saying that 'some part at least of my cutting is that I give myself permission to be nice to myself afterwards' and that this was also an important element of her SM.

For some participants who drew on this therapeutic discourse there was tension in recognising potential links between self-injury and SM, particularly when the issue of similar activities or spaces on the body were raised (as discussed above). Amelia's concerns about burning in scene being 'too close' to her self-injury was not something that she wanted to 'work through in that context'. Corrine was similarly unsure about using similar practices in SM scenes as she did in self-injuring.

> I've never tried cutting or play piercing, although I want to. [. . .] I had a bit of a mental wrangle about this just over a year ago – I felt like my desire to be marked like this in play was a contradiction, given that it could be confused with my marking from harming myself.
>
> (Corrine, Int.)

As well as maintaining boundaries between 'headspace', specific activities and particular bodily spaces then, participants also relied on boundaries of marking, specifically the aesthetics of wounding and the relationship to scarring to distinguish between self-injury and SM, as the next section of analysis will explore.

The aesthetics of wounding and scarring

One of the central issues raised in the FR was the way participants related to wounding (and consequent scarring) of their bodies. In the following extract Kath is discussing similarities between her experiences of cutting as part of self-injury and SM:

> Aesthetically there is a similarity. I like the look of having cut myself and I like the look of it having been done.
>
> (Kath, FG2)

Kath was the only participant who engaged with this aesthetic discourse for both self-injury and SM wounding. Although for most of the participants there was an element of focus on the visual appearance of self-injury (for a number of reasons, which will shortly be described), the notion of aesthetic beauty was applied only to wounding from SM. Particularly interesting here was the way participants who (like Kath) had experience of using the same act of wounding (here cutting) in both self-injury and SM contexts constructed a distinction between the two.

In a later interview, Kath elaborated on the pleasure she took from self-injury, writing

> in my case, cutting isn't just about self-injury, but also a bit about body modification, almost like a temporary tattoo. I'm not really trying to punish myself; I'm trying to control my environment and to create something new on myself.
>
> (Kath, Int.)

For all of the other participants, the idea of punishment was a strong motivation for self-injuring and this was often linked to self-loathing (Strong, 2000). Anne wrote, 'self-harm is a way to firstly stop me from having my brain tangled up in negative thoughts and emotions by inflicting sheer physical pain on my body and secondly a way to punish myself' (Int.). There was a clear focus on the visibility of wounding in terms of marking the desired release or punishment in the narratives of participants here (with the exception of Kath). Eliza described ritualised self-injurious behaviour in terms of how the cutting looked and explained, 'This was never really about feeling, but about seeing.' Like Corrine, Eliza had changed her self-injuring behaviour from less visual techniques (wrist banging) to cutting. She stressed the role of the visual marker of 'enough blood' as evidence that she could stop cutting. For a number of the participants, the act of self-cutting was partly an act of rendering visible their psychological distress (Walsh and Rosen, 1988). Eliza said in her interview: 'I cut to see the pain that I'm in, to make visible my frustration.' Describing her mother's response to her self-injury Eliza explained, 'I didn't do it to you, I did it quite *visibly* to me' (Int.).

For most participants, the relationship to cutting or other wounding from SM was different to that of self-injury, with more attention placed on the aesthetics and erotics of wounding. For example, Jemima had 'watched and photographed cutting scenes' and felt that cutting in that context was 'erotic and beautiful' in contrast to self-injurious cutting of which she wrote, 'I can't stand to watch' because it looked 'scary and uncontrolled' (Int.). Lin said,

> We do a lot of things that people think are hideous and we think of them as beautiful [. . .] when I cut somebody a lot of it is about putting my mark on them actually.
>
> (Lin, FG1)

From the perspective of Lin who principally tops (taking the dominant role in SM scenes), the wounding she inflicts is 'beautiful' in contrast to what she understands of the dominant societal discourse, which renders them 'hideous'. Emma echoes this later in the group: 'cutting, deliberate breaking of the skin is not a natural thing [. . .] it's not even a cultural thing in our culture.' Emma draws on a discourse of 'decorative cutting' and 'artistic cutting' to position the cutting she receives in SM as distinct from that which she inflicts on herself. 'Decorative' or 'Artistic' cutting is 'very deliberate and very carefully done' in contrast to her self-injury which happens in 'a kinda frenzy' (FG1).

In relation to other marking from SM (particularly bruising), participants enjoyed 'how they look' (Anne). Often this was linked to pride and pleasure in endurance. Jemima wrote, 'I like the marks and bruises I get in scenes very much too, for similar reasons – survival, and the memory of a great time' (Int.), and Eliza wrote that in contrast to her self-injury marks, 'marks made in scene I wear like a badge of honour'. In some ways, as will be argued in the final section of this chapter, the marking gained in SM functions to signify a 'real' encounter in the context of 'fantasy'. Salecl (1998) suggests that the experience of pain in SM play helps participants to bring bodily experiences into the symbolic. While SM was positioned as fantasy and 'play', the very 'real' marking from these activities was used to support narratives of desirability and identity.

Private/public scarring

Participants offered conflicting narratives of their relationship to scarring from self-injury. Corrine wrote:

> I'm not entirely sure how I feel about my scars. Sometimes I'm proud of them. They show where I've come from, where I've been, what made me what I am today. Medals of honour, of courage, of bravery. [. . .] Sometimes I fucking hate them. They're ugly. They serve as memories of the bad times, meaning that I can never forget them.
>
> (Int.)

Some participants related to their scarring as a visible marker of endurance or the passing of time. Anne said of hers, 'I do actually like them in an "I made that" type of way and also as a reminder of time passing'. Most participant narratives supported Levenkron's claim that self-injury was accompanied by 'a sense of shame and fear of social stigma, causing the individual to attempt to hide scars' (1999: 25). Eliza wrote that her decision to self-injure only on her thigh was partly because 'I do not want the pity that might come with scarred arms, nor do I want the assumption that I'm desperate for the attention of my peers' (Int.). Eliza was careful to avoid scarring from self-injury because

> I couldn't bear to look at myself if I ever get in inverted commas 'better' and look back going 'yeah but look what you used to be like, look what you did, you were one fucked up girl'.
>
> (Eliza, FG2)

For Eliza then, a narrative of healing involves getting 'better' and having self-injury 'all behind' her. Levenkron writes that scars 'become the most visible and explicit stigma for the recovered cutter to deal with' (1999: 242) and Eliza's discourse of 'recovery' or ('in inverted commas') 'better' requires that she avoids scarring and 'the pity' or social stigma that might come alongside that. Kath felt in contrast that scarring from self-injury was more socially acceptable than that from SM, writing,

> I'd prefer not to have any scars at all [. . .] I don't hate them, I just slightly wish they weren't there I prefer the ones from SI to the ones from scening – possibly because SI seems slightly more socially acceptable than cutting for pleasure?
>
> (Int.)

Eliza draws on a boundary construction of 'inside your own social group' compared with the broader social discourses drawn on by Kath above. In that context she feels that being assumed to have engaged in SM is more desirable than self-injury, saying 'I would much rather have someone think that I had been getting up to something a bit dodgy than I'd been self-harming' (FG2).

In relation to publicly visible marking from SM, participants offered similarly conflicting narratives. As Eliza said, 'it depends on whether you are inside your own social group or not' (FG2). Some participants expressed concern at publicly displaying marks from SM because of the way that they might be (mis)understood by others, Jemima said:

> I am not scared of people thinking I am doing SM; I'm just scared of people thinking I am being beaten up or am in an abusive relationship. I am scared of people worrying about that, that I might be, you know, in a situation that's really bad for me whereas obviously the SM is entirely positive for me.
>
> (FG2)

Conclusions

The 'mainstreaming' (Weiss, 2006) of SM representation has, despite the tendency to 'ultimately reinforce boundaries between protected and privileged normal sexuality, and policed and pathological not normal sexuality' (Weiss, 2006: 105), broadened the range of possible discourses for constructivist identities to draw on. However, I have argued that the representation of self-injury and SM found in *Secretary* is seen as problematic by those participants who engaged in both practices principally because of the link it draws between them. In relation to their own self-injury and SM practices, participants drew boundaries that were emotional, physical or bodily, and relational. Self-injury was marked by 'noisy' headspaces and 'emotional distress', whereas SM was marked as 'massively positive' and as only taking place when participants were in a 'good' headspace. Participants drew embodied boundaries, with self-injury and SM wounding taking place on separate parts of their bodies and often with different types of wounding or implements. Finally, participants maintained self-injury as private, with SM taking place within a relational dynamic. Some participants had less clear boundaries where a discourse of 'healing' was drawn on but tensions were evident here in their discussions of self-injuring by proxy.

The central issue raised here has been the aesthetics of wounding and scarring in both self-injury and SM. Generally participants privileged the visible wounding of self-injury as a private expression of relief, endurance or punishment but expressed anxiety about that marking being seen by anyone. The visible marking of SM was used to evidence similar experiences, but were less tensely related to within participants' own social contexts, worn as 'badges of honour' and cherished as reminders of desirability. Some similar discourses emerged in narratives of self-injury and SM, marking and scarring from both was evidence of having endured – 'a mark of survival' (Jemima, FG2). Hart argues that '[t]o a certain extent, the controversy over whether s/m is "real" or performed is naïve, since we are always in representation even when we are enacting our seemingly most private fantasies' (Hart, 1998: 91). In representing (via inscribing on the body) the performative practice of SM outside of the scene in which the marking was gained, perhaps participants are able to maintain the sense of endurance, desirability and power that they have experienced within it. Participants contrasted this with marking from self-injury, a form of 'rendering visible' about which they felt shame. These boundary settings allowed participants to counter narratives that pathologised SM by linking it to self-injury and the suggestion that SM might be used to self-injure 'by proxy'. That countering enabled participants to maintain discourses of desirability in relation to SM, either as a 'therapeutic' exploration of the negative emotions associated with self-injury or as something 'diametrically opposed' and 'massively positive'.

Participants drew different boundaries between self-injury and SM according to recognised dominant discourses either within their subcultural group or in broader social settings. The boundary setting outlined in this chapter is produced within a particular (marginalised) (sub)culture and the fact that participants construct differences between self-injury and SM may say more about the way in which they perceive these behaviours are viewed by those 'outside' that culture than how separate they actually are. Hart suggests that the tension in these issues is that 'the struggle is not to avoid repetition but to repeat with differences that are transformative' (1998: 160). In the narratives presented here there is the discursive possibility for participants to transform the experiences and emotions associated with self-injury through SM, but that transformative potential is tempered by the need to construct differences between SM and self-injury in order to counter discourses which link and pathologise both.

Notes

1. Self-injury is a practice for which many of the available labels are value laden, for example 'self-mutilation' (Babiker and Arnold, 1997) assumes that such behaviour is mutilating the bodies of the women who engage in it. I use 'self-injury' to describe self-inflicted harm to the body (many participants used the term 'self-harm').
2. I use SM to describe consensual and erotic power exchange with the giving and receiving of sensation which can include the exchange of painful sensations (which might or might not be constructed as 'painful' by the receiver). Just as with self-injury, terminology for SM is value laden with the legacy of pathologising discourses of psycho-sexuality. I choose to use SM rather than S/M or S&M here because SM is grounded in a relational exchange of power, thus elements of sadism and masochism are inextricably linked.

6
Making the Moves: Masculinities, Bodies, Risk and Death in the 'Extreme' Sport of Rock Climbing

Victoria Robinson

There are many, diverse reasons why people participate in sporting activities. For those who do, their sporting identities are closely linked to issues of pleasure, self-esteem and agency, but also, at times, to pain, risk taking and obsession (see Rinehart and Sydnor, 2003; Wheaton, 2004a). This chapter will examine a specific masculine identity in relation to the body, injury and pain, risk and death, as well as aspects of sexuality, in relation to the extreme sport of rock climbing. As well as looking at sporting masculinity in relation to gender relations, the chapter will also explore aspects of difference, for instance, age and (hetero) sexuality, constructed in relation to risk, pain and danger in rock climbing and mountaineering. For instance, what causes some rock climbers to risk (or even seemingly 'seek') injury or pain in pursuit of achievement? How does this connect up to a heterosexual sense of self, for example? The chapter will also be concerned with theorising the ambiguous nature of pain and injury in a specific sporting site. Therefore, approaches which see men's experience of injury and pain as purely a masculinising experience will be problematised. Further, participating in some extreme or adventure sports can mean there is a real possibility of death. Studies of sport and literature on masculinities have largely not explored how a so called death risk takes on its meaning in relation to masculine identities. How rock climbers negotiate potential death reveals much about the construction of gendered identities in the context of wider society's attitude to risk, and will be explored here. The 'erotics' of death and the body will also be considered.

The chapter, therefore, is concerned with masculine identity in the context of what has been termed 'lifestyle' or 'extreme' sports, and not more mainstream sporting practices, such as football, for example. The chapter will also be informed by empirical data which has emerged from an ethnographic study of UK-based rock climbers. The study was comprised of 47 semi-structured interviews with male climbers and a number of their personal female partners from across the UK (some of whom also climbed). The participants were aged from their early 20s to 70s. The climbers could be characterised as either elite rock climbers who climbed at a high level, with some of them being sponsored, or the non-elite men who usually climbed less frequently than the elite, and not at as hard a level. While some of the interviewees worked in the outdoor pursuits industry, for instance, at indoor climbing walls, or adventure pursuit shops, others were lecturers, ran their own business, were students, health workers or were unemployed, for example. Of the women interviewed, some were climbers and not having any kind of relationship with any of the men interviewed, some were climbers and were in a heterosexual relationship with a male climber in the study, and some women were non-climbers, but having a heterosexual relationship with a male climber in the study. Rock climbing is one of the fastest growing extreme sports in the UK. Though more men engage in climbing, it is a risk sport that is participated in by both women and men. Recent figures from the British Mountaineering Council (BMC) (2007) reveal a notable increase in female members.

There is debate by theorists and sports participants over what terms best describe such sports as rock climbing, windsurfing and skateboarding, for example (see Dant and Wheaton, 2007). Some of my participants rejected the label of 'extreme' to describe their sporting activities, seeing it as too media fuelled to be able to have any purchase on their experiences. This was felt particularly when rock climbing was seen to be a complete way of living, or an actively chosen lifestyle where participants' social and personal lives as well as sporting activities were interconnected. Others felt differently, as this 44-year-old climber said when asked if he thought his climbing practices could be considered 'extreme': 'Well, I am pretty extreme I suppose. What I do when I am climbing sure beats me working for a living!' In addition, though many theorists continue to refer to such sports as 'new' or 'alternative' in contrast to mainstream sports such as rugby, many of these practices now have a sporting history, with a number of them becoming institutionalised through commercialism, sponsorship or via regulation by sporting bodies (see Donnelly, 2003).

In relatively recent times, theoretical attention has turned to men's participation in sport from different perspectives, including within the fields of sociology, cultural, feminist and leisure studies. Additionally, a critical studies perspective on men and masculinities, or more broadly the field of masculinity studies, has also theorised sporting masculinities. Connell (1997) has linked sport with masculinity and power, where hegemonic masculinities are embodied through sporting practices and relationships. He argues that 'Sport has come to be the leading definer of masculinity in mass culture' (p. 233). Further, sporting prowess has been conceived of as providing a regular and routinised forum for the promotion and expression of learned and generated masculinity (Horne et al., 1999). There have been an increasing number of studies done on men, masculinities and identities in relation to sport, particularly in terms of how sport can be seen to reflect and create hegemonic masculinites (see, for instance, Messner and Sabo, 1990; McKay et al., 2000; Mangan, 2000). The hegemonic model of masculinity has also been seen as heterosexual (see Carrigan et al., 1985). There has, however, been criticism of the conceptualising of masculinities as hegemonic (see Whitehead, 2002; Hearn, 2004; Moller, 2007). However, this concept continues to have purchase on how masculinities are theorised in a number of different disciplines (Connell, 2005).

Further, Connell (2005) has developed the concept of hegemonic masculinity by identifying the existence of multiple masculinities. Therefore, he sees that this diversity of masculinities can lead to some men attempting to challenge traditional gendered relations. These insights have been applied to the area of sport. For instance, Messner (1992), in an attempt to problematise the construction of a dominant, sporting hegemonic masculinity, puts forward three reasons why sport does not construct a monolithic masculinity. Firstly, men are seen as paying a price for being involved in sport, for instance, in terms of the damage done to their bodies through constant injuries. Furthermore, men have diverse experiences of class, race and sexuality in sporting contexts and, lastly, more women entering sport and becoming proficient in different sporting practices can challenge a dominant heterosexual masculinity. Thus, theorists have argued that some men's behaviour in specific sporting sites can be seen to challenge dominant conceptions of a heterosexual, hegemonic masculinity.

Additionally, McKay et al. (2000) have argued that feminists in the 1980s and 1990s stressed the negative aspects of men playing sport, and highlighted issues such as men's misogyny, their capacity to manage pain and injury as part of a masculinising experience and the fact that homophobia was prevalent in different sports. Because of this, the diversity and complexity of sporting activities, as well as any possibilities for disruption and resistance to masculinity or gender relations through sport, were not acknowledged or were minimised. Conversely, more recently Abdel-Shehid (2005) has critiqued a masculinity approach to sporting masculinities, which he feels has limited analysis of sport by an insistence on defining sports, such as football, as essentially patriarchal in nature.

In contrast to the theorising of traditional, organised sports, there has been research done on more alternative or individualised sports such as windsurfing (Wheaton and Tomlinson, 1998; Wheaton, 2004b) and skateboarding (Beal, 1995, 1996, 1999; Borden, 2001). Many of these studies have argued that sports which are not as institutionalised as more mainstream pursuits potentially allow more room for stereotypical gender relations and performances to be transformed. Such sports have been termed 'lifestyle sports' (Wheaton, 2000a, 2000b), 'whizz sports' (Midol and Broyer, 1995) or 'extreme sports' (Rinehart and Sydnor, 2003; Robinson, 2004, 2008). These sports have also been theorised by Lyng (1990, 2005) within the term 'edgework', which refers to a number of diverse, high-risk activities, including sport, which can be seen as sites where norms and boundaries are transgressed. In general, such individualistic sports are also perceived to be more inclusive of both women and those men for whom traditional sports are not seen as welcoming places, in that they are seen to be too defined by status and competition, for instance (Wheaton, 2004b; Robinson, 2004).

Lifestyle or extreme sports have also been seen to embrace risk and danger and are largely white, middle class and Western in composition (Rinehart and Sydnor, 2003: Wheaton, 2004a; Laviolette, 2007). However, there are differences between some extreme sports in relation to the participants engaging with real danger or life-threatening activities, as opposed to those who are not likely to suffer serious injury, or where death is not a possibility. Clearly, the sport of rock climbing is one where participants literally, at times, risk life and limb when engaged in this pursuit. A 35-year-old climber in my study demonstrated this, when recollecting a near fatal accident which left him incapacitated for a long period of time: '[h]uge piece of rock came away with me on it and all the gear started pinging out and I went about a 100 foot down the side of this mountain, and was fairly smashed up really.' Moreover, Rinehart and Sydnor (2003) posit a view that extreme sports stand in opposition to mainstream sports as they are usually not institutionalised with governing bodies, but are at the same time increasingly becoming commercialised. Additionally, Wheaton (2004a) argues sports such as rock climbing and windsurfing call for a commitment in time and/or money and a style of life that builds up around the various pursuits in terms of social identities, attitudes and collective expression.

These sports are usually also further characterised by creative, performative and aesthetic factors.

Regarding the transformatory potential of these sports, I have argued (Robinson, 2008) that, specifically in relation to rock climbing, there are possibilities when women and men climb together. For example, gender relations can be more equal. This can be seen, for instance, when women enter the world of climbing and achieve at the same level as men, and so women's sporting performances are taken more seriously. Further, traditional sporting masculinities, which can be characterised by expectations on men to display bravado or not express fear, can be challenged when men are forced to show what have been seen as traditionally 'feminine' emotions, if on a climb where they feel afraid, or vulnerable. However, much of the research on such lifestyle sports has revealed that any meaningful changes to masculinity or to gender relations can be contradictory. For example, the potential for any shifts in male sporting identities has been problematised, as men can still be concerned with status and competition and not always welcome women's entry into these 'new' sports (see Palmer, 2004; Robinson, 2008). By examining key aspects of male rock climbers' experiences, that is, the sporting body, including the sexualised body, risk and death, it is possible to explore any such potential shifts in masculine subjectivities and identities in a nuanced way.

Bodies, pain and injury

When discussing the sport of boxing, Woodward argues that 'At one level, the relationship between the body and identity might appear relatively simple' (Woodward, 2006: 68). However, as she goes on to recognise, the embodiment of masculinities which are forged through sport can be seen as pre-emptive masculinities '[w]here the centrality of the body and its practices provide a means of securing the self' (p. 69). Along with Hall, Hockey and Robinson (2007), I have made a distinction between 'the body' as it has been conceived of within the social sciences, from feminist theory to medical sociology, and 'embodiment'. Much of the work on the body is about the body we have, the object body that we might alter in some way, whether via diet and exercise, tattooing or piercing and cosmetic surgery. Through the body identities may be claimed or imposed, via the materialities of clothing or body modification. It is also the body which is subject to the scrutiny of others – colleagues, employers or partners – as well as of the State, the media, and for my purposes here, the sporting peers of the rock climbers in my study (see Nettleton and Watson, 1998; Williams and Bendelow, 1998 for further discussion of these issues). The concept of embodiment, however, takes us towards the body that we are and, as such, provides a fruitful starting point from which to investigate processes of (masculine) identification.

Nettleton and Watson (1998) argue that, despite the centrality of the body in relation to everyday life, there has been little empirical research into how humans experience their bodies, particularly research which is informed by the subjective experience of people in different contexts. This includes, therefore, gendered differences in terms of how women and men use and conceive of their bodies. In addition, Nettleton and Watson conclude that in our day-to-day lives the body is often absent or taken for granted and it is only when we become ill or we are in pain that we become aware of our bodies. Therefore the narratives of the male rock climbers I interviewed can be explored through a discourse of pain and injury to investigate if, through their sporting experiences, they are able to reflect on this 'taken for grantedness' in ways which illuminate men's diverse relationships to their bodies. Furthermore, the body as objectified, scrutinised or regulated remains an important aspect of embodied subjectivity in that particular kinds of male bodies play a part in who men think they are. Men's bodies, when engaged in sport, are constantly under scrutiny from others and themselves. Male climbers are often, consciously or not, performing for different audiences. This can be other male climbers who are concerned to see how well their 'competitors' manage to climb, to the (hidden) male gay gaze and female partners. The male climbing body is therefore able to be conceived of as an object of desire and sporting relationships can therefore be erotically charged. Moreover, such scrutiny can bring identities into self-doubt and insecurity, as older men's sporting performances are looked upon by younger, up-and-coming climbers who often possess more youthful, fitter bodies better suited to climbing success. A male climber in his 50s illustrated this when he said, 'There's always someone younger at the crag than you, their body's in better shape, they train more, 'cos they got more time on their hands. You can't compete with that, you know?'

Thus different aspects of sport, including risk, competition, violence and injury, have all been looked at in relation to masculinity and identity (see, for example, Curry and Strauss, 1994; Young et al., 1994; Dyck, 2000). Pain in sport can be hidden or ignored, downplayed or instill pride and reflects complex and various constructions of gender. The embodied experience of sport is therefore ambiguous (Dyck, 2000). Young and White (2000) argue that injuries occur because of the financial emphasis on winning at all costs, but they also occur because of a connection between getting hurt and the masculinising of participants that this represents. Therefore, theorising on sport, men and the body has been concerned to investigate how men deal with pain, and injury as part of this masculinising process.

Messner (1992: 121) has conceptualised the male sporting body as a 'tool' or 'weapon'; male athletes become alienated from their own bodies by 'brushing aside' injuries or taking drugs to cover them up. For athletes (and manual workers) Williams and Bendelow (1998: 166) cite studies such as Kotarba (1983) where pain for such groups is a familiar feature of their '*normal*' everyday lives (their emphasis). Athletes often risk pain and injury through competition and have to consider the social costs and benefits of admitting pain before any decision to publicly disclose such pain is taken. This is supported by Watson (2000) who explores how men conceal injury and manage pain in the course of their everyday lives. Lilleaas (2007), in her work on athletes and their reactions to their own bodies, found that they accepted pain as part of the sporting experience, keeping their bodies under a constant surveillance in the process. These theories can be useful in exploring men's experiences of pain and injury in different risk sports. For example, in the context of skateboarding, Borden (2001) is concerned with young male skateboarders talking about the pain, danger and bodily injury involved in a 'new' sport, as opposed to one that is mainstream. He conceptualises their experiences in terms of the 'competitively collective nature of the group' (2001: 53). This collectivity is formed by participants having a set of individual attitudes and actions which are characterised by an acceptance of bodily injury. Male bonding is therefore, in Borden's view, created by such injuries through these masculine practices.

A number of the men in my study spoke about their acceptance of sporting injury as an integral and even necessary part of their being a rock climber. This ranged from accepting the immediate injuries gained through climbing, for example a sprained ankle, to expressing a stoic attitude to their need to manage more long-term injuries such as a chronic back injury. They would often 'climb' through the pain and therefore serious injury was framed as a masculinising experience in that how they were seen to deal with the pain added to a reputation for not complaining or for being 'brave'. The mountaineer Greg Child (1998) refers to contemporary climbers as 'the ibuprofen generation' (p. 41) in that through taking painkillers climbers can manage the aches and pains collected over a lifetime of climbing. One male climber in the study spoke of continuing climbing, despite injury and intense pain, until his 'hands bled'. Further, he did not miss out on his training routines in an effort to ensure he could climb at the standard required by himself and his sporting peers. Some of the rock climbers, when asked about previous sporting injuries, also confirmed Young et al.'s (1994) viewpoint that privileging forceful notions of masculinity were integral to their sporting practices. One non-elite man, aged 32, was proud of his ability to handle the pain he felt after scraping his hands continually over harsh grit stone rock, even going so far as to take pleasure in this experience. Other climbers in my study either accepted, minimised or ignored sporting injuries to allow them to continue to climb. This male climber in his 30s said, 'I usually have about three months where I get ridiculously strong and then start climbing really well and then I get injured. So, the most I climb is for six months.' However, despite these recurrent injuries he sometimes started to climb again before his body was fully recovered. Another man in his 20s admitted to it being 'absolutely horrible' if he could not climb due to injury, but accepted that this was 'part and parcel' of the whole climbing experience. A male climber in his 40s demonstrated and substantiated Messner's (1992) view that men 'brush aside' sporting injuries when he said, 'I've had a few broken ribs, and I've got a broken bone in my hand and I've sprained ankles and stuff like that, but I've had nothing really serious.'

However, this all raises the question of whether men can relate to their bodies in sporting contexts in ways which do not necessitate pain and injury being paramount to their experiences. Monaghan (2005) finds that Connell (1995) and Watson (2000) are among the few sociologists who have researched male bodies and health using an embodied perspective, but he also asserts that Watson's work, though grounding men's experiences in relational and processual bodies, does not consider how men may perceive their bodies in constructive ways. Therefore, in more individualistic and less commercial sports such as rock climbing, do men's relationships to their bodies challenge views which see men's sporting bodies destructively as 'weapons' or as necessarily constructing a hegemonic masculinity? If, as Young et al. (1994) argue, it is the norm in male-defined sports such as athletics to value a willingness to risk injury as highly as demonstrating pure skill, does this view have full purchase on 'extreme' sports? Young and White (2000) also theorise that men expose themselves to injury because of the rewards of hegemonic masculinity, despite the attendant dangers connected to this. Their viewpoint needs to be explored in 'new' sporting contexts to see whether all men subscribe to these masculinising processes. Further, Young and White's viewpoint can be further scrutinised if men's sporting experiences are seen across the life course.

Williams and Bendelow (1998) argue that it is becoming increasingly difficult to grow old and not be concerned with maintaining the body as a way of masking ageing, for example sagging flesh and a lack of muscle tone. This leads to a stress by society on the need to conserve the body, not because of any risks to health, but because 'Aging, in short, like death itself, comes to be seen as a "disease" in need of cure' (p. 76). Despite such pressures, in his study of men's feelings about their bodies as they aged, Watson (2000) found that most men finally give up on exercising, and thus were no longer in touch with their bodies through physical activity. For instance, on being in a stable relationship or on becoming fathers, the 'taken for granted' body becomes the dominant way of recalling their younger body. They often resigned themselves to getting fatter or not being as fit as they used to be. In addition, the men in Watson's study who exercised experienced their ageing bodies as not recovering as quickly when engaged in sporting practices. Further, family and work responsibilities were seen to further distance men from their embodied selves. Therefore, if male identity in relation to the body is seen in terms of the life course and men's relationships to others, in the context of wider everyday life, then we can gain a more fine-grained perspective on their embodied selves.

The male rock climbers responded to their ageing bodies in a number of ways. Some continued to train and preserved their weight at the level it was when they were younger and made sure that their physical skills were such that they could still climb at the standard they wanted to. Other older climbers took pleasure in eating what they now wanted and were comfortable in climbing at a lower overall standard than previously. Thus the diversity of the experiences of the male climbers I interviewed can be used to question some of these assumptions about the inevitability of this trajectory of male bodies across the life course discussed earlier. One climber in his 30s had suffered a major climbing accident which had left him in hospital with memory loss and near fatal injuries, the experience of which affected him both physically and psychologically for some time afterwards. He said, 'After the accident, I kind of started to realise that I need to spend more time with Rosalind [his partner]. And, I knew that, with myself, I was climbing too much. I wanted not to be doing it as much, want to do other things.' It was through a sporting injury that he was able to reflect on both the effect his climbing was having on his partner and on whether the extent and frequency of his climbing was preventing him from pursuing other aspects of his life. Similarly, another male elite climber aged 39 reflected on his risking bodily injury when he spoke about not wanting to expose himself to further injury when climbing: 'I don't want to carry on doing dangerous routes because it's a numbers game. My life's changed. I have a full-time job. I can travel more and there's a lot more things to do than I used to.' His previous sporting injuries and the danger he was often in precipitated a different attitude to his participation in the sport, and his horizons are now wider than before. Further, it is a new relationship with a girlfriend which has been the catalyst for these changes in his identity.

Sexualised bodies

As well as injury, pain and the body being important issues that emerged in my study of male rock climbers, the sexualised body was also apparent. Horne et al. (1999) argue that men's sporting bodies are becoming more sexualised in a manner previously reserved for the spectacle of women's bodies. Whitehead (2002: 182) confirms that 'there are new scrutinies on men, in terms of body shape, style and deportment'. He speculates, as others have done, whether men's current concern with the body is due to a 'crisis of masculinity' given that it has been argued that this is one of the last places that men can 'exhibit their true masculine self' (ibid.). Certainly, a large number of the climbers interviewed had been openly obsessed with weight gain in relation to their climbing performances, especially the elite climbers. Many of them had dieted at different stages in the life course, particularly when they were in their 20s and 30s. For some men this body consciousness was due to a need to lose weight to be able to climb harder, as having less body weight gave them more power to make dynamic climbing moves. For others in the study the fear of being overweight was about being concerned to maintain a self-image of a toned and 'fit' sporting male. Some of the male climbers revealed, albeit in a contradictory manner, the secret pleasure they gained from seeing photographs of themselves in climbing magazines where their muscled and tanned bodies were on display. These climbers expressed dismay if they felt they had gained weight, or were not 'as ripped as I used to be', that is, as lean and toned as they wanted to be. One young climber in his early 20s spoke about how important it was when in the company of other male climbers to be able to take off his top and display his body without thinking he was less 'fit' than the others.

At one level, therefore, such examples could be interpreted as revealing these climbers' need to buy into an image of the sexualised, heterosexual sporting male. Further, as Abdel-Shehid (2005) illustrates, Pronger's (1992) view, in keeping with other masculinity theorists, is that men's participation sport is fundamentally indicative of a 'homoerotic paradox'. This is because sport is one of the last areas in society that is separated on gender lines, but it is also often an arena where any expression of homosexuality has to be either punished or concealed. Sport can therefore be seen as constituted of bodily carnal practices, and thus men's sport can be seen as an erotic sphere. These half-naked and narcissistic rock climbers were all heterosexual, and rock climbing as a sport is largely dominated by straight, white men, as are many extreme sports (Rinehart and Sydnor, 2003). However, Abdel-Shehid also concludes that any consideration of sport as an erotic realm needs to reconsider any automatic connection between sport and heterosexual masculinity. The heterosexual men in my study took pleasure in their own bodies and those of other climbers. For example, they commented positively on seeing friends using their bodies in physical ways to perform difficult sporting moves on a climb. In addition one man in his 40s, speaking about coming back to climbing after trying other sports, said, 'I chose climbing because it was more physical, more grunty. So you can share a lot more with other men in climbing as well.' Such appreciation of other men's bodies by these men and their attendant physicality does not have to be seen as homoerotic for it to be meaningful.

Moreover, in terms of broadening out how heterosexual masculinities have been theorised in masculinity studies and studies of sport more generally, a consideration of gendered sporting relations allows for a consideration of heterosexual desire where women and men are partners in everyday life and compete in the same sport. In this respect, the views of some of the female climbers interviewed for the study shed interesting light on heterosexual relationships, eroticisation and desire. One female climber in her 20s whose male partner was also a rock climber admitted to 'enjoying going out watching him' and that she found his 'fit and toned body' attractive. In contrast, an older woman in her 50s had a different view about her male climbing partner. When asked why she was attracted to him she replied it was because 'It was just that he was such a nice person' rather than the fact he had a sporty body. Feminists have argued that we need to theorise heterosexuality in more complex ways than has traditionally been the case, so that heterosexual relations are not always constitutive of women's oppression and men's power (Hockey, Meah and Robinson, 2007). A 'new' and alternative sport such as rock climbing allows women to demonstrate agency through increasingly challenging men's sporting prowess with their own achievements when they participate. Arguably, this means that heterosexual desire can at least potentially be more equitable given that women and men, in this context at least, are sometimes able to negotiate their personal and sexual relationships from a position of (sporting) equality.

Risk and death

Another aspect which emerged from my study of UK-based rock climbers was whether climbers take risks in their sport and how the potential threat of death affects masculine subjectivities. Laviolette (2007) describes sports such as rock climbing as appealing to people because sport reintroduces the risk that modern society has obsessively controlled, allowing participants the possibility of confronting risk anew. However, Tulloch and Lupton (2003) state that, although the concept of risk has become important to the social sciences, and that the number of people who participate in high-risk 'extreme' sports has grown (Stranger, 1999), there is still relatively little empirical work on the meanings people give to *voluntary* risk taking. They further argue that voluntary risk taking is done for a variety of reasons, for instance for thrills and excitement, to overcoming personal fears, for personal agency, as well as for emotional engagement, control and self improvement. Tulloch and Lupton (2003) endorse Lash's (1993, 2000) plea for an investigation into how members of diverse cultural subgroups respond to risk in different ways. Lash posits that people have complex and ambivalent attitudes to risk. They also draw attention to the fact that theorists such as Lash are concerned with how judgements about risk are taken through collective understandings and anxieties, which go further than mere 'risk-taking'. For Lash in particular this is people's concern with the 'terrible sublime' of death. This of course has particular resonance for the 'extreme' sport of rock climbing.

Lyng (2005) argues that people risk death because extreme sports, among other activities, are seductive and fun experiences. He also asserts that to understand this phenomenon we need to employ a complex theory of structure and agency. In this way, we can seek to comprehend risk-taking activities as either a kind of escape from the pressures of an institutionalised world or as a mirror for the main cultural and institutional aspects of the changing social order. It has been argued by Smith (2005) that those involved with high-risk activities try to maximise the risks involved, as that is part of the attraction of such pursuits as extreme sports. Similarly Child (1998: 8) asserts that life and death 'are the coinage with which the climber gambles'. However, few of my participants spoke openly about taking risks which could be considered foolhardy or unnecessary, though a number of the elite, younger climbers patently took risks if it meant they could climb a harder route or gain a reputation in the climbing community as a serious climber. One elite man in his 20s said risks in climbing needed to be minimised, yet also said, 'You know, the more serious, the more intense everything is and the more memorable.' Caught between rationally realising that risks need to be controlled, at times he actually put himself in potentially fatal danger while climbing in order to have a more intense and eventful sporting experience. Additionally, older men in the study were not immune to being seduced by the pleasures of risk-taking, as this 71-year-old man attested to: 'You take calculated risks. That is part of the excitement. And controlling them.'

Further, some of the men in the study indulged in an excess of drinking and sexual encounters influenced, it could be argued, by their high-risk sporting activities, particularly if they are seen as evoking Lash's 'terrible sublime' of death by participating in a risk sport. However, the notion that extreme sports participants are needless or unthinking risk takers can be challenged. As one man in his early 40s said about climbing as a pursuit: 'It's risky, but it's about minimising your risks isn't it? Ascending the rock in a safe manner.' Another younger man, aged 34, when asked if he liked the element of risk involved in climbing replied, 'Strangely, no! I think you get an adrenaline rush from actually succeeding at something and still being here.' These accounts from the rock climbers substantiate Laviolette's (2007) thesis that sporting participants do not necessarily take risks gratuitously and that these risks need to be understood in the context of the other, diverse risk activities that people are engaged in, for instance sexual activity or coping with modern day catastrophes.

How then does risk-taking take on meaning in relationship to masculine identities in this wider, structural context? On the one hand, rock climbers and mountaineers enjoy a certain public cachet as daring individuals who risk life and limb, either for country and empire (Bayers, 2003) or to test the limits of human endurance and physical capabilities (Watson, 2005). However, media reporting of extreme sports participants such as climbers and mountaineers can also present an image of summit-driven, selfish and glory-seeking individuals (Maley, 2006). In addition, media accounts of explorers, adventurers and mountaineers often present people's desire to participate in diverse, life-threatening sports as illustrative of them being crazy, risk-taking pleasure seekers. Grice (2007) summed up the British adventurer Bear Grylls' next venture, to paramotor over Mount Everest, thus: 'Everest still holds him in its magnetic field of attraction' (2007: 1). The same article also quoted him as saying, 'I take pleasure in doing things that people say can't be done. My blood just pumps weird' (p. 2). Alternatively, Vidal (1999) suggests that more people want to experience controlled risks in an extreme sports environment to escape an increasingly tame and regulated Western urban existence. (Or, it could also be argued, to gain a more immediate experience of control in an increasingly 'risky' world, as we become aware of the possibility of global catastrophe, for example.)

Thus, against this wider discourse which posits the risk-taking sporting male as a hero, a fame-driven ego-maniac or a needless risk taker, men strive to achieve an individual sporting identity. By placing individual decisions to risk life and limb in a wider social, economic and political context, this need for men to climb mountains or scale rock faces 'because they are there' takes on a greater significance. Furthermore, many of the climbers I interviewed indicated that climbing for them became progressively more mundane over the life course. Indeed, it was the mundane, everyday practices of climbing and not the death-defying exploits often represented in the media that gave them a meaning and purpose to continue climbing, sometimes over a lifetime. In my study, as I have shown, it was when men had families or entered long-term heterosexual relationships that they began to reflect on the implications for others of their agency in taking risks. Therefore, the same man's subjectivity can be closely connected to risk-taking activities in traditionally masculine ways when he is younger, but at different stages in the life course his attitude to risk shifts.

Moreover, for some of the climbers interviewed the threat of death, or potential death, was not seen as alluring or heroic, but rather in terms of sorrow when they recounted the deaths of friends through rock climbing or mountaineering accidents. Most of the participants knew of another rock climber or a mountaineer who had died while climbing or, at the very least, had been seriously injured. This climber in his early 60s said, 'I mean, I have had doubts about climbing, and I think anybody who's climbed as long as I have, and seen some of the terrible things . . . and lost friends in the mountains.' Another man in his 40s spoke about pursuing climbing explicitly as resistance to death: 'This slow realisation, when you come into your 40s, that this is it. Your body's not gonna get any younger and you're going to die. Actually, something of climbing is resistance to that, there's some sense of denial. Maybe it is a little bit of, erm, capturing of youth when you climb.' Far from eroticising or glorifying death in the context of an extreme sports pursuit, these male rock climbers chose to engage in everyday, extreme sporting practices to manage fears of ageing, or, indeed, questioned their engagement with a sport which had been responsible for the death of friends or other loved ones.

Conclusion

Through exploring men's diverse experiences of participating in the extreme sport of rock climbing, through pain and injury, and their attitudes to risk, theoretical ideas about men's relationship to their bodies can be both explored and problematised. In relation to the male body, Stephens and Lorentzen (2007) argue that there has been a shift away from theorising about 'the body' as a monolithic entity 'towards analyses of specific instances of male corporeality' (p. 5). In this way, we can see that the relationship of the male body to masculinity is contingent and varied. As I have demonstrated, men's (extreme) sporting bodies can speak not only of pain and injury but also of pleasure, of being scrutinsed, and of taking pleasure in other men's bodies in ways which do not fit into the 'homo-erotic paradox'. Furthermore, through extreme sports, participants can be seen in their risky behaviour to be transgressing of the boundaries between life and death (Lyng, 1990). In this, men's need for authenticity and self-realisation through pursuing the sport of rock climbing can be seen as something which is characteristically masculine, in that death can be embraced and gambled with in pursuit of sporting status or achievement. However, in learning to manage risks and overcome fears it could be argued, as Laviolette (2007) does, that extreme sports participants are actively learning to manage risks and are developing personal skills which are of use in the rest of their lives. The men in my study also revealed that they are capable, over the life course, of being able to reflect on and even change their risk-taking practices to take account of their involvement in heterosexual relationships. It can be seen, therefore, that male identities in the context of an extreme sport such as rock climbing are complex, varied and shifting in relation to bodies, injury and risk.

7
Transformations of Pain: Erotic Encounters with *Crash*

Anthony McCosker

While less zealously pathologised in recent times, a broad array of sexual practices and expressions loosely defined as sadomasochism (SM), or under the broader rubric of Bondage, Discipline, Sadism and Masochism (BDSM), remain marginalised. Despite this, and perhaps as a direct challenge, literary, film and new media images have proliferated. Themes of BDSM are at play in films such as *9 ½ Weeks* (1986), *Wild at Heart* (1990), *Quills* (2000), *Secretary* (2002), and most interestingly, *Crash* (1996), as well as a wide range of television programming, advertising, websites and music. Indeed there is ample support for the claim that the turn of the twenty-first century can be described as 'a time for stories of dominance and submission' (Langdridge and Butt, 2004: 35). Behind the more mainstream images, performance art since the 1960s has led the way by tapping the body's potential for modification, and audiences' fascination with the aesthetics of 'body mutilations' (Kuppers, 2007; Jones, 1998; O'Dell, 1998). The focus of this chapter is the cinematic image of masochism in David Cronenberg's film *Crash*, which provides an important and enduring insight into the broad cultural challenges posed by the sexualisation of bodies traversed by wounds, markings and violent forces, and boundary modifications.

For more than a year after its initial screening in 1996 *Crash* attracted some of the most sustained media scorn in recent times, particularly in the UK where censorship pressure was coordinated through influential newspapers. The film was derided in the news media as a symptom or catalyst for the transgressions of contemporary obscenity and sexual depravity. But it has also inspired wide-reaching academic analysis, theorisation and debate. Reviews portrayed the film as an autoerotic exploration, linking sex, death and cars to plumb the depths of a 'perverse' subcultural sexuality (see, for example, Dick, 1997; Dery, 1997). Some scholars have analysed the film using psychoanalytic concepts such as the death drive (Arthurs, 2003; see also Adams, 1999), while others see it as an expression of a particularly postmodern form of amoral sexuality, or as a manifestation of cyberculture, illustrating the posthuman as the context of everyday life.[1] And the film and the reactions it provoked have been a central focus in explorations of 'crash culture' that survey the broader context of crashes within everyday life (Arthurs and Grant, 2003). As a media event, *Crash* moved well beyond the entertainment pages and programmes becoming a headline controversy (Barker, Arthurs and Ramaswami, 2001).[2] Through all of this discussion, *Crash* remains a heavily contested site attracting competing discourses that attempt to define, theorise or rein in its expressions of bodily pain in the context of sexual pleasure.

Both the public controversy and the content of *Crash* itself afford the chance to rethink the general notion of sadomasochistic sexuality as the erotic reversal of bodily pain and mass media experience. In the film, disaffected lovers James (James Spader) and Catherine Ballard (Deborah Unger) meet Vaughan (Elias Koteas) while James is hospitalised after a horrific car crash. Vaughan leads a group of crash victims compelled to explore the 'productive potential' of car crashes. The characters derive sexual pleasure from the violent forces of the crash, the damaged surface of cars and the wounding and marking of human flesh. Though sexual sensibilities change over time, this movement from bodily damage, disfigured flesh and car wreckage towards erotic, sensual bodily pleasure grates heavily against the hetero-normative sexuality of mainstream Western culture. It is clear that the image of violence, pain, sexual arousal and pleasure retain an uneasy status in the public domain of Western liberal cultures. But *Crash* also reminds us of the pliability of the image of pain, and the uneasy viewing experience it can command.

Whether *Crash* is considered an obscene expression of perverse and socially damaging sexual behaviour or as a productive cultural event, it is clear that it successfully employed cinema's ability to affect audiences in intense and complex ways, and benefited from the broader media's ability to carry and magnify those feelings in the form of a *controversy*.[3] There is a fundamental juxtaposition here between what we should *see* as tragic – as mournful, for example, as the site of the wreckage of Princess Diana's crashed car – and what we can feel as erotic. With its eroticised wounds and scars, *Crash* is distinguished precisely by its attempt to find and mobilise erotic pleasure in everyday objects and events normally experienced as tragic, violent and traumatic. The forces of violence are on the whole external to the characters of the film. This creates a purer form of corporeal masochism through sexual experiences premised on wounding, injury and pain decoupled from the figure of the sadist and the interplay of dominance and submission.

Undoubtedly, the thought of violence paired with sexuality left unregulated will continue to terrify some. The image of masochism presented in *Crash* is bound up in this terror. As I explore in more detail below, a corporeal, aesthetic masochism emerges out of sexual encounters that derive their affective intensity from the interaction between damaged cars, penetrable bodies, and wounded, tattooed and scarred flesh. The challenge of the masochistic aesthetic is exactly this wilful transformation of violent and painful forces to new ends. In this context, 'we cannot readily differentiate the processes by which pleasurable intensities are engendered from those by which painful intensity is produced' (Grosz, 1995: 199). This is where we can locate the unsettling instability and erotic pleasure of the image of pain in *Crash*, and its enduring cultural significance. It is important to note here that any description or analysis of a film is never entirely innocent or free of moral or political agenda, theoretical perspective or libidinal interest. My account of *Crash* focuses on its cultural and libidinal context in an attempt to demonstrate the workings of corporeal masochism within the film, in the unsettling viewing experience it seemed to provoke and in the broader media event that amplified its apparently disturbing effects.

A radical confrontation: *Crash* and the public ire

To a much greater extent than J. G. Ballard's 1973 novel,[4] Cronenberg's cinematic version of *Crash* stirred a lively history of public and critical controversy. Fierce scrutiny surrounded its release in Britain where it was banned by some local authorities on the grounds of 'sexual depravity'. This reactive context is quite telling. Firstly, there is something in the visuality of the cinematic version, in the *images* of sexual pleasure derived from crashes, that raised the ire of the public and press. Secondly, although contempt and scorn were levelled at the content of the film (and occasionally at Cronenberg himself), it is clear that the perceived threat also lay beyond the content. It was more specifically the notion of a corrupted spectator who may actually find sexual pleasure in its apparently unsavory images, or be incited to act out violently in search of new sexual pleasures.

Alexander Walker (1996a), for example, challenged the British Board of Film Censorship (BBFC) to ban *Crash* before it was released. Walker's review, written in response to its screening at the Cannes Film Festival in May 1996, was a scathing reaction echoed in newspapers around the country. His condemnation focussed on sexuality, describing the film as containing 'some of the most perverted acts and theories of sexual deviance I have ever seen propagated in main-line cinema' (Walker, 1996a).[5] The headline to Walker's article, 'A movie beyond the bounds of depravity', although added by a subeditor rather than Walker himself, became a catch phrase for the film. It was endlessly restated in the public debates that followed. Taking up the crusade for the *Daily Telegraph* (London), Nigel Reynolds's article 'Violent, nasty and morally vacuous' also helped set the scene for a bitter debate over the role of film censorship (Reynolds, 1996). Reynolds was celebratory in his outrage at what he saw as the *depravity* of *Crash* and its *obvious* social danger. He touched on a fear echoed by many others at the time: 'The atmosphere hangs with deeply unpleasant menace; his weirdos and freaks set out wilfully in their cars to crash in pursuit of death, sex and thrills. They masturbate over images of dreadful injury. They get off on mutilation' (Reynolds, 1996). The pathologising inherent in Reynolds's words extends by inference to the viewing experience, to a viewer who might follow the film's characters into the erotic pleasure of injury, scars and the exciting forces of the crash.

Media articles around the world reiterated this sense of moral outrage and asserted that the film's sexual perversity posed a broad social threat. In an Australian newspaper, Juliet Herd described *Crash* as 'a fairly unsavoury little film depicting all kinds of sexual permutations and mutations including near-necrophilia, sadomasochism, fetishes involving handicaps and deformities, homosexuality and lesbianism' (Herd, 1996). More interestingly, Adrian Martin described the film as 'polymorphously perverse', arguing that 'the categories of male and female, gay and straight, are utterly blurred by the story's end' (Martin, 1997). The common theme in both news media and public reactions to the film for Jane Arthurs (2003: 69) was that 'the car crashes and injured bodies were regarded as a potentially dangerous incitement to road rage or sado-masochism'. Each article evoked the 'video nasties' debates about the supposed corrupting effects of violent cinema on society's vulnerable (Barker, 1984), but drew attention specifically to the sadomasochistic sexuality as a social threat.

More than the content of the film itself, these commentators were worked up by the threat of viewers *en masse* getting off on, or masturbating over, images of erotic encounters with scarred bodies and crashed cars. It is the threat of *participation* in the so-called perversion presented. This threat is posed in terms of the contamination of unsuspecting and, by implication, heteronormative populations, with images of an aberrant sexuality based in the experience of pain as erotic pleasure. The public ire does, however, also confirm the affective potential of the film's rendering of pleasure in sites conventionally conceived as painful and tragic. It affirms the intensity of the images, and indeed their success as a vision of masochism. That is, as a cinematic study of the masochistic potential of the body affected by the forces of the car crash, the film also became a supercharged media event capable of extending that affective content, that masochistic experience, well beyond the theatre.

The masochist's conviction

There are, of course, a wide range of genuine sexual practices derived from the interplay of bodily pain and pleasure. But sexual practices defined as sadomasochistic continue to hold an uneasy status in Western culture. The legitimacy of SM was not debated, or was simply positioned as perversion or psychopathology, in the moralising surrounding *Crash* at the time of its release. Nonetheless understanding the practices associated with the transformation of physical pain into sexual pleasure is essential to understanding any encounter with the film. Clinical discourses delineating sadism and masochism have defined the terms as dual elements of a form of sexual pathology since von Krafft-Ebing (1886), and later Freud (1974 [1905])[6] and Reik (1941).[7] It has been only in the latter half of the twentieth century that sexual practices associated with consensual sadomasochism (SM) have begun to gain a more legitimate, if still marginalised, status (Langdridge and Butt, 2004).[8] Whatever theoretical model is used to define sexual experiences and practices in which pain is turned to sexual pleasure, the terms sadism and masochism remain heavily coded, even for practitioners.

In focusing on the notion of sadomasochistic 'roles' or 'modes', as Stoller (1991: 14–17) puts it, the common sociological and psychological approaches downplay or even dismiss the importance of the body to forms of sexuality described as sadistic or masochistic.[9] Most emphasise, what Chancer (1992) calls, the 'sadomasochistic dynamic', which encompasses the broader phenomenon of relations of domination and subordination wherever they are found. This dynamic, however, is expressed purely as a relation of domination and subordination that could encompass, by Chancer's admission, virtually any form of power relation. And 'masochism' retains negative connotations of powerlessness. For some, masochism is a dangerous symptom of the triumph of violence over the vulnerable; but the concern is usually with the concomitant promotion of sadism. Radical feminists in particular have criticised the notion of consent central to SM practice (Pateman, 1988), and the celebration of gendered power difference in the SM dynamic (Jeffreys, 1996), or for extending the possibilities for violence against women (Noyes, 1997: 3). Looking at the experiences of Internet-based SM communities, Langdridge and Butt (2004) demonstrate that sexual 'pathology' is rejected and 'sexual citizenship' sought as a way of challenging and extending the norms of sexuality (see also Langdridge, 2006). A similar sense of belonging through sexual practice appears to connect the characters of *Crash*, their community of practice lying just outside the bounds of the law and of legitimate citizenship.

Theoretical discussions of the practices, experiences and expressions associated with SM have attempted to deconstruct the sadist–masochist coupling, demonstrating the relative incompatibility of the two sexual modes (Deleuze, 1994; Silverman, 1992; Chasseguet-Smirgel, 1984).[10] In his literary analysis of von Sacher-Masoch's *Venus in Furs*, Deleuze emphasises the role of the contract in circumventing the Oedipal drama as it is established within Freud's sadist–masochist framework. *Crash* also challenges notions of *sado*masochism that emphasise the dynamic of domination and submission, by largely eliminating the figure of the sadist. The film stages masochism as '*techne erotike*' (Noyes, 1997: 5). That is, it appropriates technologies of everyday life – medical apparatuses and support devices, roads, traffic, the car with its encapsulating and body-extending surfaces – and turns them back on the bodies they transport or support to become the machinery of sexual energy and pleasure. The forces of both violence and pleasure in *Crash* arise from the machinic and industrial context itself and from the physical calculus of the crash and its appropriation by each of the characters.

The more duplicitous character of Vaughan is the only figure to overstep these boundaries in his overly violent sexual encounter with Catherine in one scene later in the film. Her bruised and marked flesh is man-made, and it is far more ambiguous whether her violent sexual encounter is consensual or not. Despite the duplicity of Vaughan as path-breaker and potential sadist, the characters seem to disturb audiences because they are able to turn the violent forces of the car crash and its resulting pain and scarification towards heightened eroticism and sexual pleasure. Ostensibly, the masochistic encounters in *Crash* are designed to support what Beckman has found of his masochist interviewees, that a lot of practitioners are interested in the exploration of the dimensions and potential limits of their 'lived bodies' by means of these unconventional 'bodily practices' (Beckman, 2001: 94). There's no clear villain or sexual monster in *Crash*.

Negative reactions to *Crash* are not surprising, and the reasons may go well beyond contested standards of sexual morality. It is well understood that in media culture the sight of the mangled, torn open wreckage of a car, train carriage or plane fuselage, for example, stands in indexically for the human carnage that has occurred within.[11] It connects with it physically. But the thought of such a pain event shifting to pleasure abhors perhaps because we understand the vulnerability of the pain image. Even if we accept Stoller's (1991: 8) point that 'there is no sadomasochistic perversion; rather, there are many sadomasochistic perversions', the centrality of pain, and by extension bodies, in understanding these sexual expressions and experiences should remain paramount in any attempt to avoid overgeneralisation, reduction or pathologisation.[12] Corporeal specificity is crucial. What the masochist knows is that the libidinal field can extend across the whole body and beyond it into other surfaces and objects, bringing about a limitless array of couplings, sensations and feelings.

Some theorists take bodily experience and affective intensity as a starting point in their account of practices associated with sadism and masochism. Elizabeth Grosz follows Lingis, Lyotard, Deleuze and Guattari in analysing the forces that move through the body melding pain and pleasure in the masochistic sexual encounter:

> Sadism and masochism intensify particular bodily regions – the buttocks being whipped, the hand that whips, bound regions of the body in domination practices – not using pain as a displacement of or disguise for the pleasure principle, but where pain serves as a mode of corporeal intensification.
>
> (Grosz, 1995: 199)

Sadism and masochism in their own ways seek to move beyond the regular and habitual acts and countenance of the body to intensify sexual pleasure. Bodily zones, areas of flesh, muscle, appendages and sensitive surfaces can be affected and intensified through unanticipated and unusual conjunctures and interactions (Grosz, 1995: 198). Within this 'corporeal' framework, the practices associated with sadism and masochism can be understood as methods for seeking out and utilising the body's libidinal potential in the quest for sensual intensity. To pathologise, regulate or censor such acts is to control the production of pleasure itself.

Lingering over impact and injury

In *Crash* cinematic techniques and visual forms bring the erotics of bodily pain to audiences not merely as spectacle or representation, but as experience, sensation, affect. Images of James in his hospital bed early in the film present his wounded body in extreme close-up. We see in close detail his damaged and heavily braced leg, as the camera pans slowly up to the deep, stitched gash on his neck caused by the seatbelt, pausing there for a few seconds before moving up to his face, focusing on a stitched cut on his nose. A side-on view of James in the hospital bed shows his whole side and torso, legs in traction, but eroticised through the exposure of naked flesh with only the curve of the bed sheet lightly covering his groin. Confusion of the erotic with the immobility of serious injury establishes the beginnings of a sensual transformation of bodily states and affects. Soon after, we see James with Catherine on his apartment balcony, peering at the immense flows of traffic below on the crisscrossing super highways. Again, the camera pans up the erotically exposed flesh of his scarred leg. At that point, James starts to explore the erotic potential of the forces of the car crash, its impact on his sense of the world around him and his sexual relations with others.

Psychoanalytic theories of spectatorship analyse cinema in terms of the heteromasculine and patriarchal norms that structure spectatorship and work to produce viewing subjects by providing dominant and subordinate positions through which to identify. While the scopophilic aspects of cinema are tested in interesting ways in *Crash*, the psychoanalytic approach does not account for the affective potential of the film's corporeal masochism. Alternatively, in line with Deleuze's approach to cinema and painting, Marks (2000) distinguishes between optic and haptic visuality in theorising cinema and spectatorship. The eyes, she argues, function as tactile organs, attaining a sensorial relationship and dynamic with the image. Instead of a relationship of representation and identification, Marks, like Deleuze, emphasises the neuroaesthetic functions of cinema and art, enabled through textures, surfaces, bodily impulses, actions and affects. In the case of *Crash*, haptic visuality is composed of injured, tattooed and wounded flesh, and in the crumpled metal of cars, the solidity of concrete and asphalt. All of this provides the framework and material substance for an aesthetic and corporeal masochism, sexual pleasure derived from and in relation to the affective states of injury or their trace in the scar.

If there is something unsettling in watching *Crash* it is the way in which excitement, sexuality and crashes are more carefully and completely aligned than we are used to seeing in popular film or television.

Within the film, James carries this sense of uneasy excitement. After his release from hospital, Vaughan shows him a compilation of photographs of crashed cars and injuries. James confesses uneasily that 'it's all very satisfying. I'm not really sure why'. His uncertainty acknowledges a resistance to the excitement or pleasure and gradually overcomes it as he extracts more from the productive potential of the car crash. Interestingly, in their analysis of the film, Botting and Wilson (1998: 189) read into the film a sense of the *disappearance* of excitement or sensation from the car crash. Critically, they see this as an aspect of the film's 'generalised automation', an effect of its emptiness and its characters' banality: 'Stylistically and technically, *Crash* refuses to evoke or simulate the sensational and spectacular effects that one would expect from a film that draws an equivalence between sex and car crashes' (Botting and Wilson, 1998: 189). They go as far as to deny the presence of 'characters' at all in the film, seeing only 'scar-screens', or 'empty units of visual identification'; and they point to the lack of excitement in the crash: 'There are no big bangs, no sensuous slow-motion smashes, no romantic chases or erotic duels on the open highway' (Botting and Wilson, 2003: 85).

More accurately, however, the energy of excitement is harnessed and transformed in order to explore something different. Freeway duels and confrontations compliment crashes that are infused with a strange calm; but they are certainly not emptied of affective intensity. As well as detailing the mechanical impact, the scenes deliberately *linger* over bodily wounds and mechanical damage. If the film takes on something new here, it is in its more detailed pursuit of the sensate qualities of pain and pleasure in the crash, and the possibilities of these for alternative forms of sexuality. Cars damaged in various degrees are coupled or confused with the blood and fracturing of bodily injuries. Scars and disabilities are constantly framed in close-up and become the point of contact between characters, and the focus of their sexual experimentation. Something in the image of wounding shifts ground, becoming a force for a highly charged, uneasy and yet pleasurable viewing experience.

One carefully arranged display of the subtle texture of the car crash occurs early in the film. For the pleasure of a small group of crash enthusiasts Vaughan stages a 'real life' re-enactment of the crash that killed the actor James Dean. As Vaughan and his fellow 'stunt' drivers speed towards each other in their replica vehicles, we see subjective camera angles from the cars, and we also see the spectators watching tensely. At the moment of collision the camera shifts to the inside of one of the cars to convey the inertia and the suddenness of the impact of metal on metal. With this close-up framing, we are offered a jarring and lingering view of the texture of the crash. The details of the cars coming together in collision, and the bodies thrown violently inside the cars are clear. We see this from within the cars as well as alongside and from the point of view of those gathered to watch the event. Here, the texture of crushed metal and machinery, physical injury, wound and pain are deliberately brought together with the excitement and pleasure in the rush of the spectacle. But it is the moment of impact, where the point of view shifts to the inside of the car, that attempts to transform us from remote spectators to participants in the corporeal milieu of the car accident.

Vision, perception and tactile experience imbue each sexual encounter and each crash, seeking discomfort there and encouraging an uncomfortable viewing experience. In an early provocative scene, James is lead by Catherine to uneasily explore the erotic and seductive texture of the car crash. Catherine had previously explored the erotic potential of the idea that she might crash while flying and that James could wake up with her in the bed next to him. And so she too begins to probe the stimulating potential of the crash, and the power of its disruption of their deadened lives. She sits next to James and begins to masturbate him in a rhythmic, mechanical manner. In a sensual, serene and aroused voice she describes the state of the crashed car:

> Both of the front wheels of the car and the engine were driven back into the driver's section or in the floor. Blood still marked the hood like little streamers with black lace running toward the windshield wiper cutters . . . The cabin was deformed and there was dust, glass, plastic flakes everywhere inside. The carpeting was damp and stank of blood and other body and machine fluids.

The destructive event of the crash enters their imagination and the viewer's in a moment of rhythmic, mechanical sexual stimulation. Two forces, erotic pleasure and the pain of severe injury, are brought together. All the usual pain and trauma of a car accident are transformed through the seductive tones and the sexual act. We are left with the image of the accident, the idea of a crushed car full of machine and body fluids, as sexual pleasure, a somehow potent yet unsettling turn-on. The film is propelled in this way by the violence and injury of the car crash but the pain disappears from these, shifting into pleasure or the possibility of once again experiencing pleasure.

The expressive oscillation between pain and erotic pleasure is pursued in many ways throughout *Crash*, but particularly through damaged and scarred flesh. Most notably, tattoos of wounds and scars feature as intensified erotic regions of Vaughan's and James's bodies in a scene later in the film that finally brings them together in a sexual encounter. Rather than an abnormality, or *dis*figuration, the scar in this scene is experienced as an intensified source of erotic energy – approaching Vaughan's stated 'project': the exploration of the fertilising, rather than the destructive potential of the car crash. In this sexual encounter, Vaughan's and James's tattoo scars are both icon and index; they are not only impressions of car parts as wounds but also stand as wounds in themselves, in the bruising and blood from the stylus's penetration of the flesh. For Vaughan, the large scar he has tattooed to his torso overlaps the rippled flesh of actual scars. With James's tattoo the puncturing of the flesh is also emphasised when Vaughan slowly removes the dressing tearing delicately at the hairs on James's inner thigh. In the close-up we see what looks like the traces of blood on the white cloth of the dressing, and its removal seems to be experienced by James ambiguously as either pain or pleasure and, ultimately, as an expression of sexual excitation. When Vaughan delicately kisses James's tattoo-scar, and lifts his shirt to let James kiss his, sexual pleasure is found in the marking and violation of the flesh.

To aid in developing a masochistic viewing dynamic, a structure of repetitiveness underscores the film. It conforms to what Linder Williams describes as the cinematic essence of masochism, its role as an instrument for 'staging dramas of suspense, supplication, abandon, and relief that enhance or substitute for sexual acts' (Williams, 1989: 195). Masochistic encounters are repetitive and ephemeral: 'This repetition . . . produces the intensity of affect, pleasure and pain, but can never repeat its initial occurrence' (Grosz, 1995: 199). Scene after scene of unusual sexual encounter allows *Crash* to mimic the striving for sexual pleasure or orgasm in a narrative mode, building towards an unattainable goal, constantly held back from the characters and viewers alike. This pattern has been taken as an enactment of the Freudian 'death drive' (Arthurs, 2003) but it also signals the struggle or yearning for sensation, satisfaction or ever more intense *affects*. Each encounter along with the logic of the film as a whole serves to find new moments and forms of the production of affective intensity.

Transforming pain: Harnessing violent forces, exploring erotogenic surfaces

Masochism as sexuality has always proved provocative in texts that reach a mass audience, but the disruption of the rigid expression of pleasure in sex through its merger with pain in *Crash* takes this further by enabling the possibility of a masochistic viewing experience. *Crash* foregrounds sensual qualities and affective states through the visual play of surface, wound, injury and car crash. It accentuates the sensitivity of flesh, the tenderness of scars and the impulsiveness of sexual activity. Behind the crash, in the heightened vulnerability of injured bodies and the body's capacity for injury, there is pain. The simple strategy of the film is to transform pain into the image and experience of sexual pleasure, resulting in the full range of reactions so strongly felt by different viewers.

Playing with the boundaries of pain and pleasure, flesh and metallic surfaces, the film also exposes, it seems at least for some, even many, commentators, the terror of the reversibility of these experiential qualities. Phenomenology has provided a powerful framework for understanding these complex embodied experiences. For example, critical of the novel and what she sees as Baudrillard's (1994 [1981]) celebration of the dissolution of the body into technology in his piece on Ballard's novel, Sobchack (1991) provides a stern warning.[13] She cautions that it is 'dangerous' to lose one's bearings within *Crash*'s free-floating signs and corporeal transformations, and its denial of the legitimacy of pain as lived experience: 'There's nothing like a little pain to bring us (back) to our senses' (Sobchack, 1991: 327).[14] While also reading the novel and film through a phenomenological lens, Kuppers challenges Sobchack's criticism, referring in the process to her own experiences of the scars marking her body with the traces of accidents and medical interventions (Kuppers, 2007). Unlike Sobchack she sees the productive potential of her own scars and wounds and those of *Crash* as allowing her to experience herself as multiple, different in space and time, escaping the social and institutional constraints that regulate her everyday experiences (Kuppers, 2007: 134).

Embodied experience is central to the themes explored in *Crash*, and to the range of audience reactions to the film. However, the sensations developed in the interaction of car crash and human bodies can also be conceived as a composition of affects and percepts, to use Deleuze and Guattari's terminology (1994). It can be argued that *Crash*, like contemporary art more generally, aspires to wield its affects and percepts so as to 'cause us to see and feel in new or unforseen ways' (Rajchman, 2000: 135). The unsettling image of masochism in *Crash* is developed through what Grosz (1995: 197) refers to as 'the erotogenic surface' of the characters and cars. Indeed the film explores 'interiors' most explicitly through '. . . the body's "outside", its locus as a site for both the perception of the erotic (as phenomenology recognised) but also for the inscription and intensification of the sensitivity of bodily regions'.[15] This enables it to build a detailed exploration of the affective potential of the body. And it allows the unsettling image of masochism to extend beyond the sexual encounters and violent incidents depicted, to the viewing experience. *Crash* both re-formulates bodily pain as a site for the intensification of pleasure and experiments with the pleasure of masochistic sex as a cinematic event, as an experience in its own right.

Cronenberg himself has spoken about the emotional language of 'affect' that emerges from the experimental sexual encounters throughout *Crash*. Reacting to criticism of the film as a portrayal of emotional misfits in a cold and perverse world, he claims to be inventing a new language through which the film's characters can finally express that which is 'impossible in the language that exists':

> [T]o a small degree, I'm reinventing film language in order to allow my characters to express things to themselves in their own emotional language. I see *Crash* as an existential romance. That simply means that maybe affect – which is to say, what we consider emotion and the way in which it is expressed – needs to find new avenues, new forms in order to express the things that we need to express these days.
>
> (Cronenberg in Dery, 1997: 44)

'Affect' is used here to refer to the emotive level of experience in the film. It can be thought of more specifically as the body's potential to be *moved* or *touched* by forces or external bodies, whether car or human, and the potential of the body to move others, including an embodied viewer. A relationship is carefully established between the crumpled surface of crashed cars and beautiful but often scared or wounded bodies to transfer and transform libidinal energy.

The unsettling viewing experience can thus be traced back to this masochistic event, or to what Grosz describes as the 'coming together of disparate surfaces [where] the point of conjuncture of two or more surfaces produces an intensification of both' (Grosz, 1995: 198). *Crash* thus enables and celebrates what Lingis (1985: 81–4) sees as a lateral distribution of carnal desire across the surface of the body, across body parts not normally 'marked' as sexual. Lyotard (2004: 20) uses the term 'jealousy' to explain the pleasurable confusion of libidinal zones across surfaces – the point where the blouse meets the neck, for example, or in the violations of tattooed and injured skin. This concept is appropriate to *Crash* where the wreckage of a car body is not a metaphor of bodily damage, but *corresponds* to it somatically – car and human bodies affect each other, and in turn affect a viewer. Merging sex with the violence of the crash allows the freeing up of a range of perhaps terrifying, perhaps pleasurable affects. Bodily violation, through the crash, facilitates this redistribution of the libidinal energy produced in both metallic and physical damage. Each surface affects the other, becoming erotic at the point of violation and conjuncture, where the surfaces of scar, tattoo, flesh, metal blend to form a range of alternative sensations.

Erotic pain and uncomfortable viewing

In the dynamic formed by the conjunction of car, crash, body and sex, *Crash* realises the erotic potential of the transformation of pain and extends this potential to the viewing experience. By eroticising the crash, the nocuous or aversive quality of injury is rendered malleable and is transformed. As in masochism itself, the *pain* of injury unravels slightly, just enough to be experienced differently, taking on the characteristics of bodily pleasure. In contemporary Western culture the persistence of visual brutality in film, digital media, performance art, painting and other art forms parallels the repetition of a more sombre and perhaps more banal tragedy of everyday crash culture (Arthurs and Grant, 2003). The deliberate lingering over injured human and car bodies in *Crash* allows an unusual tenderness to emerge out of normally destructive events.

In the scenes described above, *Crash* wields the reversibility or volatility of the expression of pain to position viewers in an unfamiliar and, it seems for many, an uncomfortable position. These sexual encounters propagated through car crashes are easily interpreted as simply perverse in the everyday context of more conventional, more tragic images of road accidents of news media. But this juxtaposition is exactly the point. It gives rise to the complex masochistic affects that are the film's real goal, enabling it to present an array of bodily practices and pleasures that would be completely new to many viewers, experienced by some as exciting, by others as abhorrent. The image of masochism presented in *Crash* can only make sense by considering the film's intense impact on audiences, its ability to affect audiences so viscerally as to attract such widespread scorn, praise and analytical attention.

My account of various scenes from the film extorts certain ambiguous sensations that highlight the disturbing point at which pain is transformed to pleasure. But where I have sought to convey sensuality in images of wounding and sex, others depict the same scenes and images as threatening instances of perversity or as posthuman disengagement. Each of these is possible because through its visualisation of sex, crash and injury, and its narrative staging of masochistic encounters, familiar affects are refashioned. Injured bodies add a sense of vulnerability, heightened sensitivity and perhaps disturbing intensity to the scenes of sex. Rather than cold, disengaged, or excessively perverse, it is full of productive affect derived from the simultaneous threat and promise of the body's potential to experience pain as pleasure. In this it presents a lasting testament to the affective potential of the body, public attempts to discipline it, and the threat still thought to be posed by the transformation of pain into sexual pleasure. I would like to thank Therese Davis for her feedback and support in the development of an earlier version of this chapter.

Notes

1. Several editions of *Screen* and other cinema journals presented analyses from a range of theoretical perspectives focusing on the death drive, or the notion of the posthuman and the interface between human–technology (see, for example, Brottman and Sharrett, 2002; Creed, 1998; Grant, 1998; Smith, 1999).
2. Barker, Arthurs and Harindranath (2001) investigated the fierce public debate in the UK, Europe and the US that lambasted the film and incited pleas for bans on its release. In the UK, the catalyst articles were written by: Walker (1996a, 1996b), Tookey (1996), Reynolds (1996). In Australia, see, for example, Herd (1996), Martin (1997), Lloyd (1997).
3. Barker, Arthurs and Harindranath (2001: 11) describe the film as 'first and foremost a creature of the press' which unanimously fueled the notion that the film was 'controversial', that it was in some way harmful or dangerous.
4. The exception was the debates in the special edition of *Science-Fiction Studies* (1991), 18 (3), primarily in response to Baudrillard's piece on the novel published in that edition and in *Simulacra and Simulation* (1994).
5. Mark Kermode and Julian Petley (1997: 16) draw attention to this point in their excellent critique of the press and political campaign to ban *Crash* in Britain, and the subsequent attacks on the board of censors for allowing the film to be screened. A more extensive review of the media event, and audience responses to *Crash* was carried out by Barker, Arthurs and Harindranath (2001). I have extracted only a small portion of the discourse surrounding the film to highlight the underlying conceptions of the viewing experience and the threat *Crash* was thought to pose.
6. Freud divided masochism into three distinct forms which he called moral, feminine and erotogenic masochism; these, he thought, were bound strictly to sadism as a 'perverse' coupling of domination and submission in the search for sexual gratification (Freud, 1974 [1905]: 36–8).
7. Building on Freud's ideas and observations, and through his own clinical observations, Theodor Reik (1941: 44) also describes three essential characteristics

in masochism: the significance of 'phantasy', the factor of suspense and the demonstrative factor.

8. Sadomasochism remains reified in psychiatric discourse as a sexual 'disorder', continuing to hold a place in the Diagnostic and Statistical Manual (DSM-IV) (American Psychiatry Association, 1994). Despite this, Giddens (1998) points out that '"Sexuality" today has been discovered, opened up and made more accessible to the development of varying life-styles . . . Somehow, in a way that has to be investigated, sexuality functions as a malleable feature of self, a prime connecting point between body, self-identity and social norms' (1998: 16).
9. This is recently addressed by studies exploring the lived and embodied experiences of SM, giving a voice to the participants (Beckman, 2001; Langdridge and Butt, 2004; Langdridge, 2006; Taylor and Ussher, 2001).
10. Deleuze challenges Freud's notion that masochism is bound to sadism (Deleuze, 1994; Chasseguet-Smirgel, 1984; Silverman, 1992). Deleuze uses a literary approach to the aesthetic, philosophical and political worlds that separate the sexual sadism associated with de Sade, and the masochistic sexuality with von Sacher-Masoch.
11. Grimshaw (2003) explores this notion through the relationship between iconic body, such as Princess Diana, and the car crash.
12. The discourse has shifted towards analyses of the lived body and lived experiences of SM practices and sexualities. Beckman (2001), for example, identifies five discourses or motivations for participating in sadomasochistic practice, understood and experienced as an alternative to 'normal genital sexuality'; 'safer sex', an exploration of the 'lived body'; a means for transgressing gay and lesbian stereotypes of sexuality; and as a means for experiencing the transformative potentials of 'lived body'.
13. Sobchack (1991) uses her own experience of cancer surgery to argue that pleasure – or perhaps more specifically erotic desire – is inconceivable in the environment of pain.
14. In a later article, after a leg amputation and the fitting of an artificial limb, Sobchack (1998) revives the issue of the sensuality of body modification, more accepting of alternative experiences, but remaining critical of the cybernetic tradition of disavowing the body which she sees as underlying *Crash* (Sobchack, 1998: 319).
15. Both Grosz and Lingis draw on Lyotard's *Libidinal Economy*, where he similarly proposes a 'Moebian-labyrinthine skin', a 'single sided patchwork of all the organs (inorganic and disorganized) which the libido can traverse' (2004 [1974]: 4); this 'immense membrane of the libidinal "body"' 'is made from the most heterogeneous textures', all joined on a surface that is both interior and exterior at once.

8
Tortured Heroes: The Story of Ouch! Fan Fiction and Sadomasochism

Jenny Alexander

> The line between good and evil lies in the centre of every human heart.
>
> Alexander Solzhenitsyn, *The Gulag Archipelago*

This chapter is about an enduring question in the study of representation – the ethics of the shared and transmitted imagination. What 'should we' or 'should we not' do to bodies in representation? And when representations involve the eroticised body bound, the skin broken and the inducement of pain, how then may we read them? In particular I explore representations of the body under duress in fictional audience-produced texts online – in fan fiction – and their contemporary cultural meanings.

The production and reception of representations of the eroticised body under duress has, of course, varied tremendously both culturally and historically, from Christian Van Cowenburgh's painting *The Rape of the Negress* (1632) with its seventeenth-century 'high cultural' gravitas and its uncomfortable concupiscent complicity (for us moderns) to the home videos which sparked the Spanner Trial (1990) and led to the conviction of 16 gay men for consensual BDSM (bondage, discipline, dominance, submission, sadism, masochism) activities.

This chapter is concerned with not-for-profit narrative written by audiences about characters from their favourite (usually serial) film and television productions, and shared with other fans online. It is about a genre of fan fiction that has largely been passed over by scholars – fan fiction of a sadomasochistic nature. That is to say, stories by fans in which a central and graphic part of the *mise-en-scène* involves a body or bodies deliberately wounded and/or apparently stressed in an eroticised context. Here you will encounter, for example, Batman and Alfred ritually cutting the bat symbol into Robin's chest, Stargate's Colonel Jack O'Neil dipping a ball-gagged Daniel Jackson in hot wax for his birthday, Xena and Gabrielle using leather whips on one another for pleasure, and the entire Fellowship of the Ring willingly trussed up in an S 'n' M dungeon.

For present purposes I am considering fan fiction with a serial screen canon in the science fiction and fantasy genres only. There is a much higher prevalence of sadomasochistic fan fiction associated with science fiction and fantasy canons than with narratives set in the 'real world'. There are far more 'Captain Jack Harkness ties up Dr Who and teaches him Raxacoricofallapatorian rope bondage'-type stories than there are equivalents for the on-screen lovers Jean-Paul and Craig from *Hollyoaks*. It is possible that this is because the mythical and intergalactic settings of science fiction and fantasy canon afford fan spin-off creatives with a distancing effect – not to mention durable superhuman or alien bodies which can be stressed and restressed and miraculously rehealed.

Fan fiction censorship

How should we think about sadomasochistic fan fiction? What are we to make of stories such as 'Forbidden feelings' by ksevfansd? Tagged 'BDSM, slash,[1] beastiality [*sic*]', a nominee in round four of the 'Multifaceted Harry Potter fan fiction awards' 2007 under the award category of 'Best extreme fic'. In this story, Lucius Malfoy ensnares the werewolf teacher Remus Lupin and our heroine Hermione ties up the latter and coerces three-way oral sex, while Hermione, despite her distress, fantasises about having sex with Lupin in his wolf form. And what of *ansereg*, the cultural practice of 'consensual elvish BDSM' created by one Tyellas within an extended *Lord of the Rings* universe?

Such 'extreme' fan fiction has been the subject of recent moral panics, perhaps part of the broader anxiety surrounding Web 2.0 and 'user-generated content'. In 2007 a group called Warriors for Innocence, based in the US, contacted Six Apart, the company that owns LiveJournal (LJ). LJ is at present one of the most popular sites for fandom blogs online. It has some social networking features, and many fan fiction writers maintain a presence there. Warriors for Innocence state (on their website) that their purpose is 'hunting monsters on the web' and 'hunting pedophiles where they fester'. They demanded that Six Apart remove journals with content that they deemed offensive. Six Apart reacted by taking down around 500 journals. Many fan blogs and fan communities were removed from LJ on the basis of the courtesy-tag warnings that routinely accompany fan fiction. In this case, tags indicating content such as 'slash' (misunderstood as an act of violence rather than a reference to a male/male pairing) 'incest' and 'non-con' were picked up for prohibition.

So many LJ users expressed outrage at this development that Six Apart's chief executive was compelled to publicly apologise a month later. The majority of fandom and fiction journals have gradually been restored since. This did not satisfy Warriors for Innocence. An article on their site entitled 'It's just fiction' (2 June 2007) comments:

> Writing child sex/rape stories is . . . sick and disgusting, but technically not illegal . . . While child rape/sex stories may not be illegal, they are pedophilia . . . Pedophiles are sexually attracted to children, they often write child sex stories. They get off on these stories and pictures of children. The more 'stories' they read and 'enjoy', the more they fantasize about children. REAL CHILDREN.

This article is cross-listed under 'Fandom, Fanfic, LiveJournal' and 'Pedophile'.

The blogs on LJ taken down as a result of the Warriors for Innocence complaint included fandom journals, survivor journals and consenting-adult age-play journals, as well as 'in real life' (IRL) journals that described or sought illegal sexual activity. *Harry Potter* fan fiction was particularly affected. The slash and femme-slash (i.e. same-sex narratives only) Pornish Pixies, a self-described 'smutty' fan fiction and fan art community set in the *Potter* universe, was locked down until the weekend of 4 and 5 August 2007. Weasleycest is devoted to stories containing Weasley family (sibling to sibling) incestuous pairings. The first member of the Weasleycest LJ community was the Lady Feylene (in 2003) who describes herself as 'a fandom and cosplay nut . . . nice person . . . main fandoms Fullmetal Alchemist, Ouran High School, Host Club and Babylon 5 . . . IRL I'm a disabled lesbian well over legal age who spends far too much time gaming'. Fey writes:

> I'm always amazed at the people who assume if you like something in fiction/write something/whatever, you must be into it in real life. I saw a lot of nasty, nasty shit in the Harry Potter fandom over it. People freaking out because people who were writing cross-gen or non-con or kids in sexual relationships were, gasp, *mothers*! And clearly anyone who writes about kids having sex, kids in incestuous

relationships, kids doing drugs, drinking, whatever totally endorse it in real life.

(http://theladyfeylene.livejournal.com/ (8 July 2007))

Pornish Pixies is populated by writers like Fey, and others called Electricandroid, Tarnationawaits and Femmequixotc who type stories such as 'Stigmata' (tagged 'NC-17'), in which arch-rivals Harry Potter and Draco Malfoy are involved in a love/hate fisting scene. According to Wikipedia, LJ's membership is two-thirds women, mostly aged 16–25.[2]

Why might teen and twenty-something fans of *Harry Potter* be writing stories at the present time exploring (among many other things) restraint and duress, non-consent and taboo, same sex intimacy, passionate attachment and loss? Will these authors embark upon careers as predatory sadists and paedophiles? Does the sharing of their narratives online with one another encourage a culture of harm?

Parent cultures

I begin answering these questions by situating the sadomasochistic fan fiction of Pornish Pixies in its broader contexts. There are elements in much of the sci-fi and fantasy film and television of the last 20 years that reference and draw on fetish and BDSM culture, and this has, I would suggest, predisposed the development of sadomasochistic fan stories in these genres. This evident contemporary on-screen sci-fi/fantasy fetish aesthetic draws on the campier erotics of earlier science fiction shows such as *Buck Rogers in the 25th Century* (Film 1979, TV Series 1979–81) *Star Trek* the first (Television 1966–9) and *Flash Gordon* (Serial Cinema 1936–40, Television 1954–60, Film 1980). Who can doubt that the huge collars of Ming the Merciless, the body-sculpted shiny black garb of Hawk or the faux-lycra of the Trek uniforms reveal a certain 'kinky' quality? Indeed, this fantasy fetish aesthetic, given a big-screen boost by the Wachowski brothers' *Matrix* trilogy (1999–2003), has almost become *de rigeur* on North American sci-fi and fantasy television shows. Acres of moody leather and skin-fitting zips have squeaked across the sets of *Andromeda* (2000–5), *Mutant X* (2001–4), *Buffy* (1997–2003), and *Angel* (1999–2004), *Farscape* (1999–2003), *Dark Angel* (2000–2), *Relic Hunter* (1999–2002), *Xena* (1995–2001), and the like in recent years. Even the military shows, where the 'good guys' wear uniform, have aliens prone to appear in leather or pvc and zips, the cylon Six in Ronald D. Moore's reimagined *Battlestar Galactica* (2003–ongoing) for instance, or the con-woman Vala in *Stargate SG1* (2004–7). Nor does the Harry Potter canon remain innocent. The character of Severus Snape, played by Alan Rickman on-screen, whose bitter brooding sadism in the classroom is matched by all-black attire, from his shiny boots to his high-collared cloak, is a sardonic and sartorial gift to s/m fan fiction. Undoubtedly, this relationship between fetish and sci-fi/fantasy has a long (pre-moving images) history, and has arisen because one of the preoccupations of other-worldly narrative has often been sex with strange, exotic and 'magical' others, and the heightened and taboo qualities this presents.

Mark Winokur provides an excellent history of 'fetishism' in Hollywood horror and science fiction, suggesting that, as rooted in European anthropology:

> The fetish was originally an attempt to orientalize the visible material culture of the unknowable other in such a way that the other's culture can exist only in monstrous form . . . [and that] . . . the monster in American film – and special effects more generally construed – is a conspicuous representative of the racialized fetish, a creation of the racial and ethnic others as fetishes.
>
> (Winokur, 2004: para. 12)

He reads earlier silent horror, fantasy and science fiction films such as *The Leprechaun* (1908) and *A Trip to Mars* (1910), 'in order to establish the ubiquity of this genre's fetishised interest in conflating the fear of race and femininity from almost the beginning of the American film industry' (Winokur, 2004: para. 23).

This history is important. Ming the Merciless, when first drawn in the *Flash Gordon* comic strip in 1934, had many of the ethnic characteristics (surname, shape of the eyes, etc.) of a Chinese villain as much as an extra-terrestrial one. This resemblance was resignified somewhat in later retellings (as in the 1980 film) as a partial cultural awareness of the undesirability of racial stereotyping began to permeate the genre. Without question contemporary North American and British science fiction and fantasy screen canon (which I shall henceforth take to mean texts of the last 20 years) has inherited these earlier representational significatory systems in relation to a fetish aesthetic, albeit in modified forms, for example the well-explored relationship to what Barbara Creed (1993b) calls 'the monstrous feminine'. However, these representational systems have not remained static. As Milly Williamson points out in her discussion of Polidori's sympathetic vampire Lord Ruthven (*The Vampyre*, 1819) and James Malcolm Rymer's equally appealing *Varney the Vampire* (1847), a fascination with (and fetishisation of) otherness has encoded such alien fantasies, even before the advent of cinema, with an empathetic identification as well as abjection and objectification:

> From its entry into the novel, the popularised image of the vampire in Europe and the Anglo-American world had become fused to Byronic images of glamorous outsiderdom, morose fatalism, sexual deviancy, and social and artistic rebellion.
>
> (Williamson, 2005: 294)

SM and kinky fanfic

Some of the ways in which these fetished and gendered histories of desire continue within contemporary sci-fi and fantasy film and television, and then are reworked in the associated fan fiction, I will come on to later. But what precisely do I mean by 'sadomasochistic' (s/m) fan fiction? I am using 'sadomasochistic' as an umbrella term to include consensual and non-consensual stories which involve some combination of sexualised restraint, fetish, pain, humiliation, coercion and power differentials. Both BDSM and 'non-con' stories (including rape and incest stories that are non-consensual rather than staged consensual fantasy scenarios)[3] are sometimes filed under the heading BDSM on fan fiction sites, although some sites do not accept 'non-con' and some do. This blurred demarcation differs markedly IRL where there is a clear separation between BDSM (consensual bondage, discipline, dominance, submission, sadism and masochism) and non-consensual sexualised violence, namely, rape, abuse, torture, assault and so on. However, this blending has a significant literary history.

The 'syndromes' of sadism and masochism were coined by nineteenth-century German psychologist Richard von Krafft-Ebing in his study *Psychopathia Sexualis* (1885). Krafft-Ebing drew his definitions from the names of two authors of works of literature – Donatien-Alphonse-Francoise de Sade, commonly known as the Marquis de Sade, an eighteenth -century French aristocrat, and Leopold von Sacher-Masoch, a nineteenth-century Polish professor. De Sade's work contains a phenomenal catalogue of acts of sexually motivated torture and cruelty, while Sacher-Masoch's most famous work *Venus in Furs* (1869) is the story of a young man, Severin, desperate to be enslaved to a cold, domineering, cruel mistress (Deleuze and von Sacher-Masoch, 1989). Neither of the scenarios described fit contemporary BDSM criteria for safe, sane and consensual play. The sexual tortures imagined by de Sade are inflicted on suffering and unwilling victims, although the torturers are filled with erotic glee. In Sacher-Masoch's novel both Severin the masochist and Wanda the sadist participate willingly, but according to Sacher-Masoch's wife Aurora von Romelin, IRL he coerced her into playing the role of his cruel *Venus in Furs* by threatening her with financial destitution if she did not cooperate.

In the realm of non-fictional sadomasochism, BDSM today refers not simply to a collection of bodily acts and behaviours that may include bondage, spanking, caning, whipping, needle-play, blood-play, sex toys such as nipple clamps, 'water-sports' (urine play), role-play with power differentials (doctor/patient, teacher/pupil, officer/grunt, master/slave) and appropriate dressing-up. It is also attached to subcultures of its own that are distinct from those of most commercial straight male sadomasochistic pornography and its associated misogyny. Contemporary British and North American IRL BDSM subcultures developed in the gay underground of the 1960s and 1970s. They have inherited in their foundation the liberationist and radical politics of that era, including significant input from 'sex-positive' Second Wave feminism (Wiseman, 1997). Participating clubs and webspaces adhere to a code of ethics whose basic mantra is 'safe, sane and consensual' (SSC) or 'risk aware consensual kink' (RACK). In the 'real world', BDSM subcultures do not condone or participate in non-consensual sadomasochism. Within these, BDSM is not about putting the minds/bodies of others under duress for erotic gratification without their consent; on the contrary, BDSM has a very strong ethics of care (see, for example, http://www.nightofthesenses.com/book_delights_08b.html).

BDSM, as presently culturally encoded and practised, is about trust, and concerns mental, emotional and sensation play. Its goal is the creation of heightened physical/psychological states in a safe environment. It is 'erotic, consensual and recreational' (Weinberg, 1995: 290). All the words, restraint, pain, humiliation, coercion, torture, that one might use as descriptors within this framework need to be 'quote marked' in our understanding, because these are played with but never in actuality forced. The one who is mentally or physically 'on their knees' in a scenario always ultimately has control, and may stop play at any time using a 'safe word' (which is never 'no' or 'stop' because people frequently mutually enjoy playing with the pretence of non-consent and force) (Wiseman, 1997; Miller and Devon, 1995).

S/m fan fiction incorporates agreed and forced scenarios. It runs the gamut from the gentle and consensual, such as 'Discipline' by Kate Andrews in the new *Battlestar Galactica* universe, which is tagged 'PG-13, mild BDSM content', to the more coercive, such as 'Latitude and

Longitude' by A. Manley Height in the *Babylon 5* universe, which is tagged 'NC-17, BDSM, borderline non-con, m/m sex and violence'.[4] However, from my travels in the worlds of fan fiction online, I would say that a clear majority of sadomasochistic fan fics follow BDSM IRL codes and involve consensual scenarios. An example would be 'Exposure/shameless Sunday' by Fangrrl, which is tagged as 'NC-17/Adult slash, d/s, cross-dressing'. It follows BDSM IRL codes meticulously. Set in the *Dr Who* spin-off *Torchwood* universe, this involves an erotic scenario between canonical characters Jack and Ianto where Jack is 'forced' to wear stockings and suspenders by his teammate, and is gagged, spanked and then hit with a belt through the accompanying silk underwear in the ensemble. Jack fully consents to this, enjoys it and looks forward to more at the end. Yes, it pushes his limits – the story tells us that he feels vulnerable, exposed and somewhat shamed and humiliated throughout, but in the narrative he himself enjoys travelling through these sensations. They are challenging and erotic for him and ultimately 'held'. In other words, Jack is safe because Ianto cares for him and takes responsibility for his well-being within the 'scene'. Such is the role of a 'top' with respect to a 'bottom' in BDSM. The story follows the conventions of an IRL BDSM scenario in relation to the body – Ianto takes care to build the intensity of sensation slowly so that endorphin release builds also. He doesn't hit Jack cold with a belt buckle. He waits until the pain parameters of the body have shifted after 'warm-up' (gradated spanking) so that the belt produces a pain/pleasure 'rush' sensation. And then Ianto is gentle and strokes the burning skin of his 'victim'/lover.

Not all sadomasochistic fan fiction is written, as 'Exposure/shameless Sunday' is, within the BDSM codes adhered to by associated IRL subcultures. 'Non-con' stories, as I said earlier, may or may not be listed under BDSM as a fan fiction category. For example, 'Prowlers' by Princess Jade Plum on her own website is listed as 'NC-17, DARK FIC (language: Rape/Torture)' and as 'BDSM, Unconsenting'. This story is set in the *Buffy/Angel* universes with a cross-over reference to the horror film *Cat People* (1942, 1982). It is set in 1889, which in the *Buffy/Angel* canon means that the hero-vampires Spike and Angel are both soulless and evil at this point. Angelus (evil Angel) has captured a 'were-leopard' woman in the Egyptian desert. The story consists of his torture and rape of her, with Spike's reluctant participation:

> Angelus has been merciless in his courtship. Her lithe back and pert buttocks are striped, cut with a ruthlessly well-placed cane. Many of the stripes are already in a rapid healing stage. Lycanthropes heal

> bodily damage fairly quickly if the injury isn't done with silver weapons. Part of me wonders why Angelus isn't using silver on her. Her ass is a perfect cloven heart shape mottled with switching and handprint bruises and bite marks. I smell the injury of her bound wrists. Although Angelus used a strong silk rope she's still fought the bonds so hard they chaffed and blistered her wrists. I know her arms and shoulders must feel wrenched and sore from working and tugging, straining for freedom to escape. Angelus snarls at me as I take in the sight of the prone bound woman. Angrily, he steps out of the shadows and wrenches her slim legs open. She winces and bites back her cries as he probes her cunny, then draws his fingers out, disgusted, 'Dry as a bone!' he rages.
>
> (http://www.geocities.com/princessplumjade/plumjadeprowlers.html)

This piece, which was probably written sometime in the early 2000s, is listed as having won a number of fan awards (fan fiction awards judged and run by other fans), for example, *the Buffy/Angel* fan awards Fancy Me Yours, Best Crossover Fic in 2003, which means that it was accepted and judged to be a good and enjoyable piece of writing by a considerable number of Princess Plum's peers.

Sadomasochistic fan fiction is variously treated online, on the innumerable sites, web rings and communities where fan fiction is uploaded, linked and shared. Some sites do not permit it. Some specify boundaries of various sorts, for instance, 'Slashspank', hosted at LJ states that it is a space for 'loving, consensual m/m spanking stories'. It is an 'outsider genre' to the extent that the more mainstream a site the less likely it is to accept sadomasochistic stories. FanFiction.net, one of the largest-known fan fiction sites online and probably one of the most well known in the mainstream media, has an 18+ rating but does not upload BDSM fiction. The first corporate-run site for fan fiction, FanLib.com, which caused considerable controversy in the world of fandom with its launch in 2007 in association with various commercial partners such as HarperCollins and Starz Entertainment, has two ratings categories, 'All' and '13+'. There are 'Angst', 'Romance' and 'Hurt/Comfort' categories, but no 'Darkfic'[5] or 'BDSM'. 'Kink' as a term amalgamates the consensual and the non-consensual. The Titantium Whip awards, created by Azure Chaos, are devoted entirely to 'Kink-fic'. Azure Chaos, also known online as Nathaniel and 'slave-prince', is, according to the Titanium Whip and his own LJ pages, 'predominantly gay', living with multiple sclerosis and with his two boyfriends, a submissive BDSM practitioner, who has survived chemotherapy and IRL sexual abuse. He writes in his LJ profile that he is

> a brother, a delinquent, a sweet thing, a lover . . . angelically evil . . . perpeptually horny . . . a poet who sometimes loses his words . . . submissive yet no doormat, strong willed yet unable to stand tall . . . wounded, trapped, yet healing and free.
> (http://slave-prince03.livejournal.com/profile)

His slash story, 'Meaning of rings' set in the *X-men* universe, wherein Warren and Scott become lovers, like Fangrrl's 'Exposure/shameless Sunday', is infused with 'real-world' BDSM ethics and an associated knowledge of related technologies of the body:

> Scott slowly began to build the sting of the whip, hesitating after a particularly sharp snap and seeing an earlier red mark that stayed on the skin even after two more lashes.
>
> Warren couldn't believe how those stings would fire up his spine then down to his dick, making it pulse and leak . . .
>
> 'Warren?' Scott asked, 'Do you want more? It can cause an adrenaline high just like a jogger's high.'
>
> 'Yes . . . oh god . . . please . . . ' his voice was shaky and full of need.
>
> Scott began to move the whip strikes further up and down Warren's back and legs, carefully avoiding the kidney area and starting with lighter stings to build them up to match the color of his ass.
>
> 'Does it feel good, Warren?' he asked as the redness leveled out.
>
> Warren was gasping in lungfuls of air as the heat and sting in his back felt like a raging fire, he'd never felt so completely alive. It was incredible and he felt too incoherent to put into words just how good it felt. 'Yes . . . ' He groaned loudly. 'So . . . good!' He didn't want the intense pleasure-pain to stop.
>
> Scott continued the whipping slowly building the intensity and careful to spread it out and not concentrate in one area.
> (http://azure-chaos.pbwiki.com/MeaningOfRings#Chapter 8)

I suggest it is not the case that those who have been physically or sexually abused are condemned to reproduce and reiterate an unhealthy dynamic within BDSM. Survivors such as Azure Chaos, in its safe, sane and consensual culture, whether IRL or fictional, may find space to rework old powerlessness and suffering.

New pornographies

Sadomasochistic fan fiction, whether adhering to IRL BDSM codes or not, participates in the pornographic. One of its significant functions is erotic and masturbatory. It is designed to be sexually stimulating. Following recent adventures in censorship, Pornish Pixies has in fact defiantly subtitled itself 'the community you wank off to'. Writing challenge categories on Pornish Pixies include 'non-con', 'three kink', 'bondage', 'come shots' and 'porn in motion'. Elsewhere I have argued that the subcultural world of online s/m fan fiction constitutes, at the present time, what we might call an emergent post-phallocratic pornographic space (Alexander, 2004). What I mean by this is that this space, as currently constituted, has a number of characteristics that combine to overturn the pornographies of the mainstream. And in so doing, it is creating new (and to my mind, hopeful) worlds of intimate, communicative and erotic possibility.

Masculine vulnerability in science fiction and fantasy screen canon is significantly more evident than it once was, but is still frequently located in 'nerdy' male characters, for example Daniel Jackson in early seasons of *Stargate SG1* or British Nigel in *Relic Hunter*. With respect to central male hero figures, physical and mental vulnerability often continues to be reserved for times of extreme danger. But if masculine vulnerability is highly contained in the canon, the fetishised 'phallic' woman is ubiquitous. From the robot Maria in Fritz Lang's *Metropolis* (1927) to the cyber-converted Lisa in the new *Dr Who* spin-off *Torchwood*, the sci-fi and fantasy canon is littered with imaginings of the pneumatic cybernetic dominant alien sex-woman. On screen there is no recurrent male equivalent quite so fetishised in costumed bondage as she. In the accompanying fan fiction, this is reworked. Within sadomasochistic fan writing (at this historical point in time) it is the male body that is predominantly fetishised.[6] Male weakness, need and pain, still often governed by strict codes in the parent culture, is the desired forbidden object. S/m fan stories write that vulnerability onto the male body, as Freud's (1991) classical fetishist wrote the absent penis of the mother onto the female body to create a ravenous all-powerful monster woman, the antithesis of ideal Victorian femininity.

Sadomasochistic fan fiction is produced within a young (teens to thirty-somethings) female-dominated environment with a significant queer presence, where the culture is often dedicated to overturning and questioning gender norms. It is predominantly the bodies of the canons' heroes that are put under duress in s/m fan fiction, mostly by one another, in scenes grounded in passionate attachment. This is applied enthusiastically to both the male and female heroes of on-screen canons, depending on the preferences of individual writers, lists and archives. However, while the on-screen rise of the female action hero in the 1990s has been accompanied by a concomitant rise in femme-slash (girl-on-girl action)[7] in fan narratives, sadomasochistic fan fiction taken as a totality does not offer a vista of entirely equal opportunities bondage.

While the fetishised vulnerable male body is put under duress, it is not engaged with as a piece of meat to be debased, as de Sade's female bodies frequently are. Fan writers love the characters they work with, and as readers and *betas* (volunteer critics and editors) they share that affection with one another. Their representations are populated by emotional attachments rather than with anonymous flesh. This is not a space of reverse misogyny (misandry), although I do not wish to do a disservice to de Sade by misrepresenting the complexity of his work (Carter, 1979). Many s/m fan fiction writers are involved IRL in BDSM subcultures, and import the 'ethics of care' these communities promulgate into their writing, as the stories by Azure Chaos and Fangrrl discussed earlier make clear. Non-consensual and rape narratives, when they do occur, are underpinned by these collective ethics.

At present 'non-con' fan fiction stories are generally being written within a culture framed by ethical responsibility, supported by fan writers' shared knowledge about BDSM codes of consent. Frequent discussion about the reasons for writing 'non-con' and the problematics of doing so appear on the associated blogs and comments that accompany the fiction. For example, this comment from Orin, who notes that she has most enjoyed writing in the *Sailor Moon* and *Harry Potter* universes, on her website 'Dark Tangent':

> I can get squicked writing non-con sex. So unless there's an honest-to-god justification, I really do NOT write rape. And rarely condone writing it.
>
> (http://www.darktangent.com/faq.htm)

Or the following remark by Lorelie Jones which, by contrast, comments on her choice to write such fics:

> Now, if I read a rape or non-con story, does that mean I condone rape in real life? Not even close. What it does mean is that a rape story can

> touch certain of my emotions that no other type of story can, and that those emotions, like all the others, need to be felt . . . I may write about subjects deemed as immoral, but I view my very writing as a moral act. I am endangering no one, and I am maintaining my own mental health. Rather than unleashing unexamined or unacknowledged feelings on my loved ones, I let them spill forth onto the page, or I project them onto the characters I'm reading about. I still find release, but I'm not taking it out on the undeserving. Personally, I consider that the most decent thing I can do.
>
> (Jones, 2007)

Sadomasochistic fan-fiction narratives can be compared with commercial visual sadomasochistic pornography available online in abundant quantity. The erotics of playing with denigratory speech are well understood within BDSM; nevertheless it is notable that a significant amount of visual pornography for the straight-male market continues to be framed by language that describes women and femininity within misogynist and patriarchal economies.

Bodily limits, cultural excess

The fetishisation of the vulnerable male body by women as producers of sci-fi and fantasy representations is a new development, and one still marginal in the canon on screen. This is perhaps unsurprising as the industry continues to be male dominated. But the torture of the hero is not new. We have only to think of the naked torso of Saint Sebastian pierced by arrows or the endless suffering of Prometheus, his liver ripped out night after night by the wrathful eagles of Zeus to be certain that the heroic figure bowed, bruised and bloodied has held a fascination for eras previous to our own. As Aristotle observed in tragedy, catharsis and the physically suffering hero body has provided a representational point for the collective experience of (displaced) suffering and endurance, from Beowulf to Buffy. However, unlike Joseph Campbell (1949), I am not proposing that all hero stories can be simply reduced to a 'monomyth', one underlying and universal human narrative. What *precisely* is codified within the body of the tortured hero – what values; what shared cultural events and experiences; what moralities; what gender, 'race', class and erotic paradigms – remains culturally and historically variable.

In contemporary sadomasochistic fan fiction the 'active audience' augments the torture of the hero/heroes, physical and psychological, always already present in the screen canon, and overtly eroticises it, in pursuit of what we might call the mastery of excess. What might that excess be? Foucault (1988: 210) argued that 'Sadism is not a name finally given to a practice as old as Eros, but a massive cultural fact which appeared precisely at the end of the eighteenth century and which constitutes one of the greatest conversions of Western imagination.' He meant to suggest, I think, that as social control extended into bodily and psychological spheres in increasingly overdetermining schema, so subjects emerged acculturated to managed technologies of staged and restrained cruelty. The sadomasochistic imagination, in other words, was inaugurated as a strategy – one perhaps desirous of and/or compelled to work through, subjectivity *subjected to* increasing microtechnologies of surveillance, control and coercion.

John Noyes (1998: 146) proposes that

> S/M [by which he means here consensual BDSM] is not an expression of violence, it is a socially determined strategy for dealing with violence, a set of codified performances and rituals. These rituals play on the violence inherent in the social codification of subjectivity, dramatizing the moments when this violence becomes visible. If we are to understand sadomasochistic performances, we have to map them onto the landscape of social conventions they are intended to negotiate.

This nuanced approach seems to me far more successfully applicable to the consideration of the production and circulation of sadomasochistic representations (whether fictional or IRL) than either blanket condemnation or blanket approbation.

Margo Weiss (2006: 108–9) has written on the 'mainstreaming of kink' in the last 20 years in the US, from fetish outfits in advertising to the success of the film *Secretary* (2002). Why has this taken place? The popularisation of sadomasochism in contemporary culture may indicate the collective need to negotiate, in some manageable way, the oppressive Orwellian double-speak of the state. Could mass cultural representations of sadomasochism be attempts to express the collective psyche through the staged, enacted and managed experience of violence – a defiant parody of autonomy, or rather an autonomy of the body personal in the face of alienation from the body politic?

While the parent culture produces Mel Gibson's sadistic *The Passion of Christ* (2004) and takes up high-street handcuffs and blindfolds in unprecedented numbers (available, for instance, in Anne Summers shops), consensual BDSM narratives of restraint and bodily duress, as well as sadomasochistic 'non-con' and rape stories, are being typed with enthusiasm by myriad British and North American teens and twenty-somethings, noticeably, within *Harry Potter* and *Lord of the Rings* fandoms, two of the most popular collective narratives of our times. The sexual self-determination of young people is problematised and denied, and yet youth is highly sexually commodified. Coincidence? I think not. The rise and rhizomatic spread of sadomasochistic fan fiction online may be read not as moral decay within a spectrum of violence linked to IRL abuse, but rather as a complex playground of imaginative coping strategies for contemporary lives filled with restraint. From SATS (school testing in the UK) to the search engine cookies which track and store every web interaction, building intimate profiles for future marketing, young British and North Americans are monitored by state and corporate panopticons on a 24/7 basis. And for the past five years they have also lived with the violence of the Iraq War, ever-present yet somehow bizarrely sublimated in their country's domestic consciousnesses.

Complicating moralities

Rather than allowing blanket and dangerously simplistic cause-and-effect arguments regarding sadomasochistic and otherwise 'extreme' pornographic representations to materially prevail, it is important to ask more complex questions. It is not enough to prejudge what sadomasochistic representations in general 'do' in the minds of recipients. This denies diversity. A better question would be to ask what ideologies are being codified (by producers and consumers) in relation to specific sets of representations. But this needs to be extended also. What cultures and contexts (productive and interpretive) are particular sadomasochistic representations circulating within? How are these representations materially produced? What are their ethical frameworks?

Debates on these issues take a different shape in different national contexts despite the increasingly transnational nature of representation. For example, in the UK a proposed new Criminal Justice and Immigration Bill is at present in passage (2006–8 ongoing). If it becomes law, it will make it an offence for a person to be in possession of an 'extreme pornographic image'.[8] Various civil and sexual liberties groups have joined forces in order to attempt to complicate the premise on which the UK government is working, which appears to be that 'extreme' pornography is necessarily equivalent to violence and therefore necessarily promotes violence, particularly towards women (http://www.backlash-uk.org.uk/index.html). This particular governmental approach not only fundamentally misrecognises consensual sadomasochism and its representations, but appears to apply a simple cause-and-effect model to representations and IRL behaviour. While the Bill focuses on images, not on written representations, the argument that there is a sure and certain relationship between 'extreme' representation, its production/consumption, and criminal IRL non-consensual activity is similar to that of Warriors for Innocence.[9] In short, not all sadomasochistic economies are equivalent.

Matt Hills warns us not to romanticise fan culture (Hills, 2002: 15); nor should we. Nevertheless I regard s/m fan fiction as constituting a very interesting social and sexual space at present. Sadomasochistic fan fiction online, as a collective emergent post-phallocratic pornographic space, brings an explicit awareness of power dynamics into the realm of desire. Its predominantly young, predominantly female audience-producers persistently play with and make sexually manifest the hierarchies of the canon and of the culture. And they do so in highly self-reflexive and ethical contexts.

As Foucault pointed out, it is no accident that de Sade's writing was during the Terror in France. Nor is it surprising that consensual BDSM cultures were developed within the gay community at a time when homosexuality was socially stigmatised and gay liberation was brewing. These too are Sadeian times. Yet the choice is not between violence and vanilla. In my view, putting the body under duress, whether IRL or in fantasy and representation, can be healing and emotionally intelligent, just as it can be damaging. It depends on the kinds of cultures we create – mutual, connected and empathetic, or indeed their opposites – in which to express the stress and endurance of the times.

Fan fiction

'Ansereg'. http://www.ansereg.com/of_the_laws_of_ansereg.htm (accessed 15 July 2007).

'Discipline'. Kate Andrews 'PG-13, mild BDSM content' http://www.fictabulous.com/discipline.php (accessed 5 August 2007).

'Exposure/shameless Sunday'. Fangrrl 'NC-17/ Adult slash, d/s, cross-dressing' http://fangrrl-squees.livejournal.com/47606.html (accessed 20 July 2007).

'Forbidden feelings'. ksevfansd 'BDSM, slash, beastiality' http://multifaceted.creative-musings.com/nominees04.htm (accessed 5 August 2007).

'Latitude and longditude'. A. Manley Height 'NC-17, BDSM, borderline non-con, m/m sex and violence' http://www.skeeter63.org/~allaire/LatitudeAndLongitude.htm (accessed 5 August 2007).

'The making and breaking of Nathaniel'. http://slave-prince03.livejournal.com/ (accessed 10 July 2007).

'Meaning of rings'. Azure Chaos http://azure-chaos.pbwiki.com/MeaningOfRings (accessed 6 August 2007).

'Prowlers'. Princess Plum Jade 'NC-17, DARK FIC (language: Rape/Torture) BDSM, Unconsenting' http://www.geocities.com/princessplumjade/plumjadeprowlers.html (accessed 17 July 2007).
'Stigmata'. Underlucius 'NC-17' http://community.livejournal.com/pornish_pixies/149100.html (accessed 7 August 2007).

Websites

Ansereg, Adult Tolkein Fan Writing by Tyellas http://www.ansereg.com/ansereg.htm (accessed 15 July 2007).
Backlash http://www.backlash-uk.org.uk/index.html (accessed 9 August 2007).
Criminal Justice and Immigration Bill 2006–07 to 2007–08 http://www.publications.parliament.uk/pa/pabills/200607/criminal_justice_and_immigration.htm (accessed 5 August 2007).
Dark Tangent http://www.darktangent.com (accessed 9 August 2007).
Fancy Me Yours http://www.firepretty.com/fmya/ (accessed 25 July 2007).
The Fanfiction Glossary http://www.subreality.com/glossary/terms.htm (accessed 9 August 2007).
The Fanfic Symposium http://www.trickster.org/symposium/ (accessed 9 August 2007).
FanFiction.net www.fanfiction.net (accessed 4 August 2007).
FanLib.com www.fanlib.com (accessed 5 August 2007).
LiveJournal www.livejournal.com (accessed 3 August 2007).
Motion Picture of America Association (MPAA) http://www.mpaa.org/AboutUs.asp (accessed 3 August 2007).
Multi-faceted Harry Potter Fan Fiction Awards http://multifaceted.creative-musings.com/index.htm (accessed 5 August 2007).
Night of the Senses http://www.nightofthesenses.com/ (accessed 21 July 2007).
Pornish Pixies http://community.livejournal.com/pornish_pixies/ (accessed 6 August 2007).
Princess Plum Jade's Fan Fiction http://www.geocities.com/princessplumjade/plumjadefics.html (accessed 5 August 2007).
Slashspank http://community.livejournal.com/slashspank/ (accessed 2 August 2007).
The Titanium Whip Awards http://titanium-whip-awards.pbwiki.com/ (accessed 5 August 2007).
Warriors for Innocence www.warriorsforinnocence.org (accessed 3 August 2007).
Weasleycest http://community.livejournal.com/weasleycest/profile (accessed 2 August 2007).
Wikipedia http://en.wikipedia.org/wiki/LiveJournal (accessed 6 August 2007).

Notes

1. Slash refers to a same-sex sexual and/or emotional pairing. Girl-on-girl slash fiction is usually tagged 'femme-slash'.
2. From Wikipedia statistics on LiveJournal at http://en.wikipedia.org/wiki/LiveJournal.

3. In s/m fan fiction 'non-con' differs from rape because 'non-con' encompasses a whole range of eroticised acts (non-consensual in this instance), such as blindfolding and whipping, which do not necessarily involve the genital or anal insertion by which rape is usually defined. 'Non-con' as a fan fiction category tends to indicate that such acts are taking place in a sexualised context.
4. Most fan fiction is 'rated'. Frequently, stories written in English have followed the official Motion Picture Association of America (MPAA) ratings system, from G to NC-17. However, the MPAA served 'cease and desist' notifications to FanFiction.net and some other fan-fiction sites for violation of trademark in 2005, and since then many sites have developed their own ratings systems (although others still use MPAA). As well as ratings, stories also tend to contain warnings in their descriptor headings.
5. 'Darkfic' is a fan-fiction category defined on 'The fanfiction glossary' as 'involving a large amount of death/pain/trauma being inflicted on the characters' (http://www.subreality.com/glossary/terms.htm) (accessed 9 August 2007). It is not necessarily sadomasochistic (i.e. the trauma is not necessarily sexualised).
6. Academics have noted that fan fiction is a female-dominated space where intimacy is staged between men. However, most have focussed on romance themes and emphasised a process of cross-gender identification. The idea that this is an arena for female-generated masturbatory material has, until recently, been elided by the impossibility of attributing a truly pornographic (i.e. orgasm-focused) imaginary to women.
7. Femme-slash writing began in significant quantities as attached to the *Xena Warrior Princess* television series (1995–2001), and *Sailor Moon* anime series (1992–7) imported from Japan to the US. *Buffy the Vampire Slayer* (1997–2003) also inspired considerable femme-slash. These canons had active female heroines involved in close friendships with one another from which femme-slash fan fiction could springboard imaginatively.
8. At this point 'extreme' is defined in the proposed legislation as sex (or in each case the appearance of sex) involving animals, corpses, threat to life (hanging, strangling, threat with a weapon) and injury, specifically to the breasts, anus or genitals http://www.publications.parliament.uk/pa/pabills/200607/criminal_justice_and_immigration.htm.
9. At the same time, attempting, as J. K. Rowling's literary agents and lawyers for Warner Brothers did in 2001–3, to censor s/m fan fiction for its supposed corrupting influence on 'innocent children' focuses in fact on the creative autonomous sexual expression of young people in a shameful display of our parent culture's hypocrisy. When Warner Brothers bought the film rights to Harry Potter in 2001 they served 'cease and desist' notices to several fan-fiction sites for infringement of copyright. Fans organised and forced a climbdown (Jenkins, 2006; see also House, 2003).

9

'Oh Spike you're covered in sexy wounds!' The Erotic Significance of Wounding and Torture in *Buffy the Vampire Slayer*

Viv Burr

The television show *Buffy the Vampire Slayer* (*BtVS*) ran for seven seasons (1997–2003) and was broadcast in the USA, the UK and other European countries and Australasia, acquiring an enthusiastic and dedicated fan base which gave it cult status. In addition to generating much fan activity, it has attracted considerable academic attention.[1] For the purposes of examining the relations of sex, violence and the body, it may be argued that *BtVS* is a particularly rich source. It is a show with a hybrid generic make-up, combining elements of gothic/horror, teen drama and soap opera; as a show aimed principally at a teen audience (but in fact drawing viewers from a much wider demographic range), a central focus has been personal relationships and sexuality. But its gothic/horror elements mean that these issues are frequently played out within narratives that involve violence. When the violence is meted out to vampire characters, the indestructible nature of their bodies (with the exceptions of stakes through the heart, decapitation and fire) means that injuries that would kill a human can be sustained and recovered from. *BtVS* therefore provides narratively and generically legitimate opportunities for viewing acts of wounding and torture, and the possibilities for an erotic reading of these are enhanced by frequent implicit and sometimes explicit references to BDSM (Bondage, Domination, Sadism, Masochism) practices.

This chapter examines selected scenes from *BtVS* involving wounding and torture, and aims to understand the source of their erotic power. Their erotic appeal certainly owes something to their cinematic construction; however, this explanation alone does not suffice. I argue that an appreciation of the dynamics of eroticism in the real world gives us a more complete understanding of why such scenes are erotically powerful. This is in principle what film and television theorists have done in incorporating Freudian psychodynamic theory into their analyses.

However, I argue that the debates around spectatorship and the gaze that have arisen through the application of psychoanalytic theory to film and television indicate that this theoretical framework, when applied in this area, has become untenable. Instead, I apply a quite different framework, that of the humanistic existentialism of Sartre. I argue that this analysis offers a more parsimonious account of the erotic, particularly in the context of wounding and torture.

Reflexivity

My analysis is inevitably shaped by my own reading of the selected scenes and my reading will further be affected by my own biography, social position and viewing history. As a middle-aged, middle-class heterosexual woman who grew up at a time when classic Hollywood films were staple television viewing, my reading may be very different from that of people with different biographies; there is certainly a difficulty in claiming that certain scenes simply 'are' or are not erotic, or that they have particular significance for female viewers, and I acknowledge this. The difficulty lies not in the inevitable partiality of one's reading but in claims that media images have universal meanings. I therefore offer my own reading here in the knowledge that it is one of many possible readings of these texts. Nevertheless television and film images are unlike real life events; they are representations and heavily promote certain readings through their techniques of construction. My analysis therefore includes the argument that some events are treated erotically and that they therefore invite a sexual reading by the viewer.

The premise of the show

Buffy Summers lives in Sunnydale, California. Built on the site of the 'Hellmouth', it is an opening to the underworld and draws to itself all kinds of demons and monsters, including vampires. The mythology of the show states that throughout history there has always been a Slayer, a girl who is given special strength and skills for killing demons and vampires. Buffy executes her demon-fighting duties with the help of her friends, principally Willow and Xander and her younger sister, Dawn. Other central characters are two men who have been Buffy's sexual partners: Angel and Spike. Angel is a vampire with a soul, forced to live with the torment of the atrocities he earlier committed. Spike, a long-time adversary of Buffy, later falls in love with her. At the height of his obsession in season 5, he commissions the building of a robot Buffy lookalike and sex toy, dubbed the 'Buffybot'. Spike seeks to become good through the return of his own soul at end of the show's sixth season; the path of his redemption is a major narrative arc of (the final) season 7.

Selected scenes

Given the premise of *BtVS*, it is no surprise that characters are routinely injured and killed. I will not discuss these 'everyday' injuries, but focus on instances of wounding and torture. Almost exclusively, such wounding and torture is inflicted by beautiful, powerful but evil females upon young, attractive males. Specifically, I will look at scenes where such wounding and torture appear to be erotically charged. In order to tease out some of the relevant issues, I will also look at further scenes where the wounding/torture arguably does *not* have erotic appeal.

'What's My Line? Part 2' (2: 10)

Angel has been captured by (evil) Spike and his vampire girlfriend Drusilla. We learn that Drusilla is weak and in order to restore her to full vampire health they must perform a ritual for which they need the blood of her sire: Angel. The scene is set in a bedroom, featuring a lace-festooned four-poster bed, giving the scene a sexual flavour. Angel, naked to the waist, is tied to the foot of the bed, his arms stretched between the posts creating a cruciform image. Spike allows Drusilla to 'play' with Angel for a while before the designated time for the ritual arrives.

As Jowett (2004) has noted, this scene conflates sex and violence. The lighting is soft, and Drusilla's tone of voice very sensual. As she tortures Angel by pouring holy water over his naked torso, we see a long shot of them. Drusilla is leaning between Angel's spread legs, an explicitly sexual image. The camera lingers on his smooth body, and Drusilla too lingers over his body, dribbling the holy water down his chest, burning his flesh. He cries out and throws his head back, echoing the appearance and sounds of sexual ecstasy.

'Intervention' (5: 18)

Spike has been captured by the powerful Hell-god Glory, who is searching for the identity of a mystical 'key' which will allow her to literally send the world to Hell. Spike knows that the 'key' is in fact Buffy's sister, Dawn, and his love for Buffy prevents him from giving Glory this information. The scene takes place in Glory's apartment room which contains a large circular bed. The scantily clad Glory seizes Spike, whose hands are tied behind his back, and throws him down on the bed. She leaps on top of him, straddling his body. This already highly sexualised scene then becomes brutally violent and further sexualised as she thrusts her finger deep inside his chest, saying 'Let's see what's inside'.

A little later we find that she has strung him up from the ceiling, his hands and feet bound, a long tear in his T-shirt. In a close-up shot, we see his chest bears the wound from her earlier assault and his face shows evidence of beating. Glory further tortures Spike. She grinds a broken glass into his face, then advances towards him with a large knife saying 'Know what vampires and apples have in common? Let's see if I can do you in one long strip', and slashes his chest with a long, diagonal cut.

Spike escapes and in the final scene of this episode, we see his battered body laid out in his crypt. Buffy, who does not yet trust Spike, visits him 'disguised' as the Buffybot in order to get him to tell her what, if anything, he has revealed about Dawn's identity. As her eyes alight on his mutilated face and torso, she utters the words from which I have taken my title: 'Oh Spike, you're covered in sexy wounds! Do you wanna ravage me now?'.

The eroticism of the earlier torture scenes is absent here, despite the explicit sexual reference in the dialogue. Spike rests on a cold, stone tomb, not a bed, and his broken body is hard to look at. Buffy's words (as the Buffybot) are a paradox. Spike's wounded body is not erotically appealing, and the dialogue serves to suggest that humans would not find his battered body arousing.

'Never Leave Me' (7: 9)

In season 7, Spike has regained his soul and is fighting on the side of good. He is kidnapped by the Bringers, agents of the First Evil (FE), in order to use his blood to open the seal over the Hellmouth. Although not strictly torture, since the wounds inflicted on Spike are not made for the purpose of inflicting pain, it is ritualistic. The FE, taking the human form of Buffy, says, 'excuse the spectacle', a direct acknowledgement that Spike's body is here being treated as visual spectacle in the cinematic sense. In a knowing reference to the fan appreciation of displays of Spike's body, the FE (as Buffy) says, 'I was going to bleed Andrew [a more minor character] but you look better with your shirt off.' She delegates the actual cutting of Spike's body to the Bringers, remaining as a spectator. But although we see the knives and other tools, the camera shows us not the Bringers but the observing Buffy/FE and Spike's body.

We see a close-up of Spike's face and then a view of the implements that will be used. Spike, naked to the waist, is strapped to a mediaeval-looking wooden wheel with leather thongs, importing BDSM associations.

Illuminated by candlelight, the scene is soft and shadowy. We do not actually see the cutting, but it is implied as he throws back his head in pain and makes a throttled sound. The focus is on his face, then the camera draws back to reveal the cuts in his chest, in the form of symbols. He is winched up and rotated until facing downwards, spread-eagled on the wheel, blood pouring from his wounds, the scene echoing a crucifixion. Spike's chest heaves with emotional effort but says nothing.

'First Date' (7: 14)

Xander goes on a date with Lissa, a girl he has just met, who turns out to be a demon. She too intends to open the seal over the Hellmouth, this time using Xander's blood. The scene invites a direct comparison with the earlier treatment of Spike, for both the viewer and the analyst. We find that Lissa has bound Xander to the same apparatus described above, however this time the bindings are not mediaeval-looking leather thongs but modern nylon rope. Like Spike, Xander is naked to the waist, but in contrast to Spike's silence, Xander talks nervously and almost constantly. There is no lingering torture; instead, Lissa stabs him in the belly with a knife. In contrast to the previous scene, this scene is arguably not erotically charged.

What makes it (not) erotic?

Character and narrative arc

It seems unlikely that wounding or torture can serve to eroticise any character at all. However, it is hard to judge this as it is only certain types of characters (and their wounding/torture) that are typically eroticised. So the degree of erotic meaning in a scene depends to some extent on narrative and character arcs, and scenes cannot be understood in isolation from these.

The four literary and mythological archetypes of romantic hero, sacrificial deity, warrior and courtly lover are to some degree helpful in analysing the characters of Angel and Spike. Angel is principally represented as a romantic hero. He is tall, dark and good-looking. He is mysterious, says little and broods a good deal. Buffy is irresistibly drawn to him, falls in love with him, and he returns her love. But images of him, as described above, also draw on the sacrificial deity. Cultural historians have written extensively about the pervasive belief in a saviour god who is sacrificed for the good of the world (see Frazer, 1922). It is a fertility myth that has shaped Greek, Roman and Christian beliefs. Angel is also coded as a warrior; the warrior in myth, literature and popular culture has an aura produced by his reputation. For both Angel and Spike, their reputations go before them.

Spike is the courtly lover, on a journey of self-improvement motivated by his love for Buffy, a woman who is his moral and social superior, and is ultimately stirred to noble actions. The quest for his soul, involving the endurance of trials, bears comparison with the heroes of medieval, Arthurian and Renaissance romances. However, in season 7 he is strongly represented as a warrior, Buffy's right-hand man in battle. Spike too is represented within the imagery of the sacrificial deity. In 'Beneath Me' (7.2) he drapes himself over the cross in a church, and we see his flesh burning and in 'Never Leave Me' (7: 9) his blood is the sacrifice that will open the seal over the Hellmouth. By contrast, Xander's status is as Buffy's helper. Although he plays his part in the fight against evil, he is not presented as either a Romantic Hero or Warrior and in fact is rescued from peril by Buffy on numerous occasions throughout the series.

Religious iconography and sexual ecstasy

Although there is little explicit reference to religion, religious imagery abounds in *BtVS*. The quasi-crucifixion scene is a recurring motif and certainly evident in three of the scenes described above.

According to Silverman (1992: 198), 'Christian masochism has radically emasculating implications and is in its purest forms intrinsically incompatible with the pretensions of masculinity.' From this argument, it might appear hard to see how references to Christian images of saintly suffering could work to increase the eroticism of these scenes. The religious iconography, if anything, should serve to de-eroticise these images. However, religious iconography sometimes undoubtedly carries erotic meaning and has frequently portrayed religious ecstasy as carrying sexual overtones. I will briefly present two such examples.

St Sebastian was a Roman soldier executed for his Christian faith by Emperor Diocletian in 288 AD. Diocletian ordered his men to bind Sebastian and shoot arrows into his body. St Sebastian became a very popular, often eroticised, subject of Renaissance and Baroque art (see Figure 9.1) and subsequently became a gay icon (Kaye, 1996).[2] A further example can be seen in the ecstasy of St Theresa by Bernini (see Figure 9.2). St Theresa of Avila spoke of her experience of being visited by an angel who repeatedly pierced her body with a burning arrow, resulting in 'sweet pain', and in this sculpture she appears to be in an ecstatic swoon.

Figure 9.1 *St Sebastian by Guido Reni (1615–1616, Génova)*

In the two quasi-crucifixion scenes in which Angel is tortured and Spike cut and his blood sacrificed, the response of these characters shows clear similarities to sexual ecstasy. Although Xander in 'First Date' is also prepared as a sacrifice, there is no echo of sexual ecstasy; in fact, his suffering is quickly over and presented only briefly to the viewer.

Images of sexual excitement and religious ecstasy may indeed map on to each other to some degree. They share a number of visual and psychological qualities, such as nakedness, submission, loss of subjectivity and the bodily signs of ecstasy/climax. The spectator is then subject to a web of significations that simultaneously refers to the sexual subject, the violated body in pain and the religious icon, so that they are each infused with the meaning of the others. The relationship between the

Figure 9.2 St Teresa of Ávila, in the Cornaro Chapel, Church of Santa Maria della Vittoria, Rome. Gian Lorenzo Bernini, 1646

psychological significance of wounding and torture and of sexual ecstasy is something I return to later in my discussion of Sartre's existential humanism.

Who is looking?

The torture scenes are eroticised through the use of cinematic techniques such as lighting and use of the camera, which lingers on the suffering bodies. The erotic appeal of such scenes is even announced by intertextual references ('I was going to bleed Andrew but you look better with your shirt off'). In addition, it is noteworthy that these scenes almost exclusively involve an active, aggressive and evil female character and a passive, good male character. This focus on the passivity (and seduction) of the male body is also characteristic of one strand of mainstream pornography (Moye, 1985). As Alexander (2004) says, 'In the kinky register of the Buffyverse canon the show's queer and feminist sensibilities stage and eroticise the bodies of the tortured and dominated as almost exclusively male, whilst positioning participating women almost exclusively on top.' Such scenes therefore draw upon a heterosexual discourse and invite the viewer into the position of female spectator, with the male as sexualised object. This reversal of normative gender positions is an issue which deserves considerable attention.

The gaze and spectacle in film theory

Gender relations and sexuality have been a focus of concern in film studies (and later television studies) since the publication of Mulvey's (1975) influential paper which sees gendered power relations and anxieties around sexuality as central to Hollywood cinema traditions. Her analysis of the dynamics of spectatorship is argued to reveal the operation of gendered power relations, and she claims that these can be understood in terms of a psychoanalytic approach to sexuality, an analytical framework that has since come to dominate film studies and, to a lesser extent, television studies.

According to Mulvey (1975), the position of the spectator is inevitably masculine, reflecting patriarchal society. Through the cinematic gaze, women, or rather parts of their bodies such as the face, become a spectacle; they are bathed in soft light and the camera lingers on them for an extended period, interrupting the flow of the narrative.[3] Like Berger (1972), Mulvey says that women connote 'to-be-looked-at-ness' and the spectator always necessarily occupies the masculine position. Mulvey (1989) later allowed that women could occupy the position of spectator, but only by adopting a masculinised position, seeing themselves and other women through the masculine gaze.

Doane (1990) later argued for the possibility of a 'feminine' female spectator, putting forward two 'routes' her subjectivity may take. She may identify with the objectified and scrutinised female character, which effectively leads her into a masochistic subjectivity, taking perverted pleasure from the 'punishing' male gaze; alternatively, she comes to narcissistically desire the woman on screen, whose femininity is so exaggerated that this allows the female spectator to distinguish herself from the image and then desire it.

In summary, then, female spectators may therefore be 'temporary men', masochistic perverts or captivated by femininity. Writers since Mulvey have argued convincingly that it is not only women whose bodies may be 'on display', but the spectator here is still regarded as male. Neale (1983) agrees with Mulvey that the gaze is masculine, but argues that the male body too can be subject to the gaze and become a 'spectacle'. However, the possibility of homoeroticism that this raises is deeply troubling to many men, so that the potential eroticism of this 'looking' is repressed or disavowed. Thus, if the male body is displayed (for example naked or partially clothed) this must be accounted for by the demands of the narrative. For example, male characters wounded in battle have good reason to remove their clothing; the wounded male body is 'disqualified' as an object of erotic contemplation. Furthermore, such wounding of the male body is taken to symbolise a punishment which it deserves for arousing male desire. In a similar vein, Tasker (1993) argues that action films legitimate looking at the male body.

Neale acknowledges that there are moments in film where the display of the male body is presented as the object of erotic looking. But he argues that on these occasions the male body becomes 'feminised' on account of occupying the position normally taken by a female character. I would agree with Tasker (1993), who criticises this argument, since it rests upon a stable gender binary, and seems to negate the possibility of both transgressive gender identities and cinematic and televisual productions that attempt to offer alternative subject positions and spectator–character dynamics. In addition, Nixon (1997) has supplemented such psychodynamic analyses with a broader cultural analysis of the dynamics of spectatorship.

So although film theory has incorporated into its psychodynamic framework the possibility of a female spectator and of a (homoerotically charged) male gaze upon the male body, the possibility of a female or feminine gaze has been given much less attention and virtually no attention has been given to the gaze of the female spectator upon the male body. Such a psychodynamic framework does not seem to allow for a female gaze in principle; the female spectator who views the display of the male body must, one assumes, be gaining homoerotic pleasure through her temporary identification as masculine. And when the male body is wounded, female spectators must be drawn into a punishing attitude towards the male body through this identification. The alternative, according to Neale, is that the male body necessarily relinquishes its masculinity when it becomes an erotic object. The inadequacy of psychodynamic theory to properly theorise female spectatorship in general, and in relation to the male body in particular, was drawn attention to 20 years ago (Gamman and Marshment, 1988). However, since that time there has been a disappointing lack of progress in this area, although the arguments outlined above are problematic and have not gone without criticism, as I will demonstrate.

The female gaze and the male as spectacle in *BtVS*

Firstly, the 'male (hetero?)sexual narrative' (Dyer, 1985, cited in Hearn and Melechi, 1992), in which the narrative is driven by the male hero's pursuits, is not present in *BtVS*. As Stevens (2003) observes, *BtVS* has a central strong, female protagonist whose character drives the narrative and through whose eyes the spectator sees the fictional world; Buffy 'governs' the gaze. As in action cinema, she is the central figure, but she is not a 'muscular' heroine (Tasker, 1993). She is the focus for the viewer's identification, and one that is available to female viewers without the need for their masculinisation or masochism. Furthermore, teen drama and soap elements may be seen as making *BtVS* attractive to a female audience (although the actual demographic shows a much more even gender balance). Many of those occupying the position of spectator are likely to be female, and given the fan responses to the display of Spike's body in particular, we can assume that these occasions provide instances of 'visual pleasure'. Any analysis of spectatorship and visual pleasure in *BtVS* therefore requires us to consider the notion of the female spectator and the possibility of the female gaze.

The bodies of both Angel and Spike are displayed as objects of desire (Owen, 1999; Jowett, 2004) and visual pleasure, seen through the eyes of Buffy or other female characters. Stevens (2003) argues that Spike is constructed as a spectacle and a fetish object through Buffy's gaze. His body is sexualised; it is 'openly and erotically displayed'. It glows in soft, golden lighting, carefully framed and this spectacle temporarily halts the flow of the narrative. Spike is an object of Buffy's desire at these moments and for the spectator too.

Neale's (1983) analysis would suggest that torture and wounding would disqualify the male body as an object of desiring looks. But the bodies of Angel and Spike are clearly on display as objects of desire in these scenes: 'Whilst ostensibly condemned however, these torture scenes are, in fact, designed as *pleasurable* viewing experiences' (Alexander, 2004; italics in original). Nor is the wounding of these characters 'legitimated' through action (Tasker, 1993). Instead they are passive and restrained.

Furthermore I cannot agree with those who argue for the feminisation of male characters who become spectacle and objects of desire. Spike's and Angel's 'passivity' during the wounding and torture scenes is explicit. However, it is problematic to suggest that this produces them as feminised. In Jowett's (2005) view, this positioning of the male body as 'sexual object to be looked at' feminises the character, as does positioning it as passive victim (see Creed, 1993a). Both Tasker (1993) and Abele (1997) find fault with this argument (originating with Neale, 1983); no evidence for this feminisation, other than the fact of the male occupying a traditionally female position in the narrative, is offered.

It is easier to read the wounding and torture of Angel and Spike within hero discourses of masculinity. Donald (1992) notes that the American male warrior in war films says little and endures pain. He must be able to pass the test: 'Within this structure, suffering, and torture in particular, operates as both a set of narrative hurdles to be overcome (tests that the hero must survive) and as a set of aestheticised images to be lovingly dwelt on. Relatively few studies seem to comment in any depth on the figure of the male hero in this context, pursued and punished as he so often is' (Tasker, 1993: 125).

BtVS devalues and inverts traditional models of the gendered subject in cinema and television (Stevens, 2003). It would therefore seem perverse to insist that these male bodies are on display to a masculine gaze, that they are feminised by such treatment and that the desire they stimulate is a principally homoerotic desire.

The claim that theoretical space needs to be made for a non-pathologised female spectator and for a female gaze has been made by various other writers in film studies more generally, who have also recognised that gendered subject/object positions have become increasingly 'queered' in more recent times. Tasker (1993) argues that gender identities are in a constant state of renegotiation and redefinition in contemporary film so that it is misleading to try to analyse texts as if they could reveal stable, clear categories. Saco (1992, 1994) too argues against Mulvey's claim that there are fixed masculine or feminine identifications, and notes that masculinity as object of desire is becoming commonplace. She argues that mainstream films are not always structured around the male gaze (for example, melodrama), a point endorsed by Abele (1997) and Goddard (2000). Waterhouse (1993) argues that Mulvey fails to address 'the issue of women's own positive pleasures in taking control of the gaze', and refuses to see the possibility of women's visual pleasure as pathological or politically indefensible.[4]

Saco (1994) further argues that viewers, in producing their own readings, are more active than Mulvey gives them credit for. Fiske (1987) had earlier made a similar argument with regard to television, in any case doubting the extent to which Mulvey's argument applies to television: While he allows for some of television's viewing pleasure to be derived from the fetishisation of the female body and the construction of a masculine reading position through which women see their own bodies, he argues there is space for resistance to the dominant ideology. Drawing on Barthes (1976), he advocates the notion of 'play', the pleasure in making and controlling meanings, which requires an active, creative viewer. The text therefore has a plurality of pleasures to offer, varying across readers from text to text and the reading depends on the viewer's social location. Drawing on Fiske, Hanke (1992) points out that gender and genre are related. For example, soap operas offer opportunities for women to create resistant readings, while cop shows reinscribe gender dichotomies. But in any case the polysemic nature of texts and the heterogeneity of audiences means that ideologies are always under threat. Research on audience reception seems to bear out the claim that the social characteristics and location of different audience groups radically affects the meaning that viewers draw from television texts (Morley, 1980; Katz and Liebes, 1984; Hodge and Tripp, 1986; Fiske, 1987).

Psychoanalytic theory has dominated much of film theory and Mulvey remains the point of reference for many discussions of the gaze and its effects. I have spent some time arguing for the possibility of a female gaze and for the viewing pleasures of a female spectator. I have seen no psychoanalytic analyses of the female spectator's pleasure in watching scenes of male torture/wounding. As detailed above, the very proposition of a female spectator appears to involve her masculinisation, in which case her voyeuristic enjoyment becomes a kind of homoeroticism-by-proxy. Even where writers have claimed a space for the female gaze, the dynamics of this viewing position have not been articulated, and I would argue that this is because the limits of psychodynamic theory have been reached or exceeded (Gamman, 1988). Counter arguments appear to rest on claims about the shifting nature of identity, changes/complexity in the gender positions on offer in contemporary film and television and an emphasis on the reader rather than the text. I would not disagree with these points, but they offer little help in understanding the dynamics of eroticism and desire in the scenes of wounding and torture I wish to understand.

Nevertheless my purpose is not to develop an adequate theory of the female gaze (although this work needs to be done). By demonstrating the inadequacies of mainstream film theory when applied to *BtVS* in general and scenes of wounding/torture in particular, I suggest that the importance of *gendered* power relations in understanding the workings of the gaze and its link to eroticism has been overstated. In order to reach a fresh understanding of the psychology of this eroticism, I propose a more parsimonious theoretical approach, one not based upon or making assumptions about gendered identities.

An alternative theoretical framework: The Sartrean gaze

A quite different approach to understanding sexuality that nevertheless recognises the importance of the gaze is that of Sartre (1943/2000). Sartre certainly sees 'the gaze' as fundamental in human relations and as involving threat to the individual.

As in psychoanalysis, Sartre sees the gaze as essentially an attempt at controlling the other, based on an anxiety around perceived threat. But this does not depend upon a gendering of subject/object and so requires no tortuous arguments to explain the female gaze upon the male. It may be argued that this is politically naive, and it may be that this analysis ultimately needs to take into account patriarchal relations in order to acknowledge that men may be more effective users of the gaze (and of other modes of denying the other's subjectivity). But within this view women and men are both bearers of the gaze and objects of it; the gaze itself is not gendered. Sartre does not base his analysis on castration anxiety, but on the threat of the Other to our own subjectivity. For Sartre, 'looking', subjecting the other to our gaze, is something that both men and women are motivated to do.

Sartre: Sexuality and the Other

For Sartre, the human condition is that we are 'condemned to be free' (Sartre, 1965: 41), to determine our own identity. But this identity (the 'in-itself') is fragile, because we can choose to be different at any moment. The person is a freedom (the 'for-itself') that strives to become something. But the moment it becomes something it is no longer a freedom; it has solidified into an object. It must wrench itself away from this finality to regain its freedom, its subjectivity. We therefore yearn for two incompatible states: not only to become some/'thing' but also to retain our freedom, our subjectivity. So although we yearn to become something, to have an identity and presence in the world, we are also terrified of thereby losing our freedom. We are made powerfully aware of this at the moment we feel ourselves looked at by the Other: 'The Other looks at me and as such he [*sic*] holds the secret of my being, he knows what I am. Thus the profound meaning of my being is outside of me, imprisoned in an absence' (Sartre 1943/2000: 363). We find that the power to define who we are lies with the Other.

Our response is to try to stop the Other from objectifying us, and we principally attempt to do this either by seizing and capturing the Other's subjectivity or by turning our own look upon the Other, thereby rendering the Other an object. However, Sartre argues that both of these possibilities are equally doomed to failure, and that the failure of the first precipitates us into an attempt at the second, whose failure leads us back again to the first in an 'inescapable and certainly vicious cycle' (Howells, 2000: 86). The strategies used to capture the subjectivity of the Other are love and masochism. The alternative strategy, to render the Other an object for us, is desire and sadism. 'Hatred' is the final, desperate but ultimately ineffective, attempt to escape this cycle. Although at first sight it may seem counter-intuitive to pair love with masochism (rather than desire), and desire with sadism (rather than masochism), Sartre puts forward a convincing case for doing so. I will deal only briefly with love/masochism and with hatred, as it is desire/sadism that I believe particularly applies to the scenes I am analysing.

Love and masochism

Love, for Sartre, is the attempt to take back control over one's own being by taking control of the Other's subjectivity. The goal is to mean 'the whole world' to the Other, to be the lens through which the Other must look in order to see meaning in the world. However, our status as such a special object is fragile; the Other's existential freedom to objectify us cannot be denied and when love fails we seek recourse in its very opposite; to resolve the conflict by abandoning our own subjectivity and becoming wholly an object for the Other, to adopt a masochistic position. But this fails too; the possibility of becoming nothing more than an object is an illusion. If we *choose* the masochistic position, we have thereby simply exercised our own freedom: 'The more he tries to taste his objectivity, the more he will be submerged by the consciousness of his subjectivity hence his anguish. Even the masochist who pays a woman to whip him is treating her as an instrument and by this very fact posits himself in transcendence in relation to her' (ibid.: 378–9).

Desire and sadism

This propels us into adopting the second strategy, to capture the Other's subjectivity through first 'trapping' it in the body and then possessing it through possession of the body:

> So the Other's For-itself must come to play on the surface of his body, and be extended all through his body; and by touching this body

> I should finally touch the Other's free subjectivity. This is the true meaning of the word *possession.*
>
> (ibid.: 394; italics in original)

Sartre absolutely rejects any arguments that reduce sexual desire to physiology or instinct. He also separates desire from any particular sexual practices, which vary with different social groups and are socially acquired. So desire may be manifested in a variety of ways, but at its core is the attempt to capture the subjectivity of the Other by first making it incarnate, by rendering it nothing but a body through the 'caress'. But this too is problematic. The power of the caress to draw the Other's subjectivity onto the surface of the body can only come from a subjectivity that is itself incarnate, from a mutual incarnation where bodies caress each other, where subject and object positions are temporarily abandoned. The moment that the desiring consciousness moves from caressing to seizing the body of the Other, it has once more become an agent, a subject. The incarnation of the Other's subjectivity collapses at that moment, unsustainable without that reciprocal incarnation. Thus desire fails to achieve its goal. This failure is the reason why desire can never be satisfied. We should not confuse desire with satisfaction through sexual pleasure in this respect. Although sexual pleasure may be possible, desire remains unfulfilled (cf. Krimmer and Raval, 2002, who note the conflation of death and desire, and the impossibility of the fulfillment of desire and love in Western literary tradition).

The failure of desire leads into sadism. If we cannot capture the Other's subjectivity by incarnating it through desire, we attempt to do so by incarnating it through pain. Through sadism, we incarnate the other's subjectivity by making him/her identify only with his/her body through the pain we inflict, while retaining our own subjectivity. In fact Sartre talks of the 'moment' of sadism in sexuality as the point at which the desiring consciousness becomes an agent in seizing the Other's body. However, sadism too fails. The 'look' of the victim/Other merely solidifies the sadist in that identity, rendering him/her an object of simply a different kind. Furthermore, if the incarnation is achieved and the victim's body becomes a meaningless flesh the sadist is at a loss to know what to do with the victim; any *meaningful* action demands that the victim is more than a *meaningless* flesh and the incarnation dissolves once more, the subjectivity of the victim seemingly inevitable and ungraspable. It is at this point that the sadist may once more resort to desire to resolve the conflict, to render himself/herself flesh also in a desperate attempt to find a way to seize the

Other. Thus 'Sadism is the failure of desire, and desire is the failure of sadism' (ibid.: 405).

Hatred

The final phase in this conflict is hatred, the attempt to symbolically rid the world of all Others through ridding it of one specific person. We imagine that we could at last be freed from the 'look'. But this too is an illusion. The death of the Other simply permanently fixes us once more in the identity which constituted us in his/her eyes. In terms of the rationale of hatred, whether it is the Other who dies or oneself, it amounts to the same thing. It is the attempt to permanently remove one of us from the field in order to resolve the conflict. Furthermore, the failure of this final, desperate attempt launches us once more into the whole cycle, to be 'indefinitely tossed from one to the other of the two fundamental attitudes' (ibid.: 412). Thus we are condemned to constantly flip between these alternatives in an attempt to escape the threat of the Other.

For Sartre, therefore, 'normal' human sexual relations are in principle sadomasochistic. This of course does not mean that we literally pursue a sexual relationship with or try to torture or kill all Others. We have many subtle and symbolic forms of these attitudes. We see them in flirting, kissing, teasing, badinage and in a myriad other ways. The important point is that the seeds of desire and sadism are ever present in each other.

A Sartrean analysis of wounding and torture in *BtVS*

The close link between sadism and desire is fundamental to Sartre's understanding of human relationships and needs no further theoretical explanation. This also allows us to understand the conflation of religious iconography and eroticism, since the sadism implied in, for example, images of St Sebastian, crucifixion and sexual arousal are for Sartre two sides of the same coin.

This link between sadism and desire may at first seem unlikely; after all, most people probably do not routinely wound or torture others for sexual gratification. We see eroticised representations of such acts relatively rarely in film and television and these are usually depicted as perversion. However, it must be remembered that when Sartre writes of sadism and desire he sees these as 'attitudes'; the acts we commit while in their grip may fall well short of actual wounding and torture. In addition, the eroticism of wounding and torture scenes in *BtVS* must be understood in the context of *BtVS* as a show located within gothic/horror genres. The conventions of these genres grant a license to depict such acts with relative frequency and with impunity; *BtVS* can 'get away with' a depiction of human sexuality that arguably makes more explicit some key elements of human experience than media productions in other genres allow (Burr, 2003).

Furthermore, a Sartrean analysis allows us to separate wounds from the *acts* of wounding and torture. The depiction of wounds themselves is not erotic or eroticised, for example in the images of Spike after Glory's torture of him. It is the *act* of wounding that appears erotic. Such acts draw us into the process of bringing the Other's subjectivity to the surface of the body and thereby the (illusory) promise of destroying it. Wounds themselves, within this analysis, would gain erotic meaning only by virtue of the fact that they refer to and evoke the wounding/torture processes by which they were inflicted. We may further expect, for example, a wound known to have been inflicted for the purposes of giving pain to carry more erotic meaning than one sustained accidentally. These are issues that require further investigation in order to identify the conditions under which wounding is more or less likely to carry personal or social erotic meanings.

Sartre is also able to offer a rationale for the fetishisation of both female and male bodies through spectacle. Scenes of the wounding and torture of Angel and Spike are 'spectacular'; the camera lingers over, even 'caresses', their bodies; the lighting is soft and casts them in a warm glow; the action is temporarily halted by this spectacle (although I would argue that the display of their bodies is nevertheless given 'good reason' by the narrative, in line with Neale and Tasker). However, such spectacular treatment is not, within a Sartrean analysis, motivated by castration anxiety but by the threat of loss of subjectivity that the gaze of the Other always brings; keeping the 'Other' under scrutiny seems to offer the possibility (again illusory) of stabilising subject/object relations in the desired direction.

A further issue that needs to be addressed is the extent to which this analysis applies in the same way to film and televisual representations as it would to the real world. Just as Mulvey's (1975) analysis applied psychoanalytic theory about relationships between real men and women to film, my application of Sartre's analysis attempts a similar transfer. As argued above, the notion of a relationship between wounding and eroticism in 'normal' human sexuality is, on the face of it, counter-intuitive; the sight of the damaged, mutilated body is not the focus of normative notions of desirability. Most people do not habitually gain sexual pleasure through the torture and mutilation of another's body, and I have already pointed out that for Sartre desire and sadism are 'attitudes' rather than specific practices. However, within 'consensual' S&M practices physical damage to one's partner can indeed be part of erotic power play. With the emphasis on 'consensual', S&M practices do not encompass torture, since this is by definition non-consensual although it is quite possible that real-life instances of torture may contain erotic meaning for one or both parties. This does not, however, resolve the puzzle of how to define, measure and explain 'consensuality', especially when this is within the context of relationships, perhaps especially long-term relationships, with their own gender, sexual and other power relations.

Furthermore, there may be subtle but important differences between the dynamics of eroticism in real life and media representations of wounding. It seems reasonable to assume that whereas in real life (S&M) wounding, this is likely to have erotic appeal to those involved in the act rather than to a hypothetical spectator. In film, television and art the wounding is more usually not part of what is generally defined as a 'sexual act' or shown to have erotic appeal to the characters themselves, but is erotically appealing to the spectator. Again, such issues need further investigation in order to answer questions about the relationship, if any, that may exist between real-life experiences and fictionalised wounding.

However, in my view the adequacy of this analysis, like any other, cannot rest on its internal coherence alone. I have drawn attention to the need for empirical research above. Research on audience reception (which seems to have become more established in television studies than film studies) is vital if we are to judge the explanatory power of theoretical analyses when offered up against the experiences of real viewers, both male and female. The work of Stacey (1994) in relation to the visual pleasures of the female spectator is exemplary here.

Conclusion

The eroticism of the wounding and torture scenes from *BtVS* described here may be seen to derive from a combination of cinematic, narrative and psychological processes and mechanisms. Their eroticism is certainly constructed through lighting, *mise-en-scène* and dialogue. However, although cinematic treatment may contribute significantly, this alone cannot determine an erotic reading. In some scenes the nature and narrative arc of the character seems to discourage an erotic reading or a potential sexual reading supplied in the dialogue only serves to highlight the scene's lack of eroticism. However, the eroticisation (or not) of a scene through cinematic techniques cannot be analytically separated from character and narrative arc; Angel and Spike are the characters whose bodies have been most subject to erotic treatment, but they are also heroes on a path of redemption and bear significations from earlier romantic heroes, warriors, sacrificial deities, courtly lovers and religious icons.

In terms of the dynamics of spectatorship, I have argued that a Sartrean analysis allows a more parsimonious account of the pleasures of the spectacle in general and of scenes of wounding and torture in particular, than can be gained through an application of Freudian theory. Furthermore, it does so while allowing for a non-pathologised female spectator, something which I believe to be particularly important in the analysis of shows such as *BtVS* where gender dynamics are atypical. Nevertheless it may be that Sartre's account of the gaze needs to acknowledge power differentials between men and women and to articulate what implications this may have for subject/object relations through 'the gaze'.

Notes

I would like to thank Amelia Burr, Christine Jarvis and Jeff Hearn for their invaluable help and suggestions to me in writing this chapter.

1. For a comprehensive bibliography of academic publications on *BtVS*, see Buffyology: An Academic Buffy Studies and Whedonverse Bibliography, http://www.alysa316.com/Buffyology.
2. See, for example, Derek Jarman's film *Sebastiane*.
3. See Easthope, 1986, for an interesting analysis of the female 'pin-up' from this psychoanalytic perspective.
4. Here, Waterhouse critiques Mulvey's arguments in both 'Visual pleasure and narrative cinema' (1975) and 'Visual and other pleasures' (1989).

10
Spectacular Pain: Masculinity, Masochism and Men in the Movies

Tim Edwards

'Masochism' is a term perhaps not commonly associated with men or masculinity. Similarly, movies have rarely received much serious study within the world of sociology and social science, or even sexual politics, while studies of masculinity still tend to see analysis of such popular cultural texts as films as rather small or trivial fry compared with such serious topics as work, violence and structural inequality (Edwards, 2006). This is perhaps not surprising given the legacy of over 40 years of Second Wave feminism. Masochism, in its connection with femininity for many feminists, could easily be seen as a form of justification for, even celebration of, the subordination of women (Caplan, 1993).

It is my purpose here, then, to challenge, if not necessarily overthrow, both of these notions and to demonstrate that masculinity has much to do with masochism and that movies are indeed worthy of social scientific study. The initial difficulty of this line of inquiry is that analysis of masculinity, masochism and movies often degenerates into consideration of disparate topics lying across differing disciplinary boundaries. Masochism is a psychoanalytic term evolving, like many other sexual categories, out of the development of sexology in the late nineteenth century. Conversely, analysis of masculinity emerges later through the work of Second Wave feminists and then through the rise of critical studies on men where often profeminist men have tried to consider masculinity for themselves (Hearn and Morgan, 1990). The most immediate conflict then comes from understanding masochism as a psychoanalytic term derived from sexology and analysing masculinity as, for the most part, a social construct encompassing a series of attributes, activities and politics defined as 'masculine'. Media studies have offered a degree of connectivity here, often drawing on a mix of psychoanalytic theory and Second Wave feminist theory. Yet, as the sometimes fractious debates in the journal *Screen* demonstrated, these disparate disciplines often made unhappy bedfellows, providing few answers and little resolution (Screen, 1992). The task here, then, is complex.

In an attempt to make some connections across the waters of studying masculinity and masochism there are three sections. The first covers questions of definition and understanding of the terms involved and the parameters surrounding them; the second considers media studies of masculinity and masochism more specifically and opens up their connections; and the third, through an analysis of two classical and two more contemporary films, seeks to demonstrate the ways in which masculinity and masochism do indeed relate or even meet at the crossroads of the movies. Previous discussions of such intersections have been driven almost entirely by Mulvey's (1975) analysis of gendered looking relations and its critique. My argument here is that this analysis is inadequate and out of date given the increasing sexualisation and commodification of the male body in cinema and popular culture more widely.

Who are you calling a masochist? Masculinity and masochism

Definitions of masochism are arguably a mess. The term is originally derived from the work of nineteenth-century Austrian novelist Leopold von Sacher-Masoch (1836–95). His name has since been used to describe feelings of sexual pleasure gained through the experience of pain or suffering and evidenced, to some extent, in the trajectory of his novels, his diaries and journals, and the letters and contracts he shared with his various female sexual partners (Deleuze and Sacher-Masoch, 1989). It is immediately apparent, then, that Sacher-Masoch sought neither to theorise nor categorise masochism in the way that it is commonly understood today. The more scientific and indeed categorical construction of masochism as a specific sexual perversion inversely related to its flipside, sadism, rests almost entirely upon the development of sexology in the late nineteenth century and in particular Krafft-Ebing's monumental attempt to document and label every sexual proclivity ever known, plus a few handfuls more, in *Psychopathia Sexualis* (Krafft-Ebing, 1965). Some of these ideas were then radically developed through psychoanalysis and the work of Freud in particular (Freud, 1977). The primary impact of these developments was, as Foucault has made explicit, to construct masochism primarily as a sexual category, an identity and a perversion subject to a series of formal and informal measures that sought to define, separate and regulate the normal from the abnormal (Foucault, 1978).

A couple of points are immediately worth noting. First, masochism as a concept develops out of literature, sexology and psychoanalysis and not from any form of social science. Second, its modern definition is equally entwined with the roots of sadism. The more recent work of Deleuze has furthermore sought to challenge this entrenched connection of masochism with sadism and to develop its understanding as a separate, if related, construct (Deleuze and Sacher-Masoch, 1989). His essay on *Coldness and Cruelty* is also an examination of the differing methods and lines of enquiry constructed by Sade, on the one hand, and Sacher-Masoch, on the other. Deleuze is at pains to point out that these are not one and the same and neither do they merely operate in relation to each but that they most importantly have their own mechanisms and processes. Also underpinning this is a critique of Freud's tendency to equate sadism with the father and masochism with the mother. Here the masochist identifies with the mother in seeking the love of the father, yet Deleuze overturns this arguing that the gender ordering of masochism is far more complex. Thus, for Deleuze masochism has a potentially far stronger connection with masculinity and the relationship between father and son.

Studies of masochism within sociology and social science are almost entirely dominated by the sexual political debates of the 1980s. During this period, all aspects of sexuality became heavily politicised through the rise of more radical forms of feminism within North America in particular which then rapidly spread into a polarised debate, if not stand-off, worldwide. Writers such as Andrea Dworkin, Catharine MacKinnon and Sheila Jeffreys strongly denounced all forms of sadomasochism as the ultimate nadir in the oppression of women, given the tendency to equate sadism with men and masochism with women (Dworkin, 1981; Jeffreys, 1990; MacKinnon, 1987). However, others, including most famously Gayle Rubin and Pat (now Patrick) Califia, often writing from the standpoint of sexual minorities such as gay men and lesbians, were fiercely defensive of the rights of already oppressed groups and accused the aforementioned writers of colluding with the powers of moral conservatism in controlling them (Califia, 1994; Rubin, 1984). The situation became increasingly entrenched given the backlash against gay men and other sexual minorities in the wake of the AIDS epidemic and wider conservative agendas both in the UK and the United States (Watney, 1987). Surveying this from a primarily libertarian stance, Bill Thompson further argued that the backlash against sadomasochism and indeed perhaps sexual pleasure more widely was driven by a very unholy trinity of radical feminism, political conservatism and religious fundamentalism within the United States showing often marked parallels in psychoanalysis, sexual politics and Christian theology (Thompson, 1994). Thompson's sometimes-polemical work was driven by an analysis of the historical intertwining of these apparently radically different areas.

As I have pointed out in earlier work, none of these debates were easily resolved given their dependence upon a series of wider tensions within the study of sexuality that underpinned often acrimonious analysis of topics such as pornography, gay liberation and indeed sadomasochism (Edwards, 1994). The problem for our analysis here is that none of this work did much to further understanding of masochism *per se* or indeed to unpack the relationship between masculinity and masochism given the overwhelming emphasis often placed upon the politics of masochism for women. The exceptions here were the analyses provided by gay male scholars but these were again polarised by similar tensions as to whether sadomasochism represented the ultimate liberation of repressed gay desire or merely reinforced the self-loathing of homosexuals and homosexuality (Rechy, 1977; Mains, 1984). What tends to emerge, then, is a sense in which the understanding of masochism within social science becomes hampered by its entrenchment within sexual politics.

Studies of masculinity within social science have arguably been more progressive. Masculinity, within the social sciences, at least is a term derived first from anthropology that, since Mead's famous studies in Samoa, has sought to examine and establish the cultural variability of what we call 'masculine' and uproot it from any form of crude biological essentialism; second, from varieties of sex role functionalism and sex typing theory, particularly in the United States, which sought to demonstrate that masculinity is a role, ideal and set of personality characteristics learned through primary, secondary and tertiary modes of socialisation; and third from Second Wave feminism which, in drawing on these strands, sought to politicise masculinity and demonstrate its deep and abiding connections with mechanisms of power, inequality and the oppression of women (Barrett, 1980; David and Brannon, 1974; Eisenstein, 1984; Farrell, 1974; Mead, 1977; Millett, 1971).

The 1980s saw various more or less profeminist men's attempts to grapple with questions posed by feminism and make some sense of the conundrum of men's experience – men acting, often collectively, as powerful aggressors, yet somehow never feeling that way, particularly individually. Some explanation came from psychoanalytic theory here, particularly in the work of Easthope, Reynaud and later Buchbinder (Buchbinder, 1994, 1998; Easthope, 1986; Reynaud, 1983). Little unity or consensus emerged, though, beyond an overwhelming insistence upon the social construction of masculinity as a set of attributes or practices (Berger et al., 1995). This increasing emphasis upon artifice was then taken up in media-driven studies of masculinity often in turn drawing upon wider post-structural theory which we will explore more shortly.

Setting aside questions raised by both social science and psychoanalytic theory concerning masochism and masculinity, a more fundamental question concerns how we might define masochism in relation to visual media and film more particularly. One starting point would be to define masochism in movies as the depiction of pain and or suffering as in some way positive, beneficial or pleasurable to the sufferer or audience. This is of course a broad definition that opens up many questions concerning intention and interpretation.

A second question to be raised here is how masochism within filmic media might actually be demonstrated and here we can be a little more concrete and suggest three ways in which masochism is evidenced in a movie format: first, through verbal communication such as 'I am in pain', 'Hurt him', or other verbal explications of suffering; second, through non-verbal communication – grimaces, groans, howls and similar commonly understood indicators of pain and suffering; or third, through easily recognised or obvious bodily or mental harm such as wounding, scarring, blood letting, injury, torture, starvation, confinement, humiliation or punishment. Problems are again here multiple, given the polyvalence of meaning, differing interpretations of suffering, let alone events and often unanswerable questions of directorial intention. In addition, many scenes of suffering, mental or physical, are shown which are not masochistic in that they encourage sympathy and or the experience of pain *per se* rather than pleasure in the audience. Thus, masochism within filmic media also depends heavily not only on questions of *what* is depicted but *how* it is likely to be experienced by the audience. What confuses this situation further is the relationship between character, actor and viewer. Scenes of suffering in filmic media may encourage masochism in the audience (identification *with* an actor/character) or sadism (identification *against* a character/actor) or an uneasy mix of the two.

A third factor here concerns masochism's relationship with genre or more widely its potential conflict with other elements, particularly comedy. Much slapstick or screwball humour, for example, involves humiliations, punishments and degradations of characters but is rendered funny either because it does not involve actual pain or because the pain involved is not *perceived* as real. The question of the 'un/reality' of the pain or suffering depicted is significant here as masochism depends on an ambiguous mix of elements – the pain must be real enough or otherwise it is just funny and yet must not be perceived to be so real as to outweigh the potential viewing pleasures that might also be involved. The role of action cinema here is critical as most action movies centre on plots and levels of heroics that are wholly unrealistic, yet this is also one way they may then also open up the space within which to engage audiences in sadistic and or masochistic patterns of viewing and identification (Tasker, 1993b). These are points most easily explored through an analysis of media studies of masculinity to which we now turn.

What are you looking at? Masculinity at the movies

The analysis of masculinity within film studies is premised almost entirely upon a critique of Laura Mulvey's (1975) famous essay 'Visual Pleasures and Narrative Cinema'. This has arguably been one of the most influential pieces of feminist writing in recent history that has, more particularly, defined an entire field of study ever since. That field of study is perhaps most aptly entitled the feminist analysis of viewing relations, giving its *prima facie* concern with the gaze as gendered and indeed sexualised. Consequently, the visual pleasures offered through narrative cinema for Mulvey are essentially twofold: first, scopophilia or the voyeuristic pleasure derived through looking; and second, narcissism, or the pleasure developed from recognition and identification, yet the true cut of her perspective appears when these concepts are overlaid in gendered terms. To put it most simply, men, the male subject and masculinity *look* while women, the female subject and femininity are *looked at*. Clearly such a perspective correlates strongly with the parallel development of a broader feminist imperative to expose the sexual objectification of the female and women more widely (see, for example, Brownmiller, 1984; Greer, 1971; Millett, 1971). In addition, it also resonates strongly with the more widely theorised gender dynamic that equates the male and the masculine with the active subject and the female and the feminine with the passive object. The more particular problematic that then ensues is the idea that the male and the masculine 'cannot bear the burden of sexual objectification' (Mulvey, 1975: 12). Similarly, narrative plotlines are themselves also seen to reinforce the activity of the male subject, often conceived as heroic or powerful, and the passivity of the female object who mostly serves the purpose of providing erotic interest alone while the narrative itself often enhances wider processes of sadistic pleasure given plotlines involving the heroic male conquest of suffering and frequent depictions of female distress.

Perhaps not surprisingly, Mulvey's work has since received a veritable barrage of criticism. This can be summarised as follows. First, Mulvey is seen to underplay the importance of female pleasure in looking and indeed the significance of women's spectatorship more widely (MacKinnon, 1997). Second, her analysis of looking relations is seen to be overly crude and simplistic in its emphasis upon a strictly polarised gender divide in viewing relations (Silverman, 1992). Third, the perspective she develops deflects attention away from more complex forms of identification (Neale, 1982). Fourth, following on from this, men as well as women may engage in masochistic as well as sadistic viewing relations and positions that exist *across* any strict gender divide (Neale, 1983). Fifth, the tendency to deflect the visual and sexual objection of men within cinema may be motivated as much, if not more, by the disavowal of homoeroticism as by any heterosexual male imperative to objectify femininity and women (Green, 1984). Sixth, her use of psychoanalytic theory both misappropriates some of its concepts and abuses some of its main tenets, particularly Freud's work around ambivalent identifications and polymorphous sexuality (Rodowick, 1982). Seventh, and mostly severely, her analysis is overly westernised, middle class and racialised (Gaines, 1986).

These are damning criticisms that expose the simplicity of Mulvey's analysis and question the role of psychoanalytic theory in understanding cinema more widely. Yet Mulvey's primary assertion that the *way* men and women look and are looked at in filmic media is fundamentally different still stands and has led to the formation of a now vast literature covering representations of men and masculinity within the worlds of film and cinema and, more importantly, an equally copious academic concern with the mechanisms of how we look at men (Cohan and Hark, 1993; Jeffords, 1994; Kirkham and Thumin, 1993). In sum, *how* we look is often perceived as impacting upon *what* we are looking at and *vice versa*.

As is clear, the vast majority of media and film studies of masculinity is both based on and driven by Mulvey's analysis of the gaze. Thus, it often fails to consider directly or explicitly questions of female, let alone male, masochism. What exists tends to make three interconnected points: first, that masculinity is a social construct rendered increasingly performative rather than real with film (Bingham, 1994; Creed, 1993a; Tasker, 1993a); second, that viewing identifications are rendered equally fluid (Green, 1984; Neale, 1982; Silverman, 1992); and third, that the presentation of the male as an object of the gaze is subject to much disavowal particularly in relation to its homoeroticism (Dyer, 1989; MacKinnon, 1997;

Simpson, 1994). Where does this leave us in relation to masculinity and masochism? One can argue that Mulvey's rigid casting of the male as a primarily active subject tends to annihilate the possibility of masculine rather than feminine forms of masochism and that some subsequent critiques have begun to reopen this possibility, particularly in relation to questions of multiple and polyvalent viewing mechanisms and identifications (Cohan and Hark, 1993; Kirkham and Thumin, 1993; Tasker, 1993b). The emphasis often placed upon performativity, however, would seem to render images of masculinity within filmic media to be too playful to be masochistic, a point underlined by the emphasis upon the disavowal of the male as object spectacle.

Part of the problem here is the limits of the analysis itself. Indeed it becomes arguable that Mulvey's as well as some of her follower's work on the gaze set up as many problems as it provided solutions to the questions it raised. This is a point put most forcibly by Willemen, whose eclectic yet stimulating essays on film criticism and theory seek to challenge much of the orthodoxy of cultural studies (Willemen, 1981). As Meaghan Morris (1994) points out in her introduction to a major collection of his articles, Willemen (1994) seeks to develop discussion of the monolithic gaze into a wider analysis of *looking* and consideration of inflexible subject positions into the fluid world of *frictions* between moving parts. Key within this is the concept of the fourth look. The first three looks are contained within Mulvey's essay: first, the look from the camera to create the film; second, the look from the audience to the film; and third, the look between the actors within the film. The fourth then focuses on the more abstract look at the viewer than comes from within the film. This more reflexive form of positioning centres on making the audience increasingly self-conscious of its own looking is demonstrated through a discussion of some of the films of Dwoskin.

In particular, one scene in the film *Moment* is considered. Here the camera is fixed on the face of a young woman lying on a bath mat and the audience is required to 'fill in the blanks' of what is happening to her. Her expression suggests this to be possibly intimate or sexual but it is never proven one way or the other. Thus, the fourth look of the actor looking at the audience is invoked. It is perhaps arguable that the fourth look is only truly applicable to more avant-garde film-making, yet Willemen's wider intention is to undermine the overly simplistic separation of film and audience. Interestingly here it is precisely this sense of the division of film and audience that is under scrutiny as the fourth look depends on the implosion of that division as the actor is seen to almost step out into the audience.

What is often at work here is a more philosophical, if not existential, question of the relationship between text, context and audience or to what extent any text, or even image, exists without an audience (Hall, 1997). Also what is significant for our discussion here is the way in which such a discussion also begins to inform wider questions of sadism and masochism within filmic media. Willemen's discussion of Dwoskin again begins to tentatively inform this as he argues that increased reflexivity in the audience also heightens their own sense of sadism in looking. One might also add that what begins to be invoked here is precisely its opposite: masochism. Thus, the more self-conscious the audience or viewer is in watching scenes of pain and suffering in film characters the more its sadistic pleasure in viewing twists on a knife edge into something more masochistic, yet this a point Willemen does not fully examine. This echoes my earlier point concerning the varying identifications with and against characters or actors in filmic media.

Further exploration of this point tends to depend upon a re-evaluation of the work of Mulvey and a return to the reading of Freud's work on masochism, a point explored in the work of Rodowick (1982). In common with others, Rodowick is critical of the rigidity of Mulvey's male–female, active–passive viewing relation dualism, yet what he also begins to explore is Mulvey's avoidance of sadism–masochism as a logical extension of the same dualism. Rodowick argues that the entire 'concept of masochism is deferred by the political nature of her argument' (Rodowick, 1982: 7). What is also opened up here are the differences between the complexity, and on occasions confusions, of Freud's arguments on physical, emotional and or psychological foundations of gendered identity and Mulvey's more simplistic collapse into gender binaries and essentialism. Moreover, Rodowick's way forward here depends upon a return to Freud's work on masochism, primarily through his reading of the essay 'A Child Is Being Beaten' (see Freud, 1977). Here Freud argues that masochism plays an important part in the development of gendered difference, yet, most importantly, the two sexes are kept in parallel until the final and more conscious stages of development throughout which the relationship to the father and patriarchal authority is key. Unfortunately, Rodowick does not have the scope or resource to fully unpack how masochism relates to masculinity within this context.

Work fully connecting masculinity and masochism is scant. One more thorough-going exception is David Savran's aptly entitled work *Taking It Like a Man* (Savran, 1998). Subtitled 'White Masculinity, Masochism, and Contemporary American Culture', Savran first and foremost 'constructs a genealogy of the fantasy of the white male as victim' ranging across 50 years of contemporary cultural examples from hipsters and hippies through to *Rambo* and *Forrest Gump* (Savran, 1998: 4). As with earlier cultural studies of masculinity, the emphasis is upon films as 'performance texts', yet Savran's ambition does not end here. Deeply concerned by the universalising and ahistorical tendencies of cultural studies and psychoanalytic theory more particularly he states:

> I am, in short, to write a materialist history of the performance of white masculinities . . . [seeking to] demonstrate that modern white masculinities are deeply contradictory, eroticising submission and victimisation while trying to retain a certain aggressively virile edge, offering subject positions that have been marked historically as being both masculine and feminine, white and black.
>
> (Savran, 1998: 9)

In his lengthy introduction, he critiques the origins of masochism in sexology and psychoanalysis and extends his analysis into an examination of its flagellation in particular. This is perhaps a moot point – masochism involves far more than eroticised whipping – yet the slippage from pain into sexual pleasure (and vice versa) remains crucial. His emphasis upon historical materialism also leads him to draw upon the connections between flagellation and the rise of a specifically middle-class form of childhood discipline within the modern nuclear family, as well as schools, the military and other more formal state-driven institutions. Rather peculiarly, he tends to elide the work of Foucault which shows clear relevance here and returns once again to Freud's essay on childhood masochism and its relationship to the Oedipal complex. In common with Neale and others, he also emphasises the more contemporary dependence of masochism as a mechanism for the disavowal of male homosexuality.

Thus representations of men fighting, their wounding and so forth are seen as symbolic codes for something far more homosocial if not fully homosexual. Yet in remaining unhappy with the tendency of psychoanalytic theory to reinforce, if not even construct, the fantasy of the white male victim his perspective then turns towards the Freudo-Marxism of Marcuse thus arguing: 'that the rise of the masochistic male subject is both a function of the rise of capitalism and a necessary cog in the process that reproduces patriarchal, heterosexualized relations' (Savran, 1998: 36). In the rest of the book, Savran works through a series of postwar examples from the works of Burroughs, Mailer and the beatnik generation through to Dennis Hopper's *Easy Rider* and a subsequent blistering critique of Lasch and Bly for the construction of a white male wimp (masochist) and wild man master (sadist) that never existed (Bly, 1990; Lasch, 1979). This leads him into a discussion of the notoriously homophobic film *Cruising* and gay male s/m culture more generally. Rather inevitably, Savran's parting shot rests on an equally visceral assault on the contemporary conflation of nationality, masculinity and conservatism that has dominated political terrain in the US for several decades, underpins various wars on terror, and gets played out to endless ends in films such as *Rambo* and *Forrest Gump*.

Savran's analysis is wide ranging to say the least and often incisive, yet in its dizzying zigzagging across terrains as broad as racism and Reaganism to Vietnam and feminism and from Freud and Marcuse to Sedgwick and queer theory it does strangely little to advance understanding of *how* masculinity, movies and masochism connect other than to say over and over that they do. Savran's reply to this would be to argue that such processes are driven by developments within capitalism and the rise of a more conservative political agenda, yet this really remains stated rather than proven.

Thus a full-scale study of the connections of masculinity, masochism and cinema has yet to exist. What does exist may be summarised as follows: first, understandings of male and masculine spectacle are inextricably bound to questions of the gendering of the gaze; second, there is a tendency for that gaze – however defined – to be deflected in relation to masculinity and this in turn often dependent upon wider questions of sexuality and homoeroticism; and third, such presentations of masculine spectacle are also often caught up with wider societal and political questions concerning the position of men and gendered ideologies that in turn may well relate to other factors such as race or nationality. In order to address such questions further, it is necessary to consider some examples and this forms the focus of the next section.

Masculinity as masochist spectacle: Men in the movies

It is arguable that the most fundamental of all images of male masochism comes from Christianity in relation to the sufferings of Christ, and particularly his crucifixion. This is a theme that has not gone unnoticed within film, the most recent – and arguably also the most gruesome – example being Mel Gibson's *The Passion of the Christ*. The playing out of Christianity as masochist spectacle has a far longer history within film, however, and it features in many of the Hollywood epics of the late 1950s in particular.

A prime example is Kubrick's collaboration with Kirk Douglas in *Spartacus*. The masochistic spectacle of *Spartacus* works on two levels: first, in relation to the astonishing final crucifixion scene to which I will return shortly; and second, in relation to the relentless stoicism of the lead character that dominates the entire three-and-a-quarter-hour film. Kirk Douglas, who also co-produces the film, is the original chiselled jawed and muscled torsoed actor whose distinctive blue eyes have sole responsibility for conveying every conceivable emotion he feels. As others have noted, the film also often resonates with both thinly veiled homoeroticism, particularly in relation to the attempted seduction of Antoninus by Crassus, and wider processes of sexualised and racialised repression most overtly represented through the various gladiatorial fight sequences and given license through notions of civility (Hark, 1993). The artistically talented character of Antoninus, played by the downright pretty Tony Curtis, as well as the near camp playing of Batiatus by Peter Ustinov, is also clearly offset against Kirk Douglas's relentless emotional restraint. These two themes come together in the final scene. Having lost his war on slavery, suffered deception by his arch enemy Crassus, and also been forced to murder his friend – and symbol of all things spiritual that he believes in – Antoninus, Spartacus is finally faced with the otherwise lost love of his life, Varinia, and their new born son, while waiting to die on the cross. It's enough to make a grown man cry. Except he doesn't. By modern standards, the film is remarkably restrained in its physical depiction of gore, wounding and suffering, yet as Steve Neale has written, it is this 'emotional reticence' which forms the most fundamental basis of male masochism and spectacle (Neale, 1983).

Ben-Hur is also a film all about spectacle and gigantic spectacle at that, with legendary time and expense, sets and camera work used throughout. At the heart of *Ben-Hur* is the story of a friendship turned bad as the relationship between Judah, played by Charlton Heston, and Messala, played by Stephen Boyd, breaks down. The film features two extraordinary scenes of near sadomasochistic role reversal. The first concerns Ben-Hur's enslavement aboard ship as an oarsman. This leads to a particularly tense scene where the ship's Admiral, Quintus Arrius, played by Jack Hawkins, orders a demonstration of the crew's rowing prowess. The rhythm of the rowing is beaten out by a menacing looking drummer reaching ever-increasing speed the final pitch of which, aptly entitled 'ramming speed', develops a near orgasmic intensity offset by Rozsa's evocative score and surveyed by a smirking and sadistic Arrius. As if to heighten tension further, a *coup d'etat* of sorts leads to a loin-clothed and muscular Heston swaggering over a chained Hawkins while on a raft in full sadomasochistic role reversal. The other element of the story concerns Ben-Hur's encounters with a mysteriously faceless and off-camera yet typically white, Western and nut-brown-haired Christ. I return to this theme shortly.

The second example concerns the film's most famous scene, a chariot race – a spectacle so almighty it reportedly took three months to film. The scene is in many ways years ahead of its time given the advanced camera work in lieu of computer-generated imagery and sheer scale involved. At its core is the long-awaited duel between Ben-Hur and the brutal Messala played with some considerable relish by Boyd. Pictured dressed in a suitably black outfit and repeatedly whipping his equally black horses, the temptation to read the role of Messala as sexual flagellator here is almost overwhelming. He even whips Ben-Hur himself while still riding his spurred chariot at full speed. Ben-Hur is nevertheless victorious and Messala, almost dead from his wounds, exerts sadistic glee in telling Judah his mother and sister are lepers, and pronounces their duel not to be over. Nevertheless he dies having infected Ben-Hur with an overwhelming desire for revenge. As the film progresses from here, Ben-Hur's desire for revenge increasingly teeters on something between masochism *per se* and melodrama of which his reunion with his mother and sister is a primary example. However, all of this is ultimately trumped by the heavy-handed playing out of the Christian myth, the crucifixion, and indeed the entire masochist spectacle of a still faceless and tortured Christ.

Classical Hollywood movies, and particularly the epics of the late 1950s, such as *Spartacus* and *Ben-Hur*, in many ways centrally and fundamentally construct masculinity around *heroism* which is then in turn dependent upon suffering, endurance and the spectacle of masochism for its resolution into happiness. This is often, whether explicitly or implicitly, also centred on the original biblical story of the sufferings of Christ, and most particularly his crucifixion. Given the increasing secularity of much contemporary Western society and popular culture, it is necessary to consider how such mechanisms develop through more contemporary cinema.

Media studies of masculinity in the 1980s were dominated, perhaps rather unsurprisingly, both by a consideration of classics and epics, as we have already seen, and also the new cult of action cinema and the spectacle of Arnold Schwarzenegger, Bruce Willis and Sylvester Stallone in *Terminator, Die Hard* and *Rambo* respectively (Jeffords, 1994; Tasker, 1993b). Many of the arguments have been summarised already, yet what is often overlooked in these analyses is the parallel development of work on masculinity and consumer culture, frequently through discussion of the New Man. Here, Frank Mort and Sean Nixon in particular sought to document and expose the shifting terrain of sexual politics towards a more media-driven, visual and aesthetic masculinity experienced and practised in men's lifestyle magazines, fashion, shopping and metropolitan cultures arguing that the 1980s saw the rise of an increasingly blurred and pluralistic culture of men looking at other men and themselves (Mort, 1996; Nixon, 1996). My own work re-evaluated many of these claims arguing that such developments had a far more concrete anchoring in economic shifts, marketing, advertising and the commodification of masculinity often selling a uniform rather than diverse image of men to themselves while others debated some of the wider implications of such developments for sexual politics (Chapman and Rutherford, 1988; Edwards, 1997).

There are, however, certain aspects of this work which are relevant to the analysis here. The first concerns the emphasis placed upon the importance of men looking at other men and indeed images of themselves. Although none of the authors mentioned here pays much attention to the question of cinema, their wider arguments concerning the rise of an increasingly homosocial, if not homosexual, gaze are relevant. Second, my own work and that of Susan Bordo in particular did much to challenge both the implied progressiveness of these developments and to expose their underpinnings in wider practices of the commodification of the male body in particular (Bordo, 1999; Edwards, 2006). Within the last few decades, the male body has grown to become a spectacle to be bought, sold and consumed whether through being pumped and shaped at the gym, moisturised with endless products, displayed through fashion and magazines, or viewed on television or at the cinema. These are terrains most successfully explored so far by writer and journalist Mark Simpson who most famously coined the term 'metrosexual' in his analysis of the rise of an increasingly narcissistic, consumerist self- and city-centred masculinity (Simpson, 1994, 1996). There is also an as yet unexplored and rather implicit connection here with questions of masochism for if men and the male body are increasingly objectified and sold to themselves and each other then the potential for male rather than female processes of masochistic looking – whether voyeurist or exhibitionist – is likewise increased. This is a theme which I wish to explore in relation to some more contemporary films pertaining to the theme of masculinity.

The first of these, *Fight Club*, would appear to turn male masochism into an art form claiming that the endurance of pain through bare knuckle fighting is the primary route to reclaiming lost manhood and masculinity. Its premise is essentially a sadistic critique of consumerist masculinity, epitomised by the destruction of the narrator's IKEA-filled apartment, as unfulfilling, effeminacy inducing and generally namby-pamby. The immediate parallel here with Robert Bly's Jungian fuelled pyromania concerning contemporary North American masculinity in his book *Iron John* is unmissable (Bly, 1990). The film's release in the late 1990s also coincided with the height of the backlash against the New Man – the aspirational, moisturising, designer-suit wearing, child cradling, city working yuppie of the 1980s encapsulated by *GQ* and similar lifestyle magazine titles and driven to apocalyptic and self-destructive implosion in another film of a book *American Psycho* (Ellis, 1991). Yet while *American Psycho* arguably sought to satirise and pathologise the yuppie lifestyle, *Fight Club* viscerally attacks it and offers an even more violent solution: mass-scale fighting. Similarly while *Loaded* magazine spearheaded the rise of the New Lad over and above the New Man in journalism, *Fight Club* took laddism to whole new heights, namely Hollywood (Benwell, 2003; Edwards, 2003).

Critical in this is the placing of Brad Pitt, increasingly sold as *the* iconic male sex symbol and the *über* body for a generation given his muscled and oiled bodily perfectionism, in the dual-lead role with Ed Norton. Indeed the film parades his naked torso, ripped abdominal muscles and pert pectorals at every opportunity. The images the film presents of the male body are sharply bifurcated. While many of those engaging in fight club are shown arriving at work and going about their daily business bruised, battered and bandaged, Brad Pitt maintains a gleaming presence. As the mentor of fight club Pitt also figures as the aspirational symbol for every wimp to real man wannabe, a point which is further reinforced when it is revealed that Pitt is merely Norton's alter ego. Thus the strongest playing out of masochistic male pleasure here is not in relation to the fighting at all but rather in the self-loathing and longing to be a he-man that the film so unashamedly promotes. Most fundamentally this depends upon the homosocial, in fact more truly homosexual, adoration of the male body – epitomised by Brad Pitt's naked torso that the film recurrently invokes. Key within this is the triangle set-up between Durden, the otherwise unnamed narrator and Singer. The increasingly homoerotic relationship between the two men is partly off set and yet partly also reinforced by the narrator witnessing, and clearly suffering, Durden's ferocious fucking (one can hardly call it love making) of Singer. Although most consciously understood as exposing the narrator's jealousy of Durden's conquest of Singer, the scene in its exposition of the narrator's suffering shows another level of pain, namely, his homosexual desire to have Durden for himself. The following display of Pitt in a feminine dressing gown and slippers reinforces the point. That said, the film is not half as radical as it appears to be – indeed Fincher has often been quoted as saying the film was taken far too seriously – and tends to end up as another effects-driven gimmick flick in an overly saturated action movie market.

Far more intriguing here is the lasting figure of James Bond – Ian Fleming's womanising, fast car driving and near indestructible hero immortalised in the most successful film franchise ever (Chapman, 2000). As is perhaps well known, Bond's almost stupendous mix of misogyny and heroism has become increasing parodied and indeed self-parodying since the heyday Connery's panther-like swagger in the 1960s. What is intriguing here, however, is how this process was almost completely inverted in the twenty-first Bond flick *Casino Royale*. When Daniel Craig was chosen to be the next actor to play Bond, the media could have been accused of setting up a near sadomasochistic relationship between the actor and his incumbent audience, such was the barrage of criticism he received – too short, too blond, too rough or not even good looking enough – it was as if the media was gearing itself up to rub its hands with glee at his inevitable downfall. To make matters worse, Craig was then depicted arriving at his first press conference on a speedboat wearing an incongruous and decidedly un-Bond-like life jacket over his suit, and rumours were later rife during film-making that the actor was struggling to manage some of his stunts. As it turned out, however, a singular and now globally iconic shot of Craig emerging from the waves buff, bronzed and generally bulging wearing a pair of pale blue trunks both paid gender-inverted homage to Ursula Andres in *Dr No* and put an end to his media torture in the time it took to blink. Thus before the film had even opened, *Casino Royale* and its lead actor Daniel Craig were packed full of the contradictions of masculine spectacle.

Both the film and its lead were heavily marketed to, and to all intents and purposes largely delivered, a 'back to basics' Bond that was less glossy and gadget driven, more rugged and altogether more physical. Contrary to earlier rumours, Craig was now argued to be doing many of his own stunts and having a far greater involvement in the production of the film than many of his predecessors. As if to emphatically prove the point, the film's first full Technicolor scene involves Craig hurtling through buildings and across dangerous terrain, dodging bullets and bombs, and running up a crane with nothing more to protect him than an overly thin Hawaiian shirt – he flexes, he bruises, he bleeds – but emerges triumphant.

The contrast between Craig's craggy and muscular, almost feral, virility and his predecessor's, Pierce Brosnan, suave, suited and near-mannequin-like masculinity could not be stronger. While Craig both looked like he could throw a punch and hurt a bit if he received one, Brosnan could be made to look uncomfortable by a slip in his tie-knot. The contrast is in large part between body and mind as Craig's Bond is monosyllabic to the point of Neanderthal terseness while Brosnan's delivers a sharp quip at every turn. This clearly opens up a far wider terrain for analysing sadomasochistic viewing pleasure yet, as I will shortly argue, this is only half the story.

Casino Royale was the first of Fleming's Bond novels, and the film is driven by a similar narrative showing not the Bond we have already become accustomed to but how that Bond came into being and became what we know now. Indeed the parting shot of the film is its defining moment – a stern-faced Craig dressed in an immaculate three-piece suit wielding a machine gun the size of a small planet and uttering the immortal words 'the name's Bond, James Bond'. Interestingly, part of Craig's 'becoming Bond' in the film involves his endurance of emotional as well as physical suffering. His love affair with, and subsequent betrayal by, Vesper Lynd breaks his heart and makes him Bond – cold, callous, cruel. As a consequence, the very plot line itself resonates with a sense of masculinity as premised upon masochism – mental and emotional as well as physical. Yet it is not the plot nor these classic action scenes that I wish to draw attention to here, but rather two other scenes that open up a far less orthodox set of viewing relations concerning masculine heroics and male spectacle.

The first concerns the already cited singular moment when the audience is encouraged to enjoy the spectacle of Daniel Craig as James Bond in a pair of swimming trunks. This is indeed a brief encounter not only because of the aforementioned pale blue trunks but because it lasts little longer than a second in a two-hour film. One's initial and unthinking reaction would be to see this moment as a further move towards the sexual objectification of men or the male body and as an inversion of the gendered gaze, even more so given its overt homage to scenes in earlier Bond movies involving Ursula Andres and Halle Berry. Yet this is only partially the case. As I have already said, the scene is quite extraordinarily brief, one blink and you miss it, and it is also framed by an infinitely longer panning of the camera over Bond's soon-to-be female conquest number one: Solange (Caterina Murino). Almost as soon as the camera pans over Craig's body, it swings back to her and stays there. Adding further testimony to Richard Dyer's influential article 'Don't

Look Now' Craig is seen looking away from the camera as if to higher things, he strolls manfully through the water, and his body is as hard, pumped and phallic as a male body can be (Dyer, 1989). Yet this kind of dismissal does insufficient justice to the role of the scene and indeed Craig and his body in the film. Whatever else its legacy may be, it remains the defining moment of Craig's success as Bond and of the film's success more widely. *That* picture of Daniel Craig in a pair of blue swimming trunks was used, and continues to be central, in the selling and marketing of the film to women and gay men and – to mix metaphors even further – in marketing terms it blows the rest of the film out of the water. One is left, then, with Craig as bodily spectacle and the interrogation of the gaze. While that gaze is in many ways deflected it also remains a severe, relentless and ubiquitous exposure that ultimately reduces Craig to object invoking much potentially sadistic, and masochistic, pleasure. Thus *Casino Royale* not only reinvents the masochism of heroism once again but couples it with the masochism of commodified sexual objectification. Viewing pumped and preened bodies, male or female, may not seem to be the most obvious demonstration of masochist spectacle yet in stripping both actors and characters of any real emotional experience, or even subjectivity, it thereby denies them any form of pleasure, or pain, other than through the audience's implicit awareness of the hours of endurance of physical anguish undertaken to look that way.

The second scene I wish to discuss occurs later in the film when Bond is captured by his arch rival and ruthless financier Le Chiffre. Removed of all tracking devices, a bruised and battered but still rather beautifully tuxed Bond is forcibly stripped and strapped stark naked on a chair with the seating removed. Le Chiffre then proceeds to torment him with a heavily weighted rope operating as implement for bodily punishment, yet the scene revolves not on conventional flagellation but on the whipping of Bond's genitals exposed through the open chair. As if the implied sadomasochistic tension was not sufficient already, the dialogue adds to it. Le Chiffre admires Bond's buffed and bronzed musculature remarking: 'Wow, you've clearly taken good care of your body', before embarking on a long discourse on the effectiveness of torturing male genitalia. He then begins torturing Bond who merely responds by asking, 'I've got this little itch, down there, would you mind?'. Le Chiffre then whips his genitals again. Bond now howling with pain utters 'No, no, no . . . to the right, to the right, to the right', is whipped again and then repeats 'Yes, yes, yes', laughs and then quips, 'now the whole world's gonna know you died scratching my balls!'. Arguably both von Sacher-Masoch and de Sade would be hard pressed to script a scene with more sadomasochistic tension. The blatant homoeroticism is also increased by the lighting of Craig's body which although bruised and bloody in places, literally gleams with phallic virility (the shirt ripping opening is the first of many mini climaxes here), while his performance in the scene overall shows an extraordinary degree of both suffering *and* pleasure as if to ram home the sadomasochistic sexual thrill once and for all. Further titillation is also provided when one finds out that the stunt was performed by Craig himself sitting naked on a piece of Perspex. Aside from the points already mentioned concerning the role of action cinema and the increasing sexual objectification of the male body, what this scene would seem to highlight is the sense in which the true spectacle of male masochism within cinema depends quite literally upon the *simultaneous* display of suffering and triumph, weakness and endurance, pain and pleasure. This further proves axiomatic within the film as Bond's betrayal by Vesper Lynd is soon exposed and building of Bond – emotionally, mentally and physically *as a masochist* – becomes complete. The film is arguably not the radical departure it wants to be, but the performance of Craig, and indeed his reinvention from hopeless wimp to heroic master in his role as Bond, remains a defining moment in the display of masochistic complexities of masculinity and heroism within contemporary cinema.

Conclusions: Spectacular pain

The key defining feature of male masochism as it is presented in filmic media is that it is spectacle – set up to be looked at and to encourage emotional engagement, of whatever kind, and in some more particular cases to be quite spectacularly extreme. A prime example here is the repeated torturing of the near indestructible James Bond. Discussion of male masochism within cinema has been almost entirely driven by Mulvey's analysis of looking relations and its critique. Given its reliance on the universalising, or at least rather static, tendencies of psychoanalytic theory, analysis of such phenomena within cinema has arguably not kept pace with more recent developments within wider society, particularly the commodification and sexualisation of the male body. These are processes that now extend infinitely wider than cinema to the worlds of fashion, advertising, the media and popular and consumer culture. Studies in these other areas have some, as yet rather untapped, application to cinematic representations of masculinity. The primary exception here has been the work of Mark Simpson which straddles any number of areas yet is overly reliant on journalism and barely explicated applications of Freudian psychoanalytic theory (Simpson, 1994). As I have stated elsewhere, much of the difficulty here has been sociology's rather 'high and mighty' attitude towards studying popular culture – at least beyond of the remits of variants of Marxist class analysis – often seeing it as somehow 'beneath' social science investigation and leaving it to the much maligned media studies to pick up the pieces (Edwards, 2006).

One is perhaps left with one final question. To what extent do any such images of masculinity relate to real men, women or society more widely? This is ultimately a question concerning the relationship between culture and ideology, yet what can be said with some conviction is that what cinematic images of masculinity present are ideals of manhood, gold standards by which men are set or, in short, notions of (male) heroism.

Thus, to summarise, I have argued that cinematic presentations of masculinity depend much on the notion of heroism which in turn centres on processes of masochistic spectacle whether through the display of physical, emotional or spiritual suffering in defence of honour, an ideal or self. These processes, I have also argued, are now increasingly secularised and commodified both explicitly and deliberately using the male body to sell films. This opens up further possibilities for masochistic spectacle – either exhibitionist or voyeurist – and complex patterns of sadomasochistic identification in the audience. While much of this has been in evidence since the 1950s, it is the very *ubiquity* of such display that shifts the terrain here. As such, the importance of cinematic representations of masculinity needs understanding within the context of wider patterns of consumerist and commodified masculinity that sell male spectacle and indeed the male body by the pound, dollar, euro and yen.

11
Cut Pieces: Self-Mutilation in Body Art

Ulla Angkjær Jørgensen

Using one's own image to make art is not new; the genre of self-portraiture has been an integrated part of Western art history since the Renaissance. The picturing of torment and suffering is also no news to art history. But the extended use of the artist's own real body, its flesh and blood, belongs to the twentieth century and grew to become established as a specific artistic practice during the 1960s.

In her book *Body Art/Performing the Subject* (1998) Amelia Jones picks up the thread from the tradition of self-portraiture, as she argues that body art is the postmodern way of articulating the subject as one who constantly performs her/himself in an intersubjective relationship with others. In the early years of body art in the 1960s and early 1970s there seemed to be some form of trust in the authenticity of the body (Jones, 2000: 40). However, the use of the body involves aspects other than the articulation of subjectivity as identity politics. To some artists the body presents itself as an alternative material to paint, with the tradition of painting after high modernism seen to have passed its peak performance in the 1940s and 1950s. The body is seen as actual concrete material for artistic purpose just like paint, marble or any other material, on the one hand; on the other hand, the body does carry with it existential problems of subjectivity and death, which belong to the symbolic order of things.

This chapter addresses the issues of sexuality and death coming together in the body, which are taken up in some radical body actions in the 1960s and early 1970s (Vergine, 2000). The chosen works are formed within the modern tradition of the avant-garde, which is understood to be on the front line of what it is possible to articulate given the time of production. In the mind of the avant-garde artist her work will always be one of a transforming character. This is relevant to our context because it means that, at their best, avant-garde works of art spar with hegemonic ideas of culture. They do not merely depict existing ideals or ideas; they also try to transform these ideals or ideas into new ones. The avant-garde artist believes in the visionary and transforming power of the aesthetic; by making art she takes part in the reformulation of symbols, she negotiates cultural meanings. However, no artist of today can be seen to hover above ordinary life, or stand outside history; she is just as much part of her time and subjected to the mechanisms of culture as anyone else. It is in the twilight zone of what we already know and what we are about to discover that the avant-garde artist works.

The aim of the chapter is to address how acts of self-mutilation signify differently in the case of female and male subjects as a result of sexual difference. In the case of Yoko Ono and Marina Abramovic the passive role of the sexual submissive female is challenged; in the case of Günter Brus the violent self-sufficient agency of the masculine subject is addressed and in the case of Valie Export the split character of the female subject is being investigated.

Ritual and violence

Yoko Ono's (b. 1933) *Cut Piece*, first performed at the Yamaichi Concert Hall in Kyoto on 20 July 1964,[1] ushers in practice of self-mutilation in body art. Though Ono never experienced any real cuts of her flesh, the performance demonstrates the use of the body as a site of giving/exchange and violence/destruction, which links it with the logic of ritual offerings. Seated on a stage in front of an audience, Ono invited people to come up and use a pair of scissors to cut off her suit. The performance did not involve any actual cutting of the body; it was more an act of 'giving', according to Ono herself (Rhee, 2005: 103). Eventually though, the act unveiled her naked body. However, the chosen aggressive method of cutting instead of ordinary stripping off of the clothes suggests that something far more disturbing is at stake than mere unveiling. Ono left open the possibility for viewers to cut her body. And even though no one took the opportunity, some came quite close, according to her own later comments on the event: 'One person came on the stage . . . He took the pair of scissors and made a motion to stab me. He raised his hand, with the scissors in it, and I thought he was going to stab me. But the hand was just raised there and was totally still. He was standing still . . . with the scissors . . . threatening me' (quoted in Rhee, 2005: 103).

Jieun Rhee discusses the coming together of eroticism and violation in this exchange act of giving on the part of Ono, and of taking on the part of the viewers. Rhee focuses on the differences in the reception of the piece in Japan, Europe and the United States. The element of stripping in the performance proves to have evoked strong, but also different, reactions in the different audiences. Ono's subtle 'peace-seeking' insistence on the aspect of giving, combined with some of the viewers' aggressive denuding of her body, rearranges the common notions of passive viewer and active performer in a striptease context and in pornography, but her performance also resembles what is at work in sadomasochistic practices of sexuality. Ono's own desire can therefore be interpreted as one of (masochistic) surrender (Rhee, 2005: 114). The connections made between the notion of giving and the actual denuding of the female body seem to have evoked different connotations in the different cultures, though all of them seem to invoke the uncanny yet desirable coming together of sex and violation for some. As Rhee recollects, 'what was ambivalent aggression in Kyoto seems to have become a burlesque [in New York and London] [. . .] *Cut Piece* was received as an exotic striptease' (Rhee, 2005: 110–12).

In all of her *Cut Piece*-performances Yoko Ono strikes at the heart of what Georges Bataille understands as the true nature of eroticism: its profound bonds with violation, and violence even. In this drama the naked body signifies the vulnerability of the subject, its openness to (the inevitable) otherness:

> The whole business of eroticism is to destroy the self-contained character of the participators as they are in their normal lives. Stripping naked is the decisive action. Nakedness offers a contrast to self-possession, to discontinuous existence, in other words. It is a state of communication revealing a quest for a possible continuance of being beyond the confines of the self. Bodies open out to a state of continuity through secret channels that give us a feeling of obscenity.
>
> (Bataille, 2006: 17)

In Bataille's thinking the violent and destructive nature of erotic activity is the fulcrum of human existence: the solar plexus, which connects discontinuous existence, a singular and individual subject, with continuous existence, the principle of eternal non-subjective existence. The dissolution of one existence leads to the creation of another, not necessarily a new subject, but eternal life. Therefore eroticism is profoundly linked with death; we may even speak of a death drive in Freudian terms. The nucleus of Bataille's thinking, however, is that life is not destroyed by death: '[it] *is even proved by death*' (Bataille, 2006: 21; italics in original).

The problem with Bataille seen from a contemporary gender critical perspective is that he relies heavily on a heteronormative model of sexual intercourse. In his descriptions of the sexual act the female part is seen to take on a passive role and the male part an active one. Both end up in the same dissolved state, but the violent road to the blissful state is dependent on the violent male and the submissive female (Bataille, 2006: 17). Nonetheless I have chosen to bring him in here because his idea of the violent nature of sex and his coining of the significance of the vulnerability of the naked body is to the point, when considering the character of the works in question. But Bataille is also relevant as he gives away culture's 'unconscious' abuse of the female body and also, therefore, is relevant in a gender perspective. His book was first published in 1957, only seven years before Ono's first *Cut Piece* was performed, and the works of Ono, Abramovic and Export (see later) must be understood historically in the context of the second feminist movement: *they* react to culture's unconscious abuse of the female body. Bataille delivers one aspect of an explanation for culture's violation of the image of the female body. The female body must be sacrificed in order for the two (heterosexual) partners to reach a state of ecstasy.

Bataille understands (hetero)sexual intercourse as a religious sacrifice in which the two involved individuals through their opening up to eternal otherness, 'the dissolution of the separate beings, reveals their fundamental continuity [. . .]' (Bataille, 2006: 22). In religious sacrifice something similar takes place. The victim is stripped of her clothes and even her life, and the spectators are left to consummate the passage from discontinuity to continuity.

What Rhee sees in Yoko Ono's *Cut Piece* is how she by letting herself be undressed by others, makes herself open to both ethnic and cultural otherness in different settings: to ethnic otherness in the United States and Europe and to cultural otherness in Japan. Bataille, however, would argue that she also makes herself vulnerable to eternal otherness, as the ritual and violent character of the undressing links the performance with erotic activity, and hence the promise of death. The pair of scissors, the cutting away of her clothing, underline the dissolving process the subject goes through in these existential passages; the fine threshold between clothing and skin, which is constantly under threat from the scissors, marks the subject's fragile and self-containing border, which in Bataille's understanding, we have to rid ourselves of in order to enjoy continuity.

In 1974 Marina Abramovic (b. 1946) subjected herself to a similar kind of treatment. In Galleria Studio Morra in Naples, Italy, she performed *Rhythm 0* with an audience who was mainly brought in off the street and whom she invited to handle her body with different tools. She was standing passive alongside a table, which displayed 27 different objects to be used on her body; these included a pistol, an axe, a fork, a bottle of perfume, a bell, a feather, chains, nails, needles, scissors, a pen, a book, a hammer, a saw, a lamb bone, a newspaper, grapes, olive oil, a rosemary branch, a rose and other things (McEvilley, 1995: 46).

In this case the performance developed to even greater extremes than was the case with *Cut Piece*. RoseLee Goldberg recollects that '[b]y the third hour [people] had cut all her clothes from her body with razor blades and even nicked bits of flesh from her neck. Later, someone put a loaded gun in her hand, and pushed its nozzle against her head' (Goldberg, 1995: 11). Abramovic had arranged the event as a true ritual: a table covered with a white cloth on which the objects for the ritual sacrifice were displayed; beside the table, she had placed herself, the body to be sacrificed. The audience answered to, what Bataille would call, their true violent nature. Some took the opportunity to harm Abramovic and the performance was, in fact, brought to an end when some of the bystanders had had enough and took action to stop it. The eerie thing about *Rhythm 0* is that it validates Bataille's point of the persistence of humans' 'violent nature' and demonstrates the need for society's prohibitions. If we chose to read the performance in the strictly Bataillian sense, it proves both women and men's violent nature: the female artist who submits herself to this ordeal and who might find pleasure in it (which cannot be ruled out) and men who willingly – some aggressively – take the opportunity to act on the female artist's body.

Another critical point in Bataillian terminology is that his idea of the violent nature of humans is borne out of a transhistorical man-the-hunter-narration that almost automatically links the human violent agency with the male. There exists a paradox here as Bataille means 'human being' as in mankind when he speaks of 'man', but in fact he leaves the agency with the male. Consequently, I have chosen to use the term 'human' in the following when speaking of Bataille's 'man'.

According to Bataille, humans have built a society of work, or reason, in order to tame their violent nature, '[they have] worked and cut [themselves] away from violence' (Bataille, 2006: 43). However, this mostly successful mastering of chaos does not erase the violent impulses completely; they still flow as an undercurrent in the inner life of humans and break through from time to time. In modern societies science has become the regulatory force of humans' excessive nature, but before that, in pre-industrial societies, taboos acted on behalf of science. Still, modern societies observe a few rules, which originate from taboos: those on sex and death. All cultures appear to observe restrictions on the liberty of sexual conduct and the handling of the dead body. Even though modern society may think of itself as liberated, it does not allow the performance of sexual acts just anywhere; lovers do, generally at least, seek privacy. And even though we think of ourselves as modern and rational, we nevertheless handle the dead body as if it were still alive. In the Christian world we still subject to the two fundamental commandments of the Old Testament: 'Thou shalt not kill', and 'Thou shalt not perform the carnal act except in wedlock', though these are transgressed over and again.

But transgression is surely also the mechanism that keeps the Bataillian dualism going. Transgression is the tool by which people experience the greatest of pleasures; it is in transgression we lose our discontinuous selves to continuity. The destruction of the self – partially or fully – is the key to ultimate pleasure in Bataille's thinking. The Bataillian dualism, however, is not one of repression, as with the psychoanalytic one; taboos are regulatory not repressive: 'We can even go so far as the absurd proposition: "The taboo is there to be violated"' (Bataille, 2006: 64). In psychoanalysis, in contrast, culture, or the symbolic order, represses nature, the original realm of the mother's body. In order to become a subject one has to undergo development away from the territory of the mother's body (nature) into language and culture. The realm of the mother has to be suppressed in order for the subject to enter into the realm of the father. Bataille has no problem with nature; on the contrary, the subject's recurrent transgressions into violent nature are necessary in order to lose itself to bliss and continuity.

Though modern society has generally done away with archaic forms of sacrifice and taboo, we still observe social contracts for what can be done to and with the body. The performance artists in question experiment with the transgression of one of the few taboos left, that you must not violate the body. The body still seems to carry deep symbolic meaning concerning the obscure connection between life and death, in Bataillian notions it marks the passage from discontinuity to continuity. This seems to be a basic meaning of the body, which modern science has yet to map out.

From her examination of specific performance acts in the 1970s, Kathy O'Dell understands artistic self-mutilation as acts of masochism. It is her observation that masochistic performances often return to the threshold between the oral and Oedipal stages (in Freudian terms), respectively the imaginary and symbolic (in Lacanian terms), the passage which Lacan refers to as the mirror stage (O'Dell, 1998: 36). And the great contribution of masochistic performance art, according to O'Dell, is 'the efforts by artists to connect to the dynamics of the mirror stage [. . .]: the attempt to deconstruct the very notion of identity that oedipalisation tries to render inflexible' (O'Dell, 1998: 36). In going back to this significant passage in which the child for the first time experiences the separation from the mother's body, and sees itself as a split body in a world of other bodies, artists negotiate the premises of the symbolic takeover by culture, that is, the loss of the tactile and of the imaginary potential of the mother's body. The mirror stage produces the body as an object and the subject as the linguistic self. Masochism, the wounding of one's own body, then becomes a demonstration of the sensate basis of identity, or the bodily identity, if you like. When revisiting the mirror stage, artists want to reconstruct subjectivity as a uniting of body and language. But there are different roads to the goal, and different roads marked by different genders.

The skin as armour: Günter Brus

In 1968 two artists literally had to flee their home country, Austria, as a consequence of their action *Art and Revolution* performed at the University of Vienna.[2] Günter Brus (b. 1938) and Otto Mühl (b. 1925) both received prison sentences for having violated Austrian symbols, matrimony and the family, disturbed public order, and for having caused bodily harm (Green, 1999: 61). During the notorious trial Brus and Mühl declared that they were in fact painters; they had, however, freed themselves from the canvas.[3] 'Our focus is the body', they claimed (Green, 1999: 59). If art is a place to reflect the body, the body may be a place to reflect painting and take it beyond its former limits. In this context it is important to note what characterises the artists' handling of the body; the body is interesting because it possesses scandalising potentials: it is the site of taboos that continue to survive.

Brus's first action in 1964 was performed after he had tried to paint with his body directly. He was trying to get beyond what he thought was the solipsism of 'informal painting'. Informal painting was a 1950s European parallel movement to American abstract expressionism, in which abstract forms were seen to derive directly from the painter's body impulses. Brus wanted to get away from the mere idea of the mirror relationship between body and painting; he wanted the body to do the act by itself and leave the canvas behind, as it were.

He had the year before experimented with painting with both his arms and legs tied up in order to disturb painterly gestures and as a result also to disrupt the tendency towards composition (Klocker, 1989: 115). In his early actions in 1964 and 1965 he was therefore still focused on the relationship between canvas and body, for instance in the action *Ana* (1964). In this, he painted the room of the action completely white, after which he was wrapped up in pieces of cloth like a mummy and started to roll about in order to apply paint to the cloth. The action connected the body to an art historical meta-meaning, that signifies the canvas as a metaphor for skin. Brus applied the metaphor to the skin, so to speak, like a crust, which he in his subsequent actions was about to break. Even though it is said that he was not satisfied with the action, in retrospect it seems a logical link to his *Self-paintings* of 1964 and 1965. In these actions the crusted painting on the body surface fused with the skin. He appeared as cast in plaster. Still he constantly sought to mark breaks in different ways, for instance as a black, serrated, painted line down through the vertical axis of the body like the splitting of a log with an axe. In these actions the body surface appeared as akin to armour.

While he was doing these actions he was also producing drawings, in which he was preoccupied with imaginings of torture. And in 1967 he started to realise the self-mutilations in a series of actions called *Body Analysis*, one of which was *The Total Madness* (1968). In this action, he cut himself through his shirt and skin with a razor blade and urinated in a bucket. According to Hubert Klocker (1989: 120), he was now clearly preoccupied with liberating the body completely from the physical and sexual taboos surrounding it. He seemed to have entirely left painting behind and was only interested in the body and its functions. At the same time as he cut his body, he also let its secretions flow during the actions. It seemed rather easy to urinate, but he also succeeded in masturbating and emptying himself on stage, which can be seen as the last excess.

Breaking Test was his last action. It was carried out on 19 June 1970 in Münich while in exile. It is a thoroughly choreographed action, in which Brus naked and even tonsured for the occasion pressed the body to its extreme limit of pain in order to provoke consciously uncontrolled reactions. After *Breaking Test* he finished with all his body actions and turned to drawing and writing. He writes about *Breaking Test*:

> The actor is aggressive against himself and against surrounding objects, as a result of which appropriate reactions are set free: self-injury, rattling sounds in the throat, strangulations, flogging, spastic behaviour and so forth. A breaking test of nerves means the sudden change in direction of the action, the abrupt stop of an action. Shock-like impulses should be emitted, which may at first irritate the viewers but later change to a comforting conflict solution.
>
> (Brus quoted in Klocker, 1989: 143)

Pressing the body to its limits obviously means making it shed its secretions as expression of an inner bodilyness. When the secretions get over the body's edge they connect inside and outside. It is liberating that all that has been suppressed explodes out into the open. This is why the skin becomes such an important sign; it is the place through which this movement takes place.

With the help of psychoanalyst Didier Anzieu's concept of a 'Skin Ego' we can approach the mystery of the skin (Anzieu, 1989: 69ff). As a point of departure Anzieu understands the Skin Ego to be a mental image, formed on the basis of the intimate skin-to-skin relationship between the infant and its mother (or the mothering person). In this relationship the infant experiences sharing the mother's skin and on this ground it visualises a protective envelope. Anzieu maintains that all psychic activities are due to biological functions. More precisely, the Skin Ego finds support in the three main functions of the skin: The primary function is as a sac, which contains feeding, care, etc. The second function is as an interface, which marks the boundary between inside and outside, and at the same time protects against aggressions and penetrations coming from the outside. The third function, which the skin shares with the mouth, is a site of communicating with others. This makes it a transporter of meaning through sensing and percepting, and it is, moreover, an 'inscribing surface' of the marks left by others (Anzieu, 1989: 40).

Anzieu goes on to explain how this fantasy of a common skin may take a narcissistic turn or a masochistic turn. Cases of abrupt and violent shifts between, on the one hand, overstimulation of the skin from the mother and lack of mothering attention, on the other hand, may lead to masochistic tendencies, whereas overdoing the stimulation in itself may lead to narcissism. The masochistic 'jouissance' is due to fantasies of having one's skin flayed and the recovery (the bandaging) afterwards. This state is thus an eternal changing one between suffering and cure. The narcissist, on the contrary, has built a shield out of the exaggerated stimulation. The exaggerated understanding of the need for establishing signifying relations on part of the mother has led to the formation of a narcissistic shield. The child has become invulnerable. In both cases the individual has suffered a handicap in the formation of the Skin Ego, which would otherwise be a psychic envelope ensuring the well-being in the relation between the Ego and the world (Anzieu, 1989: 43–4). The masochist and the narcissist have in common a disturbance in the Skin Ego resulting in a lack of ability to feel the boundary of the body. The sensuous ability for connecting to and communicating with the world has been damaged.

The remarkable thing about Brus is that his actions express both extremes. The first actions seem to be expressions of the invulnerable narcissist; the crust of canvas and paint is like armour of plaster that cuts him off from the surrounding world and prevents his body from secreting and sensing the world. After that he flays himself: he tears off the shield and stands naked and vulnerable for his, by now, masochistic inclinations. There must be cutting, flaying and secretion in order to feel. It is a compressed process and development, which he goes through.

In analysing Brus's actions I have also found the work of Klaus Theweleit very instructive. In Theweleit's analysis of the body of the fascistic soldier we detect the same extremes of narcissism and masochism in the same body. Military drill teaches the soldier to fell joy in the bodily pain that meets him: the lashing, the repetitions, suffering of privation, the whole idea of the body's denial in flagellation. There is disciplining of the body: in the hierarchy, in punishment, in the dormitories, with cold washes, etc. The formation of the fascistic soldier makes visible the materiality of the body, its concreteness. Whatever may be left of ethereal spirit is anchored in the material. The body is understood as machine.

Something as flickering and personal as feelings are transformed into operational tools. The soldier is transformed into a body machine, whose movements transform functions such as thinking, feeling and seeing (Theweleit, 1989: 153). He becomes a steel figure, a suit of armour and a single machine part in the big army:

> The new man is a man whose physique has been machinised, his psyche eliminated – or in part displaced into his body armour, his 'predatory' suppleness. We are presented with a robot that can tell the time, find the North, stand his ground over a red-hot machine-gun, or cut wire without a sound.
>
> (Theweleit, 1989: 162)

His pent-up feelings transform the body armour into fuel for its adroitness. (Theweleit, 1989: 162). The body armour delimits the person from the surrounding world. The Ego is thus produced from outside impulses; the lashing and the disciplining which strikes against the body to build and harden it. The body armour becomes the Ego. Furthermore this takes place because the drill action absorbs the man's desire (which is always thought to be heterosexual) for women. The body armour makes him an invulnerable individual, a 'homo solus', who is not dependent on another object, or another individual. In battle, however, this situation changes in that there is another object, the enemy, who can be reached by a body who gets out of control. The soldier is characterised as an explosion of aggression; the battlefield is his body. And the goal is to penetrate the enemy's body, to tear it; he explodes against the enemy (Theweleit, 1989: 178). One paradox of this construction is that it claims to embody 'the nation' and 'the whole', meaning the community, however, this is executed best as isolated, self-sufficient subject on the look out for the flow of desire (Theweleit, 1989: 191). And strangely enough, in the heat of battle and in the moments of desire the body seems to be most split:

> War is a function of the body of these men. Strangely, however, their body remains inwardly divided in the very moment in which its functioning is most intensely pleasurable. In war, the man appears not only naked, but stripped of the skin; he seems to lose his body armour, so that everything enters directly into the interior of his body, or flows directly from it. He is out of control and seems permitted to be so. But at the same time, he is all armour, speeding bullet, steel enclosure. He wears a coat of steel that seems to take the place of his missing skin. He is collected, directed toward one strict goal; in this sense he is controlled in the extreme.
>
> (Theweleit, 1989: 192)

When reading Theweleit's description of the fascistic soldier's body, this vision constructed in Central Europe during the first half of the twentieth century, it seems striking how much it shares with the body actions of Günter Brus in Austria in the 1960s. In both cases, there are isolated subjects; there is explosion and aggression; and there is this connection between two, according to Anzieu, namely, different types of Skin Egos. Anzieu's description is very much to the point, whereas the occurrence is not. For both in Theweleit and in Brus, it seems as if the narcissist and the masochist are able to produce each other, or at least both exist in the same body. The idea of the body armour contains both the building of a shield and the stripping off of that same shield as it is, paradoxically, exemplified in the battlefield. In the actions *Total Madness* and especially *Breaking Test* Brus embodies the battlefield: he is at war. This is where he finally explodes: he is both stripped of his skin and speeding bullet.

In his book *Cracking the Armour* (1993) Michael Kaufman uses the armour metaphor in his description of masculinity in patriarchy.[4] For him, the term can be used in a much broader sense, but has its most critical occurrence in soldiers, modern ones too.[5] But as a general term it covers the urge for power (Kaufman, 1993: 30) and the suppressing of emotions necessary for this quest (Kaufman, 1993: 56). Masculinity is thus constructed as the right (and duty) to exercise power over others: in war, at work, in society, in the family, in having sex, everywhere; masculinity needs others to dominate in order to come out right:

> Even the most secure man can ultimately only experience himself as a real man, that is, as possessing masculinity, if he's able to experience someone else as possessing femininity, that is, a real woman, a child, or a man whom he sees as less than a real man.
>
> (Kaufman, 1993: 47)

In queer theory this specific interdependence of opposed positions is termed the heteronormative matrix. It takes a man, a woman and child to add up to the equation family, in which the individuals are expected to perform to a specific pattern of domination and submission. As Brus 'breaks' the armour and Kaufman wants to 'crack' the armour both want to get away from a masculinity of domination and isolation.

The textual skin: Valie Export

From the very beginning of her career in the 1960s the feminist character of Valie Export's (b. 1940) work has been manifest. She has tirelessly undertaken one experiment after another in analysing the conditions for the modern female subject in Western culture. Already in 1967 the notion of a split subject figures in her video-poem *Split-Reality*. Export visualises what Simone de Beauvoir was the first to draw attention to: woman's double position in patriarchy. According to Beauvoir, the female subject is caught between two modes of existence. On the one hand, she is a human being and thus a free subject; she is capable of transcendence. On the other hand, her female sex deprives her of that same subjectivity, because she is 'the other sex'. Her destiny is always to be under the gaze of another, which makes her an object and therefore immanent. The female position is a double position. And it is the status as an object that genders the female sex; the subject is not gendered. Gender means to be under the gaze of another. However, the woman can make use of different strategies (being the subject she also is) in order to master her ambivalent position. According to Lacan, though, we are all split subjects under the gaze of the Other, meaning we are all under 'surveillance'. However, we only experience ourselves as such in split seconds. Nevertheless to feminists like Export and Beauvoir women are constantly *aware* of being under the gaze of the Other. It is this status of the female body as an object in culture, which produces the first-hand knowledge of the condition. This knowledge seems to follow Export in almost all her work.

In the film *Syntagma* (1983) Export recollects the themes of different earlier works. In different sequences she undertakes the split quality of the female subject-reality relation. The sequences are made up of different film shots, some made up of diverging eye/camera positions, literally splitting the image in two diverging moving parts. One sequence presents the split quality of existence in shots where the picture of a moving female body in colour (to give it the quality of flesh) superimposes and interacts with metaphors of the same body, represented as fragments of black and white photographs, as to illustrate the feeling of simultaneously belonging in two realities. In another sequence a woman walks along a row of cars, the camera follows her from behind; her face is visible in the cars' side-view mirrors, though from her angle she cannot see her own image. According to Kaja Silverman, the sequence underlines the fact that our body is constantly produced as image in the eyes of anonymous others (Silverman, 1997: 215). At the same time we are experiencing the world from the site of our sensational body, we're 'occupying a point in space' (Silverman, 1997: 217). The double reality, or split reality, experience is moreover anticipated in the beginning by a voice over speaking in two languages, German and English, claiming: 'The body clearly takes a position between me and the world. On the one hand, the body is the centre of my world. On the other, it is an object in the world of the Other.'[6]

According to Silverman, '*Syntagma* is [. . .] more concerned with the ways in which we are constituted as spectacle from the place of the Other, and with the violence that often implies, than with our attempts to self-display' (Silverman, 1997: 215). It is the experience of being in the world more than the performance of the self, which is her concern. The notion Silverman uses to explain Export's efforts in *Syntagma* is 'two body paradigm', meaning there is always 'the sensational body' and 'the image body' present at the same time, my body for me and my body in the eyes of others. Like the image body, the sensational body, is also a body of language. It is no clean natural body, it is a speaking body, a body constructed of corporeal reality, whereas the image body is constructed out of representations (Silverman, 1997: 217).

We can track the sensate body from the beginnings of Export's career. Like Günter Brus she connects her skin with the canvas. She speaks of *mein Hautleinwand* (my skin canvas) (Zell, 2000: 65). This is especially so in the case of the actions *Cutting* (1967–8), *Body Sign Action* (1968), *Eros/ion* (1971) and *Remote* (1973). Export begins her skin/canvas/cut examinations already in the performance of *Cutting.*[7] In this piece, in which she dissolves the screen with the canvas and with the skin, by cutting through different materials (paper, screen/canvas, body), she demonstrates the linguistic quality of all materials, including the body, as well as the corporeal basis of language. For the first time she makes the body speak. 'The cut has something to do with parts, or taking things apart, with destroying the whole, because one wants to understand the different parts [. . .]', she says (Zell, 2000: 78). The cutting technique is thus to be understood as a method of cutting through existing meanings attached to different materials like the body is nature and therefore reality, screen and canvas belong to the cultural, or linguistic, order of things and is therefore representation. Her action is a splitting process in which she negotiates the theoretical opposition of reality and representation: the screen becomes body, and the body becomes a screen. However, to be accurate, there is yet no real cutting of the skin.

The textual quality of the skin is directly presented in *Body Sign Action*, which is a tattoo of a suspender on Export's naked thigh, as it is also a photograph of the sign. The photo shows the thigh in front with the female sex visible behind. The tattoo is a direct answer to the question: is the female body stigmatised, that is, written by culture? The tattoo furthermore means branding, or the burning cutting of the naked skin; a sign one is left to live with for life. On a file Export has written: 'Books are made from parchment', and an arrow points to: 'parchment = manufactured animal skin', and from parchment an arrow points to the words 'codex' (('man'. And then again: 'Man as codex. Man as carrier of signals.'[8] Export uses the term 'man' and probably she means human being as she obviously thinks of humans as users of language. However, given her feminist intentions to expose the double nature of the female position in patriarchy, it seems more to the point to read it as the cultural constructed position of masculinity in this context. In her equation language and body are each other's companion as the front and back of a coin. In this signifying action Export moreover intends to show the sign inscribing mechanism of culture upon the female body, which she furthermore links with another meta-meaning as she has also written 'skin canvas' on the file beside the photograph of the tattooed thigh; her body is her art material, a site from where language is derived and onto which it is inscribed.

Export performed the action *Eros/ion* on several occasions during 1971. With different stagings she rolled her naked body in hundreds of broken glass pieces. The damage to the skin was not severe; the audience did not know, though, and she was met with shouting, as they wanted her to stop (Zell, 2000: 67). From Export's position the performance was meant as a symbol against the general violence to the female body in society.

> Although some of my performances look very painful they are not. When I think about how I live, how we all must live in our society, it is painful. In performances the pain becomes a physical way to explain my attitude. If I were a writer I could express it by saying, 'This and that is painful' and everybody would look at me and say, 'That's O.K., yes I know.'But if I show the actual physical pain, the audience sees how painful it must be, then they understand what I mean.
>
> (Export quoted in Zell, 2000: 68)

Export wanted to call forth a general anaesthetised body into action and sensation. The performance was meant to be a real avant-garde ritual of transformation. By way of making contact to the forgotten sensate body, she wanted to provoke a change, to get rid of negative habitual rituals. And in order for people to really understand this, she had to provoke a real effect of empathetic pain in them.

The last of her self-mutilation acts was performed in front of a camera in the film . . . *Remote* . . . *Remote* . . . from 1973. She is seated in front of a poster-size photograph of an infant and a somewhat older child, with a bowl full of milk in her lap. The picture comes from a police archive of child abuse. She wears ordinary clothes. She cuts her fingernails with a carpet knife. Now and then she dips her fingers in the milk. There is no sound or dialogue in the film (Zell, 2000: 86–7). In a handout that followed the screening of the film she claimed that human conduct is influenced by past events and that the human psyche is formed with a parallel terrain of constant angst and guilt, and deformities, '[which] tear the skin [and] in the cutting of the skin the drama of human self-representation is performed' (Zell, 2000: 87). In all of the performances mentioned here Export made her female body talk back to culture. By cutting and afterwards healing with milk, a symbol of the maternal body, she wanted to connect language and the maternal body.

Concluding remarks

All the works discussed, however different they might be, share a common desire to overcome the presumption that the body is a piece of sealed off nature in the midst of culture. They also have in common a concept of an inner and outer body and they all share an understanding of the bodily basis of subjectivity. What they struggle to visualise is in which ways the body speaks and is spoken. The cutting of the skin seems to connect rather than disconnect layers of meaning between body, psyche and language. In this perspective Bataille provides a basic understanding for the connectedness of the naked body and violence. Cutting has a dissolving effect; it is not so much the pain itself – Valie Export claims that pain isn't the issue – but the effects that pain causes, physical in the body of the performer (Brus) and in the audience (Abramovic and Export). Violence in this context means the dissolving rather than destruction of fixed categories, in which process the subject is left open to otherness.

The performances address different conditions for the execution of sexuality in patriarchy. According to Theweleit and Kaufman, masculinity is forced to express itself as the violent execution of power in which case the way out seems to be to break the body armour as with Günter Brus. Yoko Ono and Marina Abramovic demonstrate how culture leaves the image of the female body open to not only the otherness of identity but also to the violent execution of power. And Valie Export tries to break the code by showing the split character of the female position at the same time as she tries to cut her way across the split in order to connect the separated parts. In each case the cure for violence seems to be violence itself; one wonders if there might not be another way out?

Today homosexual love can be seen as a corrective to the heterosexual bindings of a submissive female position and a dominant male position within patriarchy. Though there is nothing to prevent homosexual couples from performing according to the same heterosexual matrix of submission and domination, the mere existence of same sex relations disturbs the 'naturalness' of the heterosexual matrix.

Notes

1. *Cut Piece* was performed twice in Japan. The second time was on 11 August 1964 at the Sogetsu Kaikan Hall in Tokyo. On this occasion it was part of a larger show called *Yoko Ono Farewell Concert: Strip-Tease Show*. Her third performance of the piece was in New York at the Carnegie Recital Hall in March 1965. And her fourth and fifth stagings were in London at the African Centre on 28 and 29 September 1966, as part of the *Destruction in art* symposium (Rhee, 2005).

2. I use the term 'action' here rather than performance to indicate the active and dynamic component in these events.
3. The artists were educated painters and their artistic point of departure was the informal painting of the 1950s. The informal painting is usually understood as the European answer to US abstract expressionism. In this respect the manoeuvre from painting to space and body can also be seen as a European parallel to what was going on in the US at the time. Artists as well as art critics at the time were committed to discussing the 'crisis of painting' in connection with the actions. Painting was a problem to Günter Brus as it did not, in his opinion, leave him the opportunity to make a radical artistic gesture. In the context of Art History painting is the central medium of the visual arts and the main problem of the time seems to be a so-called historic crisis of painting, namely, how to renew it?
4. Wilhelm Reich (1897–1957) was probably the first to use the term 'armour' in describing a psychic defence mechanism. He detected it in clinic sessions, where patients were likely to put up a defence against analysis. He writes that the armour, '[on the one hand] serves as a protection against the stimuli from the outer world, on the other hand against the inner libidinous strivings' (Reich, 1969: 44).
5. Also modern soldiers learn to build up 'a suit of armour'. Kaufman quotes Victor DeMattei, an army paratrooper during the Vietnam War: 'The purpose of basic training is to dehumanise a male to the point where he will kill on command and obey his superiors automatically [. . .] First you are harassed and brutalized to the point of utter exhaustion. Your individuality is taken away [. . .] You never have enough sleep or enough to eat [. . .] Keep in mind, there is no contact with the outside world' (Kaufman, 1993: 172–3).
6. A quotation Export has borrowed from Laing's (1960) *The Divided Self* (Silverman, 1997: 215).
7. See Zell, 2000, 79ff, for detailed description. All translations of Zell from the German have been made by the author.
8. See, for instance, illustration in Museum Moderner Kunst Stiftung Ludwig Wien, 1997, 10.

12

The Loathsome, the Rough Type and the Monster: The Violence and Wounding of Media Texts on Rape

Mona Livholts

> I am the author and I have fear. But in the world I describe this word is never used. Never ever!
> Fear is nothing below the surface.
> Fear is soluble by water, dissolves.
> Fear is consumed by the element itself, becomes part of it.
> Has no name of its own.
> Has no name.
>
> (Aino Trosell, *Ytspänning*)

Media and rape: The violent authoring of sexual violence crime

This chapter seeks to engage the reader with the question of what sexualised and embodied speech, in the context of media narrative about sexual crime in the press, actually *do*. It takes media reporting of a case of serial rape, as a starting point to explore wounding in terms of violent categorisation and emotions of fear produced by dominant and sexualised speech and visual symbolism (Livholts, 2007).[1] The purpose is to analyse the violence and wounding of media texts by focusing on the forming of men and masculinity in the context of media reports and to explore the function and consequences of academic and journalist authorship. The chapter illustrates how journalists' use of language does violence to the people in the text by the way it represents them, and also how it disrupts the researchers attempt to study rape. Starting with a critical reading of the relevant newspapers, I found myself so affected by the fearful descriptions of a serial rapist who strikes in the darkness, but also the dominant and sometimes aggressive voices of the journalists, that I was inclined to end the research completely. The chapter puts forward the argument that by using a multi-methodological reflexive approach and focusing on the complex function of authoring in journalism and research, it is possible to contribute to new understandings of the violence and wounding of media texts on rape.

The starting point for critical exploration is that media constitutes an arena for the production of stories about what goes on in the world. What is reported, who gets to speak, what is spoken about and not spoken about shapes the forming of issues (van Dijk, 1995; Sjölander, 2004). Relations of power such as ethnicity and gender are part of the power structure in a media context. Minorities and women have less influence over media production and are less quoted; stereotyping representations of these categories have social and psychological consequences (van Dijk, 1995; Brune, 2003; Jarlbro, 2006), including for the reproduction of sexual violence.

Representations of sexual crimes in media are characterised by gendered and racialised relations of power and are related to different views depending on how they are categorised (Marcus, 1992; Cuklanz, 2000). Rape which occurs in public space during night-time and is committed by a man not known to the woman is often considered 'real rape' (Andersson, 2004).[2] Such rapes tend to receive much attention in the press and to construct stereotypes of the deviant maniac and even the monstrous rapist (Stanley, 1995; Sandberg, 2003; Livholts, 2007). As Wardle has pointed out, media produce the myth 'that sex crimes are committed by '"other" men, using terms such as "fiend" and "beast", which distance them from "ordinary" men' (Wardle, 2007: 273). One of the consequences related to stereotypical constructions of men, women, rapists/murderers and victims is that women continue to experience themselves as vulnerable and as potential victims. Moreover, the focus on the evil perpetrator draws attention away from institutional relations of violence between men and women.

There is no doubt that men's violence towards women and each other is extensive and has serious consequences for people's lives (Hearn, 1998; DeKeseredy and Schwartz, 2005). However, violence is a complex phenomenon, which takes a range of various forms. It may be physical and material and/or reproduced as discourse through words (Hearn, 1998). Of particular importance for this study is the relation between different categories of men, the social construction of masculinities, the body and sexual violence. As Messerschmidt (2005) has shown, the forming of masculinities and crime are intimately connected to the symbolic meaning and physical use of the body. Furthermore, the context and situation of criminal act is decisive for the production of social positioning and forming of masculinities.

According to Marcus (1992), symbolic violence in media reporting on rape occurs through the production of a 'gendered grammar language'. This language involves both the complex relations between women in regard to ethnicity and gender and also between men. Marcus argues that rape prevention is intimately connected to deconstructing what she calls the rape script in media. Hirsch (1995) calls for a broader range of understandings of how rape is related to the contexts in which they take place. In a study of US and Kenyan media reporting of rapes at a Kenyan boarding school, she found that 'rapists' and 'victims' were constructed in relation to national stereotypes. While Kenyan media spoke about sexism, violence and postcolonial relations, US media focused on traditional Kenyan culture as an explanation. Bredström (2003) found that Swedish media reporting of a case of group rape focused on the non-Swedish cultural background of the young men. Gender, ethnicity and class are thus (re)produced in specific ways in and by the media.

The case of sexual crime studied in this chapter consists of a series of attempted rapes, rapes and attempted murder committed by the so-called Hagaman (in Swedish, *Hagamannen*) in the city of Umeå in the north of Sweden between 1999 and 2006. According to the verdict in the Upper Northern Court of Appeal in Sweden, the crimes are documented as follows:[3]

- May 1999: Rape
- November 1999: Attempted rape on two different women at two different places
- March 2000: Serious rape and attempted murder
- December 2000: Rape
- December 2005: Serious rape and attempted murder

The empirical material consists of newspaper articles in the Swedish press between 1999 and 2006.[4] It is important to say that I make no claims to speak the truth about what happened, but focus exclusively on textual representation of violence. Furthermore, the study acknowledges limitations and ethical dilemmas related to the fact that it draws attention to heterosexual rapes in public space, men and masculinity, while the majority of sexual violence actually occurs in homes, and rape is part of a larger problem of men's violence against women, girls, boys and men in society. However, the intention is to problematise the categorisation and spatiality of violence and to contribute to discussion on locally and nationally produced narratives about rape. By analysing media coverage over time, it is possible to discern powerful examples of speech acts, which play an important role for the forming of the issue. This is not the same as saying that all newspapers and journalists produce text and visual symbolism in the same way, or that all readers engage or do not engage with what is written in the same way. Nevertheless methodologies used by journalist authors, such as dramaturgy, repetition and plots, shape the structure of text and produce specific narratives about the world.

The chapter begins by introducing a critical, reflexive approach to media analysis based on discourse analysis and narrative analysis, autobiography and memory work. Thereafter, three thematic narratives of marginalised and demonised masculinities are analysed. I conclude with some reflections on the question of the violence and wounding of media texts on rape.

A critical and reflexive approach to media study on rape

She is balancing the book on her fingertips to protect it from the steamy water. Now and then she interrupts reading and watches the white and grey pattern of the tile. She is reading about a researcher who began an analysis about a case of serial rape, but decides not to finish it according to the original plans. This resonates with her situation; often she would sit at her office, reading, writing, thinking and feeling tensed, watched. Fear of darkness, now included bright daylight. Sharp imprints of shadows in university corridors plagued her memories. Suddenly, a memory transfers her to a room on the ground floor at her student apartment. She has been cleaning and having a bath; the air is filled with a fresh smell from soft soap, and the new cotton curtains with white and blue stripes, looks homelike in the window. She notices a gap between them and intends to pull them together, when she looks straight into a man standing outside. Her memory is rich with details in his clothing; the folds in the dark brown jacket, pockets with a rounded lower part, metallic shining buttons, and black boots with yellow strings. In a state of confusion she pulls the curtains together, lies down on the bed, and pulls the bedspread over half her body; lies there all night in the company of a man with no face who claims access to her room.

In media studies, both discourse analysis and narrative approaches have been used to analyse the structuring effects of language and the power of story building (van Dijk, 1995; Brune, 2003; Bredström, 2003; Reimers, 2005; Livholts, 2007). The critical, reflexive approach used in this study is multi-methodological, inspired by discourse analysis and narrative analysis, autobiography and memory work. Discourse analysis has allowed me to place the conceptual practice of language and its consequences as a focus of interest; this includes contextualised meanings, associative circumference, and metaphoric meanings, contradictions, and ambiguities and silence (Sahlin, 1999). In particular I have been inspired by Sjölander's (2004) use of the function of authors in discursive media analysis. Sjölander, who uses an application of Foucaultian work, has studied the formation of the issue of nuclear waste in the media, focusing on the role of the commentary and the function of the author. The commentary relies on repetition in order to actualise things that have already been said. The function of authorship is subscribed to everybody who takes part in defining an issue. This may include experts, politicians, protest groups, individuals, authorities, but indeed also journalists themselves. On some issues journalists act as 'servants of the public' (Sjölander, 2004) – what van Dijk (1995) calls 'the humanitarian face'.

In this study, I subscribe journalists and other voices, including my own, the function of authors. The construction of narrative themes is a technique often used by the media, frequently grounded in assumptions about good and bad societies (Brune, 2003). Narrative representation may also construct, by transgression of specific genres, interweaving fact and fiction (Edström, 2006). When I reconstruct narrative themes from media coverage in the case of Hagaman, I pick up on the use of metaphors, dichotomisation and the way journalism makes use of transgressive genre by the interweaving of the case with other criminal stories.

The relationship between present and past in research and journalism is complex. As Zeiler (2008) argues, the collective dimension of memory produced by journalist authors also lives on through the involvement of the individual journalist and their writing about particular events. In this study I have developed a reflexive metanarrative approach based on autobiography and memory work (cf. Livholts, 2001b). Autobiography allows the contextualisation of how different and changeable conditions in the life of the researcher impact on and are affected by the study. As Liz Stanley has argued (1995), there are no clear boundaries between writing about lives and the process of authoring a text about someone's life. She writes about the troublesome development of her research about the so-called Yorkshire Ripper who murdered and raped women in that area during the mid-1980s. My aim has been to create what Willard-Traub (2007) refers to as scholarly autobiography, that is, a method of personal narrative in research which contributes to analysis and reflexivity. Memory work has been used as a reflexive practice related to the research process (Livholts, 2001a); the reader is invited to take part in understanding how analysis of media reporting in the present activates memories from the past.

Memory work was first developed by Frigga Haug and her colleagues (Haug et al., 1987); the methodology focused on the fragmented and situational, privileged a subject–subject relationship to the issues explored and put language, writing and the body in focus. After Haug et al.'s introduction of the method, it has been used both as a collective and individual and co-working strategy (Bryant and Livholts, 2007; Crawford et al., 1992; Widerberg, 1995). While autobiography contextualises lived experience over time, memory work allows bringing in the fragmented and contributes to altering present experience. In the autobiographical memory section at the beginning of this section, taking a bath and reading an academic text, which brings relief to a doubtful researcher, is interrupted by an unwanted memory from the past, evoked by the subject of research: rape. The feeling of being watched has already previously entered into working space through the reading of media texts and has caused emotional distress. Transgression of time and space when memory transfers the researcher to a situation in her student room many years ago, contributes to reinforcing emotions of victimisation in the present.

The creating of meaning through visual symbolisms in media texts is influential, and this study emphasises that visualisation of place through photography may constitute a powerful representation of rape. Huxford (2001) points out the power of colour, composition, size and shape of photographic images in media; not least, photographs have been used to represent truth and may promote the journalist as an expert eyewitness. Interestingly, Wardle (2007), in her examination of visual press coverage of child murders in the US and the UK during 1930–2000, shows a change in representation from focusing on the capturing of the perpetrator and the role of the criminal justice system to an increase in visual and personal portraits involving family relations and 'emotional responses of society' such as 'grief and anger' (p. 263). In the Hagaman case the media made use of photographs in particular powerful ways, not least by creating visual imagery of physical and mental wounding and pain by rape. This chapter analyses these texts and visual symbols as data. Visual symbols mainly mean photographs, in particular of places where rape happened, but can also include text which is influential through the power of metaphors, such as 'shadow' and 'monster'.

Shadows and sexual crime: A society on the hunt for the loathsome

One Sunday morning in December, when the landscape is covered by a thin layer of powdery snow and the kitchen smells from newly brewed coffee, the phone rings. She is surprised to pick up and hear the voice of a man who introduces himself as a journalist. He tells her that during the night between Saturday and Sunday, a woman has been raped at the district of Teg in the city. He knows she is working with a study on the serial rapist Hagaman and wants to talk to her about rape. Stress and fear impairs her hearing and speech, while she talks to him. A snapshot of a snowy landscape and a wounded woman's body appears before her, and all she can think of is the coldness rising from the frozen ground outdoors. Next morning she gets up early and reads the headlines in the newspaper: 'Violent rape. The woman fought for her life'. A photograph is taken of the place of crime. A blue and white ribbon with the text 'POLICE CLOSED AREA' marks that the place is a crime scene. A thin white cover of snow is lying on the ground and behind the sparse vegetation she can see the bridge and the river partly covered with ice. The surface of the water, which still dominates the river, reflects a black shady area. Despite that the place is situated in the central parts of the city, the photograph mediates an isolated and hostile landscape and she becomes painfully aware of the fact that the media rape map has yet another mark added to it.

A crime, a meeting, a travel, a room, a view; events are often related to and remembered in relation to the places where they happened. The naming of countries, regions, landscapes, cities and villages have particular narrative understandings related to them (Hagström, 2006), and the names of places where dramatic events have happened speak particularly powerfully. In the autobiographical memory section above the journalist enters the private space of the researcher by making a telephone call to her home. The information she receives on this Sunday morning places a raped, abused and wounded woman's body in her mind's eye, and the photograph published in the newspaper on Monday morning evokes emotions of isolation and hostility mediated by the connections between sexual crime, landscape and text. As a reader she is confronted with the place of rape as an abandoned scene, and wounding inflicted through sexual abuse appears as visual imagination through the researcher's interpretation of the situation. In the context of experiencing these emotions, the landscape outside changes from beautiful white winter to a cold and isolated space. The text, 'Violent rape. The woman fought for her life', reinforces the researcher's impression of a woman alone at the mercy of violence and she becomes aware that a mark has been added to what she understands as a rape map.

In the case of Hagaman, the media recurrently publish a map, most likely with the purpose of visualising the progression of sexual crimes. The place of the first rape – the district of Haga (Meadows) in Umeå – gives the perpetrator the name 'Hagaman'. In the media the name becomes a synonym for an ordinary man, based on the description of his (ordinary) looks and (Swedish) language, but also a short, brutal and baffling rapist (using much violence, cruelty of the acts). In March 2001, after the third incident of rape and attempted murder, the local newspaper *Västerbottenskuriren* published an article which used geographical space and location to illustrate the threat of sexual violence to women.

> He is called Hagaman because the attacks have happened in the district of Haga, and it is obvious that he has some kind of connection to the district, even if it doesn't necessarily mean he lives there now. Haga is also a strategic place for attacks on women, with many moving about after the pubs have closed. It is possible to select a victim there. And to strike.
>
> (*VK* 24 March 2001; my translation)

It is interesting how the description of a dangerous district at night, as in the citation above, is formed by the author function of a man from the police. It is an example of how the journalist sets the scene for the police to use the symbolism of a seeing eye of a man who looks at Haga as a 'strategic place for attacks on women', a place where it is possible to 'strike'. The word 'select' indicates that victims are more frequent here than in other places, and the description has similarities with an animal hunting down a prey (cf. Wardle, 2007). The voyeuristic gaze contributes to develop a narrative about a man who has control over the terrain. This technique of staging a voyeuristic gaze is also used in a photograph which is published twice in the local newspaper *VK*, once on 12 August 2000 and another time on 11 April 2002. The photograph shows a woman walking alone in the darkness on a cycle and walking path, which is lit only by a few lamp posts and surrounded by darkness. It is taken from an angle slightly above and behind the woman. The text accompanying the photographs talks about how Hagaman sheds new light over the city, and that people in Umeå are afraid of the dark. The dynamics of the male gaze, mediated by photographs and other descriptions, contribute to the objectification of women's bodies and a view of women as victims.

Central to the process of separating other men from Hagaman is their occupation, dress code and their engagement to protect women.[5] Indeed, descriptions of the perpetrator's body as deviant, as well as regional and class-related dimensions become characteristic for the reporting. When the first description of the offender is published, the focus is directed towards his small body and feet, and the description of cowboy boots becomes associated with a particular masculine style (*VK* 26 February 2002). Indeed, the portrait of a small body and feet is repeatedly commented upon and tend to overshadow other description. In February 2002, when a photo fit picture is published, journalists become more active in separating Hagaman from other men. In an article in one of the local newspapers, *Västerbottens Folkblad*, an interview with a university lecturer is published (*VF* 1 March 2002; see also *AB* 3 April 2006). A close-up photograph, taken in what seems to be a study at the university, shows the upper part of a man dressed in a shirt and with his sleeves rolled up. The surrounding space of the room with files, pens and calendar together with his story, where he claims to be innocent, contributes to constructing an image of an intellectual established person in working life. The lecturer shows his 'fashionable' shoes to the photographer and journalist, to differentiate his style from that of Hagaman.

A central narrative theme which introduces central authors and actors in the case of Hagaman is the hunt (*VK* 24 March 2001). The crime investigation around Hagaman is described as the most extensive ever described in the region, the media makes use of metaphoric expressions like 'the shadow'. The shadow of a perpetrator tends to fuse with both geographical space and concrete events, labelling the unpredictable and fearful scenery of rape at the same time as it claims to always be present through the occurrence of other events.[6] This is reinforced by the way journalist authors connect the crimes of Hagaman to known criminals, and compare them to violent murders in film and other fiction. In the context of discussing a reward the media refer to several other crimes, for instance, the murder of Swedish Prime Minister Olof Palme and the so-called Laserman, who shot several people with non-Swedish ethnic backgrounds (*VK* 1 February 2006).

Another example of how Hagaman is related to known criminals in a historical context is when media write that the same computer system which was used in the US during the hunt for the serial killer Ted Bundy will also be used in the hunt for Hagaman (*VK* 19 February 2000). And in the local newspaper *VK*, comparison to a violent murderer is being made by a chronicler who refers to the film *The Silence of the Lambs*, where a serial killer eats parts of his victims (*VK* 15 February 2000). By placing the crimes of Hagaman in the context of previous serious crimes, a portrait of a worthy opponent of the police is created. Even if some articles criticise the police, they are mainly portrayed as skilful investigators who make use of technology, while the perpetrator is described as an impulsive man with low intellectual capacity and with no skill to plan his crimes (*VK* 24 March 2001). With this background, journalist authors sometimes use an overbearing tone when making clear to the offender that sooner or later he will make a mistake, be caught and put behind bars (*VK* 19 April 2000). The normative discourse which constructs men's minds as rational and logical is of central use for journalists in this process (cf. Gerschick, 2005). Within this particular discourse's own terms, journalists can be seen as acting against sexual violence when they belittle the offender's bodily characteristics and intellectual capacities; but crucially, this does not apply at all in the terms of other more critical discourses.

In December 2005 authoritarian and angry voices of journalist authors increase when a rape and attempted murder took place in the district of Teg. From the occurrence of this rape and when a man was arrested and accused for the crimes of Hagaman in March 2006, previous alliances between the voices of the police and journalists become more strongly allied and intertwined. In January 2006, a journalist takes an active role in encouraging the public to take part in the hunt for 'the Loathsome'. The first time the expression, 'the Loathsome', was used was actually June 2000 (*VK* 3 June 2000) when the journalist referred to various murders in Swedish criminal history. The inspiration to use the name comes from a Swedish detective novel. The next time 'the Loathsome' was used by the journalist was the first Monday after the rape and attempted murder in Teg in December 2005. This time the headline of the reporter column is 'the Loathsome' and the journalist refers to the problem of men's violence against women in society. He asks the reader what has gone wrong and invites everybody to write to the newspaper (*VK* 12 December 2005). A few weeks later, the name occurs again under the heading 'The hunt for the loathsome concerns everybody'.

> The hunt for the brutal rapist is now at its fourth week and the questions are beginning to gather. Why has he not been arrested? How is it possible that the hard work by the police so far has not reached the wanted result? And why this silence? *The hunt for the loathsome* is really not only a matter for the police, since it actually concerns the whole society as a state governed by law, where the security for women is one of the obvious linchpins. The hunt concerns everybody.
>
> (*VK* 2 January 2006; my translation and emphasis)

Throughout the media coverage of the case it is characteristic for journalist authors to speak not only to the public but as agents *for* the public. In the quotation above the journalist asks questions related to the absence of a result in the hunt for Hagaman and what he understands as a prevailing silence. By naming the offender 'the Loathsome' in this context he makes not only a statement, but adds emotions of disgust and detestation. In other words, the journalist uses his function as an author to make a powerful dissociation, spoken as a representative of society. The basis for this is the responsibility for society to act against violence to women, which means that he benefits from the national discourse of equality when he justifies a collective hunt for the loathsome. The paradox is that the rhetoric which highlights the broader problem of men's violence to women in society does not stigmatise men as a collective; stigma is reserved exclusively for the serial rapist in public space.

Transformative acts of good and evil: The rough type and the monster

A man has been arrested, suspected of the crimes of a serial rapist. One of the newspapers has published a photograph from maternity hospital. The people in the picture – a baby, a woman and a man – have no faces. Contours of hair and the shape of their heads are framing the expression of numbness. The heads of the adults are closely together and the child is resting towards the woman's chest. The text underneath the photograph says REALITY (a common father of small children). Next to the family photograph a photo hit picture, with the text PHOTO HIT PICTURE, shows the face of (the feared) Hagaman. The arrest constitutes a starting point for media report, which seeks to explain how a man with a normal life could transform into a monster. After a few weeks of reporting she packs her research material into boxes. She may finish her study one day, but not now. Now he is an animal, with black eyes and with a smile, he attacks women. Someone speculates that underneath his clothes exists another body than just small and weak – a rough type. She wants to be out of this era of time, where journalists have turned back the clock to dictate the rules which make all of us judges in this case.

By the time a man is arrested suspected for the crimes of Hagaman, in March 2006, a media narrative has been formed around the process of categorising a criminal (mind). The power of discourse is then directed towards the body, portrayed as a surface for a ruthless mind and as the site of powerful transformations from good to evil. The autobiographical memory section above illustrates how the researcher is emotionally affected by the exploitation of the situation. The photograph from the maternity hospital, published in the newspaper, was taken several years earlier. When the photograph is used in the context of media reporting on the 2006 rape, facial expressions are removed, most likely with the purpose of protecting identities. However, the consequences of this are that such visual symbolism also constructs a form of invalidation or even punishment of those so anonymised.

One starting point for looking at how authors in the media produce embodied speech in this study is focused on journalist writing as reportage about the body, and I show how descriptions of the male body and evaluation of physical expressions are contextualised by different situations. In contrast to the photograph from the maternity hospital where facial expressions are removed, journalist authors sometimes use the opposite technique, namely close observation of bodily characteristics. One example of this is collected from media reporting from the trial. The trial is closed to the public and in June 2006, a journalist acts as an eyewitness and invites readers into the court room by writing as follows:

> Hagaman's face is red. It is impossible to know if it is he is blushing with shame, or if the beams of the sun has coloured his cheeks. However, considering the custody paleness of his arms, it is possible to make the conclusion that he is at least a bit uptight. [. . .] No, it does not seem to be shame, which has given the skin a reddish tone. [. . .] When Hagaman scratches one of his cheeks, a rasping sound can be heard. What is surprising is (X.X) physiognomy. Ever since the arrest I have believed him to be a somewhat sinewy type. But he actually looks quite rough. The neck is thick without being bully, and even if the grey T-shirt of the correctional care is hanging like a dishrag on the upper part of his body, there is no doubt that he is rather broad-shouldered. But of course, no weak men can work as sheet metal workers. It demands and develops a certain amount of muscles out of the ordinary. It is actually a bit unpleasant to imagine what this amount of muscles can be used for, other than an honest job.
>
> (*VK* 17 June 2006; my translation)

The journalist author makes a detailed visual portrait of Hagaman, including skin colour, body constitution, physical strength and other facial features. The quotation above begins and ends with a speculation. The opening speculation is grounded in an attempt to sort out why the skin of the offender is red; the journalist seeks for signs of shame, regret and remorse. The concluding speculation leaves to the reader's imagination to reconsider what the amount of muscles the offender's body can be used for, 'other than an honest job'. The word rape is not used; however, the whole article is related to the crimes with which Hagaman is charged, namely, attempted rape, rape, attempted murder. The journalist invites the reader to look underneath the clothes of the prosecuted. He assumes a scrutinising and judgemental gaze on the body, evaluates the physiognomy of the offender as 'rough' and describes the clothes from the correctional care as conspicuously lousy.[7]

The journalist author also makes assumptions about the occupation of the offender and generalises about how sheet metal workers need to be strong, in contrast to 'weak' men. The evaluation and degradation of weakness is contrasted with the dominant masculine characteristics of the strong muscular body, with the use of muscles presumed as related to sexualised violence towards women. The visualisation of the criminal body and mind and the insinuation of using it in the context of rape that is handed to the reader is an example of the objectification and sexuality of wounding afflicted to a woman's body. At the same time, journalists practise a form of interpersonal violence by the way they appoint themselves as representatives for the public with the power to act judgementally in relation to the offender. Indeed, the citation is an example of disciplining and punishment expressed by institutions – media, police, legal system – where men possess a great deal of power.

Another narrative theme is constituted around the transformation process from an ordinary Swedish man and family father to a violent merciless monster, underpinned by psychological speech as the main explanation. A journalist presents this in the following way:

> A calm and nice father of two children. At the same time a monster who has kept women in the city of Umeå hostage for eight years. On the surface, the double life of (X.X) is inexplicable.
>
> (*AB* 23 April 2006; also see *AB* 24 April 2006)

The media explicitly ask how it is possible that a man with a normal life – an ordinary Swedish guy – has committed these crimes against women and confronts the reader with this as a riddle (*VK* 31 March 2006; *EX* 30 March 2006). The riddle, in terms of what is considered to be incomprehensible in terms of rape, places normality on an equal footing with a Swedish man who lives an idyllic life and is well behaved at work. It is interesting how the most well-known situation for violence against women, their private homes, in this context constitutes a base for journalists to describe 'a calm and nice father'. Instead, the Swedish way of using alcohol is introduced as the problem.[8] This suggests drinking a lot of alcohol and acting in the way that one would not normally act – like committing systematic rape. The outcome of this presentation is that

Swedish culture is represented as good and solid, and thus never becomes a way of explaining violence against women. Indeed, this is contradictory to how journalists sometimes refer to men's violence towards women in society as the real problem. As soon as it is clear that a man who has a relationship with a woman and is a father of two children is suspected of the crimes of Hagaman, transformation from good to evil is used as explanation. In one article the journalist creates a dialogue with the offender's lawyer, who regains the function of author.

> – Have you seen the evil (X.X)?
> – No I have heard about the evil (X.X) but have not experienced him. Only the poor injured party has had to do so. I have become very close to him – unusually close to be a client. During periods we have talked to each other once or twice a day. And my question mark is very big, why?
> – Do you think that his cohabitant has experienced the evil side?
> – She claims she has not. That is the fantastic with such a double nature as (X.X)?
>
> (*AB* 15 July 2006)

The dialogue between the journalist and the lawyer makes a clear distinction between two sides of the same person: good and evil. The result is that the act of committing rape and attempted murder is taken out of the context of ordinary life; indeed several journalists write about how the good family father has transformed into an evil monster. According to these descriptions, the surface of the body shows no signs of evil, thus the monster inhabits the inner regions of the body. Transformation from good to evil is also illustrated with reference to Dr Jekyll and Mr Hyde scenario (*SVD* 9 April 2006), and in one article a voice claims that the word 'sick' is written in fire on the forehead of Hagaman (*AB* 20 July 2006). Another way by which the media construct proof of a monstrous presence is by claiming that the surface of the body actually reveals signs of evil. In one newspaper, witnesses describe how they have seen the black, staring, hollow eyes of the offender (*EX* 17 June 2006; *EX* 29 June 2006). In another newspaper, evil is equivalent of the smiling rapist (*AB* 14 April 2006; *AB* 28 April 2006). Like the loathsome, the monster is deprived of human characteristics and worth. Journalists and other authors exercise violence by violent stereotypical categorisation which makes possible to exclude the rapist from citizens of the city and society. The separation of good and evil, calm fathers and monstrous rapists, leads to demonisation.

The violence and wounding of media texts on rape – concluding reflections

This chapter has focused on the paradox that reporting about crime may also mean the exercise of violence and wounding towards people in the text, as well as towards readers. As the academic author of this text, I have entered into media texts about a case of rape in the Swedish press and interpreted representations of 'the loathsome', 'the rough type' and 'the monster'. I have shown how the process of naming, the male gaze and geographical space constructs fear of rape and reproduces general ideas about all women as victims of rape. Furthermore, I have illustrated how metaphors like the shadow create connections between geographical space and the suggestive threat of sexual violence, and how at the same time they entered into university corridors and disrupted my writing. Other names, like the loathsome and the monster, serve particular purposes of stigma, which in turn led to stereotypical general categorisations of 'evil' perpetrators and 'good' men. It is indeed problematic how media reporting of a case of rape constructs a 'humanitarian face' of a society which condemns sexual crime, while at the same time sexual violence constitutes a serious and probably increasing problem.

The violent authoring of sexual violence crime in media coverage in the case of Hagaman puts the body at the centre of wounding and violence in a particular way. An important aspect related to this is how visual symbolism is powerfully created in both photography and text. This has been illustrated in how visual journalism removes body parts symbolic for the senses, and journalists use their voice to act as witnesses, make close observations and devalue bodily characteristics of the offender. Photographs of places where rapes have taken place confront the reader with geographical spaces to illustrate the sexual crimes; photographs which show a wounded body in an abandoned landscape covered with snow represent the violent silence of discourse.

I have argued that it is important to apply a reflexive methodological approach which makes possible for the researcher to communicate with readers about the powerful narrative and discursive structures of the text. This is both an issue which concerns methodological aspects of critical inquiry and a matter of research ethics, intellectual empowerment and social change. Researchers, like journalists, always run the risk of using a voice which presents itself as authoritarian echo, deprived of emotion, doubts and difficult choices. Academic texts may appear clean when the hard-working analytical and emotional body of the researcher remains speechless or only exists in early versions of the manuscript which have been put aside or deleted. By creating a multi-methodological approach based on discourse and narrative analysis, memory work and autobiography, this chapter has sought to reconsider the relations between sexual violence/rape/wounding in the world and violence/wounding in writing/representation – in both journalism and academia.

Media texts

Aftonbladet (*AB*)

2006–04–03 'Utpekad som Hagamannen' [Alleged as Hagaman].

2006–04–14 'Hon flydde för sitt liv – Eva, 15, överfölls av Hagamannen berättar' [She fled for her life – Eva, 15, tells about how she was attacked by Hagaman].

2006–04–23 'Var är pappa? – Familjen har börjat förstå det ofattbara' [Where is daddy? – The family is beginning to understand the unbelievable].

2006–04–24 'Älskad av dagbarnen – Vår dotter hoppade av glädje när X kom' [Loved by the day care children – Our daughter jumped out of joy when X came].

2006–04–28 '"Jag var full och trött" – Hagamannens egna ord till rättspsykiatrikern: Därför begick jag övergreppen' ['I was drunk and tired' – Hagaman's own words to the legal psychiatrist: That's why I committed the assaults].

2006–07–15 'Jag var usel som åklagare – Leif Silbersky om att försvara våldtäktsmän, skriva memoarer och om jobbet han vill ha före 70' [I was lousy as a prosecutor – Leif Silbersky on defending rapists, writes his memoirs and the job he wants before 70].

2006–07–20 'Han struntade i om våldtäktsoffren dog – Hagamannen var oerhört brutal mot kvinnorna' [He didn't care if the rape victims died – Hagaman was extremely brutal to the women].

Expressen (*EX*)

2000–03–25 'Killarnas kamp för kvinnofrid. De gör Umeås gator tryggare efter våldtäkterna' [Guys struggle to protect women from violence. They make the streets of Umeå safer after rapes].

2006–06–17 'Elin: Han var som ett djur. Hagamannens första offer berättar om skräckåren efter överfallet' [Elin: He was like an animal. Hagaman's first victim tells about years of horror after being attacked].

2006–06–29 'Vittnet såg Hagamannen i ögonen' [The witness looked into the eyes of Hagaman].

2006–03–30 'X – ett mysterium. Barndomsvännen Benny: X var lugn och snäll' [X – a mystery. The childhood friend Benny: X was calm and nice].

Göteborgsposten (*GP*)

2006–06–13 'Alla spärrar försvann när han drack – Familjefadern X.X förvandlades till våldtäktsman' [All barriers disappeared when he drank – The family father X.X transformed into a rapist].

Svenska Dagbladet (*SVD*)

2001–04–01 'Han är vanlig som vatten' [He is as normal as water].
2006–04–09 'Hagamannens ödesdrama' [Hagaman's drama of destiny].

Västerbottens Folkblad (*VF*)

2002–03–01 'I förhör för sin likhet med fantombilden' [Interrogated for his similarity with the photo fit picture].

Västerbottenskuriren (*VK*)

2000–02–15 'Vårt Umeå är inte trevligt just nu' [Our Umeå is not a nice place at the moment].
2000–02–19 'Hagamannen jagas med dator' [Hagaman is hunted with computer].
2000–03–22 'Taxichaufför jagade Hagamannen' [Taxi driver on the hunt for Hagaman].
2000–03–27 'Hagamannen fortfarande fri. Nu ställer män upp som eskorthjälp åt nattvandrande kvinnor' [Hagaman still on the loose. Men support women walking in the night].
2000–03–29 'Fler poliser i tjänst i helgen' [More police men in duty this weekend].
2000–04–19 'Överfallslarm till salu' [Assault alarm for sale].
2000–06–03 'Jakten på Hagamannen fortsätter' [Hunt for Hagaman continues].
2000–08–18 '"Jag går absolut inte hem ensam"' ['I definitely do not walk home alone'].
2000–12–05 'Polisen ville hemlighålla överfallet' [Police wanted to keep the assault secret].
2001–03–24 'De leder jakten på Hagamannen' [They lead the hunt for Hagaman].
2002–02–26 'Polisens bild av Hagamannen' [Police photo fit picture of Hagaman].
2002–04–11 'Hagamannen sätter staden i nytt ljus' [Hagaman sheds new light over the city].
2005–12–12 'Ilska över våldsam våldtäkt' [Anger over violent rape].
2006–01–02 'Jakten på den vedervärdige angår oss alla' [Hunt for the loathsome concerns everyone].
2006–02–01 'Halv miljon för Hagaman' [Half a million for Hagaman].
2006–03–31 'Den stora gåtan' [The great riddle].
2006–04–01 'Tyst gömde han sig i jackan' [Silently he hid behind his jacket].
2006–06–17 '"Han ser faktiskt rätt så bitig ut"' ['He actually looks quite rough'].

Notes

1. The chapter draws upon and develops analysis in Livholts, 2007.
2. Compare Hirsch's (1995: 1024) description of the dichotomisation of 'innocent' victims and 'aggressive' rapist and the consequences of general ideas that 'pre-exist the rape itself'.
3. The summary is based on the verdict of guilty in the court of appeal the 2nd of October 2006, which sentenced the so-called Hagaman to 14 years in prison. Source: Rättsbanken: Hovrätten för Övre Norrland.

4. The period extended from 1st of January 1999 to 31st of August 2006, and the Swedish databases Mediearkivet and Presstext were used. In Mediearkivet altogether 1086 articles were found and in Presstext 298 articles. More than 400 articles were published in *Västerbottenskuriren* (*VK*), the largest circulation local newspaper in Umeå.
5. Categories of men who are referred to as 'good men' are journalists, police, taxi drivers and voluntary groups of men who offer women a safe journey home at night. For examples of such articles see: *VK* 22 March 2000; *VK* 27 March 2000; *EX* 25 March 2000.
6. Several articles pick up on the metaphor of the shadow, for example *VK* 5 December 2000; *VK* 29 March 2000; *SVD* 1 April 2001.
7. Comments about 'the red colour of the face' and comparisons to 'an unmade sleeping bag' have also been made in *VK* 1 April 2006. In that article the journalist writes about how Hagaman is 'Crouching as under the force of lashes' when he 'received the detention order from the court'.
8. The use of alcohol is mentioned as explanation to rape in several newspapers. It is brought up by the journalist, and by citing experts and Hagaman: *AB* 23 April 2006; *GP* 13 June 2006; *VK* 13 June 2006.

Bibliography

Abbott, Stacey (2001) 'A little less ritual and a little more fun: The modern vampire in *Buffy the Vampire Slayer*', *Slayage*, 3. http://slayageonline.com/EBS/buffy_studies/scholars_critics/a_e/abbott.htm (accessed 19 February 2008).

Abdel-Shehid, Gamal (2005) *Who Da Man?: Black Masculinities and Sporting Cultures*, Toronto: Canadian Scholars' Press.

Abele, Elizabeth (1997) 'The glory of Cary Grant and other girlish delights', *Images*, 5, http://www.imagesjournal.com/issue05/features/carygrant.htm (accessed 18 July 2007).

Adams, Parveen (1999) 'Cars and scars', *New Formations*, 35: 60–72.

Alapack, Richard (2007) 'Simulation in cyberspace and touch of the flesh: Kissing, the blush, the hickey and the caress', *Cyberpsychology: Journal of Psychosocial Research in Cyberspace*, http://www.cyberpsychology.eu/view.php?cisloclanku=2007070703 (accessed 10 January 2008).

Alapack, Richard, Blichfeldt, Mathilde Flydal and Elden, Aake (2005) 'Flirting on the Internet and the hickey: A hermeneutic', *CyberPsychology & Behavior*, 8(1): 52–61.

Alexander, Jenny (2004) 'A vampire is being beaten: De Sade through the looking glass in Buffy and Angel', *Slayage: The Online Journal of Buffy Studies*, 15(4.3), www.slayageonline.com.

Allen, Katherine R. and Baber, Kristine M. (1992) 'Ethical and epistemological tensions in applying a postmodern perspective to feminist research', *Psychology of Women Quarterly*, 16: 1–15.

American Psychiatric Association (1994) *Diagnostic and Statistical Manual of Mental Disorders: DSM-IV*, Washington, DC: American Psychiatric Association.

Andersson, Ulrika (2004) *Hans (ord) eller hennes? En könsteoretisk analys av straffrättsligt skydd mot sexuella övergrepp* (His (word) or hers? A gender theoretical analysis of criminal law protection against sexual abuse), Lund: Bokbox.

Anzieu, Didier (1989) *The Skin Ego* [1985], New Haven: Yale University Press.

Armstrong, Nancy and Tennenhouse, Leonard (eds) (1989) *The Violence of Representation: Literature and the History of Violence*, London: Routledge.

Arthurs, Jane (2003) '*Crash*: Beyond the boundaries of sense', in Jane Arthurs and Iain Grant (eds) *Crash Cultures: Modernity, Mediation and the Material*, Bristol: Intellect, 63–77.

Arthurs, Jane and Grant, Iain (eds) (2003) *Crash Cultures: Modernity, Mediation and the Material*, Bristol: Intellect.

Ashe, Fidelma (2008) *The New Politics of Masculinity*, Abingdon: Routledge.

AshleyUK (2007) 'The new bme personals. AshleyUK. Body Modification ezine', http://iam.bmezine.com/pers4.exe?cmd=zoom&rec=7344 (accessed 15 June 2007).

Athanassoulis, Nafsika (2002) 'The role of consent in sado-masochistic practices', *Res Publica*, 8(2): 141–55.

Atkinson, Michael (2003) *Tattooed: The Sociogenesis of a Body Art*, Toronto: University of Toronto Press.

Australian Story (2003) 'Boy interrupted', Australian Broadcasting Corporation, www.abc.net.au/austory/content/2003/s937472.htm (accessed 2 September 2003).

Babiker, Gloria and Arnold, Lois (1997) *The Language of Injury: Comprehending Self-Mutilation*, Leicester: British Psychological Society.

Balsamo, Anne (1996) *Technologies of the Gendered Body: Reading Cyborg Women*, Durham, NC: Duke University Press.

Barker, Martin (1984) *The Video Nasties: Freedom and Censorship in the Media*, London: Pluto.

Barker, Martin, Arthurs, Jane and Harindranath, Ramaswami (2001) *The Crash Controversy: Censorship Campaigns and Film Reception*, London: Wallflower Press.

Barker, Meg, Iantaffi, Alessandra and Gupta, Camila (2007) 'The power of play: The potentials and pitfalls in healing narratives of BDSM', in Meg Barker and Darren Langdridge (eds) *Safe Sane, and Consensual: Contemporary Perspectives on Sadomasochism*, Basingstoke: Palgrave Macmillan, 197–216.

Barrett, Michele (1980) *Women's Oppression Today: Problems in Marxist Feminist Analysis*, London: Verso.

Barthes, Roland (1976) *The Pleasure of the Text*, London: Cape.

Bataille, Georges (1985) *Visions of Excess: Selected Writings, 1927–1939*, ed. Allan Stoekl, Manchester: Manchester University Press.

Bataille, Georges (2006) *Eroticism: Death and Sensuality* [1957], London: Marion Boyars.

Batty, David (2004) 'Mistaken identity', *The Guardian Weekend Magazine*, 31 July, 12.

Baudrillard, Jean (1994) *Simulacra and Simulation*, trans. Sheila Faria Glaser, Ann Arbor: University of Michigan Press.

Bayers, Peter L. (2003) *Imperial Ascent: Mountaineering, Masculinity and Empire*, Boulder, Colorado: University Press of Colorado.

BBC (2000) 'Surgeon defends amputations', 31 January, http://news.bbc.co.uk/2/hi/uk_news/scotland/625680.stm (accessed 19 August 2008).

Beal, Becky (1995) 'Disqualifying the official: An exploration of social resistance through the subculture of skateboarding', *Sociology of Sport Journal*, 12(3): 252–67.

Beal, Becky (1996) 'Alternative masculinity and its effects on gender relations in the subculture of skateboarding', *Journal of Sport Behaviour*, 19: 204–20.

Beal, Becky (1999) 'Skateboarding: An alternative to mainstream sports', in Jay Coakley and Peter Donnelly (eds) *Inside Sports*, London: Routledge, 139–45.

de Beauvoir, Simone (1953) *The Second Sex*, London: Picador.

Beckman, Andrea (2001) 'Deconstructing myths: The social construction of "sadomasochism" versus "subjugated knowledges" of practitioners of consensual "SM"', *Journal of Criminal Justice and Popular Culture*, 8(2): 66–95.

Bendelow, Gillian (1998) *The Lived Body: Sociological Themes, Embodied Issues*, London: Routledge.

Bender, Eve (2005) 'Mixed message seen in major study of suicide behavior', *Psychiatric News*, 40(13): 8.

Benwell, Bethan (ed.) (2003) *Masculinity and Men's Lifestyle Magazines*, Oxford: Blackwell.

Berger, John (1972) *Ways of Seeing*, Harmondsworth: Penguin.

Berger, Maurice, Wallis, Brian and Watson, Simon (eds) (1995) *Constructing Masculinity*, London: Routledge.

Bersani, Leo (1987) 'Is the rectum a grave?', *October*, 43, 197–222.

Bindel, Julie (2008) 'The knife consultant', *The Guardian*, 11 January, http://lifeandhealth.guardian.co.uk/women/story/0,,2239034,00.html (accessed 18 February 2008).
Bingham, Dennis (1994) *Acting Male: Masculinities in the Films of James Stewart, Jack Nicholson, and Clint Eastwood*, New Brunswick, NJ: Rutgers University Press.
Blacking, John (ed.) (1977) *The Anthropology of the Body*, London: Academic Press.
Blanchard, Ray (1989) 'The concept of autogynephilia and the typology of male gender dysphoria', The Journal of Nervous and Mental Disease, 177(10): 616–23.
Blanchard, Ray (1991) 'Clinical observations and systematic studies of autogynephilia', *Journal of Sex and Marital Therapy*, 17(4): 236–51.
Blum, Virginia L. (2003) *Flesh Wounds: The Culture of Cosmetic Surgery*, Berkeley, CA: University of California Press.
Bly, Robert (1990) *Iron John: A Book about Men*, New York: Addison-Wesley.
BMC (2007) 'Climbing in the UK – popularity and participation', http://www.thebmc.co.uk/Feature.aspx?id=1422.
Borden, Iain (2001) *Skateboarding, Space and the City: Architecture and the Body*, Oxford: Berg.
Bordo, Susan (1993) *Unbearable Weight: Feminism, Western Culture, and the Body*, Berkeley, CA: University of California Press.
Bordo, Susan (1999) *The Male Body: A New Look at Men in Public and in Private*, New York: Farrar, Straus and Giroux.
Bornstein, Kate (1994). *Gender Outlaws: On Men, Women and the Rest of Us*, London: Routledge.
Botting, Fred, and Wilson, Scott (1998) 'Automatic lover', *Screen*, 39(2): 186–92.
Botting, Fred,and Wilson, Scott (2003) 'Sexcrash', in Jane Arthurs and Iain Grant (eds) *Crash Cultures: Modernity, Mediation and the Material*, Bristol: Intellect, 79–90.
Braunberger, Christine (2000) 'Revolting bodies: The monster beauty of tattooed women', *NWSA Journal*, 12(2): 1–23, http://muse.jhu.edu/journals/nwsa_journal/v012/12.2braunberger.html (accessed 3 April 2006).
Bredström, Anna (2003) Maskulinitet och kamp om nationella arenor – reflektioner kring bilden av invandrarkillar i media' (Masculinity and struggles on national arenas – reflections on the image of immigrant boys in the media), in Paulina de Los Reyes, Irene Molina and Diana Mulinari (eds) *Makens olika förklädnader. Kön, klass & etnicitet i det postkoloniala Sverige* (The different disguises of power. Gender, class & ethnicity in postcolonial Sweden), Stockholm: Atlas, 182–206.
Broch-Due, Vigidis and Rudie, Ingrid (1993) 'An introduction', in Vigidis Broch-Due, Ingrid Rudie and Tone Bleie (eds) *Carved Flesh/CS Selves,* Oxford: Berg, 1–39.
Brooks, Abigail (2004) '"Under the knife and proud of it:" An analysis of the normalization of cosmetic surgery', *Critical Sociology*, 30(2): 207–39.
Brottman, Mikita and Sharrett, Christopher (2002) 'The end of the road – David Cronenberg's *Crash* and the fading of the West', *Literature-Film Quarterly*, 30(2): 126–32.
Brownmiller, Susan (1984) *Femininity*, New York: Simon & Schuster.
Brune, Ylva (2003) '"Invandrare" i mediearkivets typgalleri' ('"Immigrants" in the media gallery of typification'), in Paulina de Los Reyes, Irene Molina and Diana Mulinari (eds) *Makens olika förklädnader: Kön, klass & etnicitet i det postkoloniala Sverige* (The different disguises of power: Gender, class & ethnicity in postcolonial Sweden), Stockholm: Atlas, 150–81.

Brunk, Doug (2001) 'Body piercing considered mainstream by adolescents', *Family Practice News*, 31(17): 29.

Bryant, Lia and Livholts, Mona (2007) 'Exploring the gendering of space by using memory work as a reflexive research methodology', *International Journal of Qualitative Methods*, 6(3): 29–43.

Buchbinder, David (1994) *Masculinities and Identities*, Victoria: Melbourne University Press.

Buchbinder, David (1998) *Performance Anxieties: Re-Producing Masculinity*, St Leonards, NSW: Allen & Unwin.

Burr, Vivien (2003) 'Ambiguity and sexuality in *Buffy the Vampire Slayer*: A Sartrean analysis', *Sexualities*, 6(3–4): 343–60.

Burton, John W. (2001) *Culture and the Human Body: An Anthropological Perspective*, Prospect Heights, ILL: Waveland.

Bury, Michael (1991) 'The sociology of chronic illness: A review of research and prospects', *Sociology of Health and Illness*, 13(4): 451–68.

Butler, Judith (1990) *Gender Trouble: Feminism and the Subversion of Identity*, New York: Routledge.

Butler, Judith (2004) *Undoing Gender*, New York: Routledge.

Butt, Trevor and Hearn, Jeff (1998) 'The construction of sexual meaning: The sexualization of corporal punishment', *Sexualities: Studies in Culture and Society*, 1(2): 203–27.

Califia, Pat (1994) *Public Sex: The Culture of Radical Sex*, San Francisco, CA: Cleiss.

Campbell, Joseph (1993) *The Hero with a Thousand Faces* [1949], London and New York: Fontana.

Camphausen, Rufus C. (1997) *Return of the Tribal: A Celebration of Body Adornment, Piercing, Tattooing, Scarification, Body Painting*, Rochester, VT: Park Street.

Caplan, Paula J. (1993) *The Myth of Women's Masochism*, 2nd edn, Toronto: University of Toronto Press.

Carrera, José María Armengol (2002) 'Gendering Men: Theorizing Masculinities in American Culture and Literature', Doctoral Thesis. Barcelona: University of Barcelona.

Carrigan, Tim, Connell, Robert W. and Lee, John (1985) 'Toward a new sociology of masculinity', *Theory and Society*, 14(5): 551–604.

Carroll, Lynne and Anderson, Roxanne (2002) 'Body piercing, tattooing, self-esteem, and body investment in adolescent girls', *Adolescence*, 37(147): 627–37.

Carroll, Sean T., Riffenburgh, Robert H., Roberts, Timothy A. and Myhre, Elizabeth B. (2002) 'Tattoos and body piercings as indicators of adolescent risk-taking behaviors', *Pediatrics*, 109(6): 1021–7.

Carter, Angela (1979) *The Sadeian Woman: An Exercise in Cultural History*, London: Virago.

Cassese, James (2000) 'HIV and the cycle of trauma in gay men', in James Cassese (ed.) *Gay Men and Childhood Sexual Trauma*, New York: Harrington Park, 127–52.

Chancer, Lynn S. (1992) *Sadomasochism in Everyday Life: The Dynamics of Power and Powerlessness*, New Brunswick, NJ: Rutgers University Press.

Chapman, James (2000) *Licence to Thrill: A Cultural History of the James Bond Films*, New York: Columbia University Press.

Chapman, Rowena and Rutherford, Jonathan (eds) (1988) *Male Order: Unwrapping Masculinity*, London: Lawrence & Wishart.

Chasseguet-Smirgel, Janine (1984) *Creativity and Perversion*, London: Free Association.
Cherry, Brigid (2005) 'Lips of blood: Female sexuality and desire in the modern vampire film', paper presented at the 2nd Gothic Conference, University of Stirling, June 1995. Posted 1 May 2005, http://www.pretty-scary.net/article261.html (accessed 15 February 2008).
Child, Greg (1998) *Postcards from the Ledge: Collected Mountaineering Writings of Greg Child*, Seattle: The Mountaineers Books.
Clarke, Julie (2000) 'The sacrificial body of Orlan', in Mike Featherstone (ed.) *Body Modification*, London: Sage, 185–208.
Cohan, Steven (1997) *Masked Men: Masculinity and the Movies in the Fifties*, Indianapolis: Indiana University Press.
Cohan, Steven and Hark, Ina Rae (eds) (1993) *Screening the Male: Exploring Masculinities in Hollywood Cinema*, London: Routledge.
Connell, R. W. (1987) *Gender and Power: Society, the Person and Sexual Politics*, Cambridge: Polity.
Connell, R. W. (1995) *Masculinities*, Cambridge: Polity.
Connell, R. W. (1997) 'Men's bodies', in Kath Woodward (ed.) *Identity and Difference*, London: Sage, 229–34.
Connell, R. W. (2005) *Masculinities*, 2nd edn, Cambridge: Polity.
Crawford, June, Kippax, Susan, Onyx, Jenny, Gault, Una and Benton, Pam (1992) *Emotion and Gender: Constructing Meaning from Memory*, London: Sage.
Creed, Barbara (1993a) 'Dark desires: Male masochism in the horror film', in Steven Cohan and Ina Rae Hark (eds) *Screening the Male: Exploring Masculinities in Hollywood Cinema*, London: Routledge, 118–33.
Creed, Barbara (1993b) *The Monstrous Feminine: Film, Feminism, Psychoanalysis*, London and New York: Routledge.
Creed, Barbara (1998) 'The *Crash* debate: Anal wounds, metallic kisses', *Screen*, 39(2): 175–9.
Croptache (2007) 'The new bme personals. Body Modification ezine', http://iam.bmezine.com/pers4.exe?cmd=zoom&rec=7342 (accessed 15 June 2007).
Csordas, Thomas (2002) *Body/Meaning/Healing*, Basingstoke: Palgrave Macmillan.
Cuklanz, Lisa M. (2000) *Rape on Prime Time: Television, Masculinity, and Sexual Violence*, Philadelphia: University of Pennsylvania Press.
Curry, Timothy J. and Strauss, Richard H. (1994) 'A little pain never hurt anybody: A photo-essay on the normalization of sport injuries', *Society of Sport Journal*, 11: 195–208.
Dant, Tim and Wheaton, Belinda (2007) 'Windsurfing: An extreme form of material and embodied interaction', *Anthropology Today*, 23(6): 8–12.
David, Deborah S. and Brannon, Robert (eds) (1976) *The Forty-Nine Percent Majority: The Male Sex Role*, Cambridge, MA: Addison-Wesley.
Davies, Dominic and Neal, Charles (1996) *Pink Therapy*, Buckingham: Open University Press.
Davis, Kathy (1995) *Reshaping the Female Body: The Dilemma of Cosmetic Surgery*, New York: Routledge.
Davis, Kathy (2003a) 'Surgical passing: Why Michael Jackson's nose makes "us" uneasy', in Kathy Davis (ed.) *Dubious Equalities & Embodied Differences: Cultural Studies on Cosmetic Surgery*, Lanham, MD: Rowman & Littlefield, 87–103.

Davis, Kathy (2003b) 'My body is my art', in Kathy Davis (ed.) *Dubious Equalities & Embodied Differences: Cultural Studies on Cosmetic Surgery*, Lanham, MD: Rowman & Littlefield, 105–16.

Davis, Kathy (2003c) '"A dubious equality": Men, women and cosmetic surgery', *Body and Society*, 8(1): 117–31.

DeKeseredy, Walter S. and Schwartz, Martin D. (2005) 'Masculinities and interpersonal violence', in Michael S. Kimmel, Jeff Hearn and R. W. Connell (eds) *Handbook of Studies on Men and Masculinities*, Thousand Oaks, CA: Sage, 353–66.

Deleuze, Gilles (1994) *Masochism: Coldness and Cruelty*, New York: Zone.

Deleuze, Gilles and Guattari, Felix (1994) *What is Philosophy?*, trans. Hugh Tomlinson and Graham Burchill, London: Verso.

Deleuze, Gilles and von Sacher-Masoch, Leopold (1989) *Masochism: Coldness and Cruelty/Venus in Furs*, New York: Zone.

Denman, Chess (2006) 'Transgressive and coercive sex', *Psychotherapy Section Review*, 40: 30–53.

Dery, Mark (1997) 'Sex drive', *21.C*, 24: 40–51.

Dick, Leslie (1997) 'Review of *Crash, Sight and Sound*', 7(6): 34.

Doane, Mary Ann (1990) 'Film and the masquerade: Theorizing the female spectator', in Patricia Erens (ed.) *Issues in Feminist Film Criticism*, Bloomington: Indiana University Press, 41–57.

Donald, Ralph R. (1992) 'Masculinity and machismo in Hollywood's war films', in Steve Craig (ed.) *Men, Masculinity and the Media*, London: Sage, 124–36.

Donnelly, Peter (2003) 'The great divide: Sport climbing vs. adventure climbing', in Robert Rinehart and Synthia Sydnor (eds) *To the Extreme: Alternative Sports, Inside and Out*, Albany: State University of New York Press, 291–304.

Douglas, Mary (1966) *Purity and Danger: An Analysis of the Concepts of Pollution and Taboo*, London: Routledge & Kegan Paul.

Dunn, Jennifer L. (2005) '"Victims" and "survivors": Emerging vocabularies of motive for "battered women who stay"', *Sociological Inquiry*, 75(1): 1–30.

Dutton, Kenneth R. (1995) *The Perfectible Body: The Western Ideal of Male Physical Development*, New York: Continuum.

Dworkin, Andrea (1974) *Woman Hating*, New York: E. P. Dutton.

Dworkin, Andrea (1981) *Pornography: On Men Possessing Women*, London: Women's Press.

Dyck, Noel (ed.) (2000) *Games, Sports and Cultures*, Oxford: Berg.

Dyer, Richard (1985) 'Male sexuality in the media', in Andy Metcalf and Martin Humphries (eds) *The Sexuality of Men*, London: Pluto, 28–43.

Dyer, Richard (1989) 'Don't look now: The instabilities of the male pin-up', in Angela McRobbie (ed.) *Zoot Suits and Second-Hand Dresses: An Anthology Of Fashion and Music*, London: Macmillan, 198–207.

Easthope, Antony (1986) *What a Man's Gotta Do: The Masculine Myth in Popular Culture*, London: Paladin.

Eckermann, Liz (1997) 'Foucault, embodiment and gendered subjectivities: The case of voluntary self-starvation', in Alan Peterson and Robin Bunton (eds) *Foucault, Health and Medicine*, London: Routledge, 151–69.

Edström, Maria (2006) TV-rummets eliter: Föreställningar om kön och makt i fakta och fiktion (The Television Elites. Images of gender and power in fact and fiction), Dissertation. Gothenburg: Department of Journalism and Mass Communication, Gothenburg University.

Edwards, Tim (1994) *Erotics and Politics: Gay Male Sexuality, Masculinity and Feminism*, London: Routledge.
Edwards, Tim (1997) *Men in the Mirror: Men's Fashion, Masculinity and Consumer Society*, London: Cassell.
Edwards, Tim (2003) 'Sex, booze and fags: masculinity, style and men's magazines', in Bethan Benwell (ed.) *Masculinity and Men's Lifestyle Magazines*, Oxford: Blackwell, 132–46.
Edwards, Tim (2006) *Cultures of Masculinity*, London: Routledge.
Eisenman, Stephen F. (2007) *The Abu Ghraib Effect*, London: Reaktion.
Eisenstein, Hester (1984) *Contemporary Feminist Thought*, London: Unwin.
Elliott, Carl (2000) 'A new way to be mad', *The Atlantic Monthly*, 283(6): 73.
Elliott, Carl (2003) *Better than Well: American Medicine Meets the American Dream*, New York: W.W. Norton.
Ellis, Bret E. (1991) *American Psycho*, London: Picador.
Farnell, Ross (2000) 'In dialogue with 'posthuman' bodies: Interview with Stelarc', in Mike Featherstone (ed.) *Body Modification*, London: Sage, 129–48.
Farquhar, Clare with Das, Rita (1999) 'Are focus groups suitable for "sensitive" topics?', in Jenny Kitzinger, and Rosaline Barbour (eds) *Developing Focus Group Research: Politics, Theory and Practice*, London: Sage, 47–63.
Farrell, Warren (1974) *The Liberated Man Beyond Masculinity: Freeing Men and Their Relationships with Women*, New York: Random House.
Favazza, Armando (1996) *Bodies under Siege: Self-mutilation and Body Modification in Culture and Psychiatry*, Baltimore: Johns Hopkins University Press.
Featherstone, Mike (2000) 'Body modification: An introduction', in Mike Featherstone (ed.) *Body Modification*, London: Sage, 1–13.
First, Michael B. (2004) 'Desire for amputation of a limb: Paraphilia, psychosis, or a new type of identity disorder', *Psychological Medicine*, 35: 919–28.
Fiske, John (1987) *Television Culture*, London: Routledge.
Foucault, Michel (1973) *Birth of the Clinic: An Archeology of Medical Perception*, London: Tavistock.
Foucault, Michel (1978) *The History Of Sexuality. Volume One: An Introduction*, Harmondsworth: Penguin.
Foucault, Michel (1980) *Power/Knowledge: Selected Interviews and Other Writings 1972–1977*, ed. Colin Gordon, New York: Pantheon.
Foucault, Michel (1988) *Madness and Civilisation: A History of Insanity in the Age of Reason* [1961], trans. Richard Howard, New York: Vintage.
Foucault, Michel (1991) *Discipline and Punish: The Birth of the Prison*, Harmondsworth: Penguin.
Frank, Arthur W. (1991) 'For a sociology of the body: An analytical review', in Mike Featherstone, Mike Hepworth and Bryan S. Turner (eds) *The Body: Social Process and Cultural Theory*, London: Sage, 36–102.
Frank, Arthur W. (1995) *The Wounded Storyteller: Body, Illness and Ethics*, Chicago: The University of Chicago Press.
Fraser, Suzanne (2003) *Cosmetic Surgery, Gender and Culture*, Basingstoke: Palgrave Macmillan.
Frazer, James G. (1922) *The Golden Bough*, New York: Macmillan.
Freud, Sigmund (1974 [1905]) *Three Essays on the Theory of Sexuality*, trans. and ed. James Strachey, London: Hogarth.

Freud, Sigmund (1977) *On Sexuality: Three Essays on the Theory of Sexuality and Other Works* [1905], London: Penguin.
Freud, Sigmund (1991) 'Fetishism' [1927], in *On Sexuality: Penguin Freud Vol. 7*, London and New York: Penguin.
Frith, Hannah (2000) 'Focusing on sex: Using focus groups in sex research', *Sexualities*, 3(3): 275–97.
Fuchs, Dale (2006) 'Costa del surgery: Spain corners market on new bodies for beach', *The Guardian*, 22 August: 5.
Furth, Greg and Smith, Robert (2002) *Amputee Identity Disorder: Information, Question, Answers and Recommendations about Self-Demand Amputation*, Bloomington, IN: 1st Books.
Gagné, Patricia and McGaughey, Deanna (2002) 'Designing women – Cultural hegemony and the exercise of power among women who have undergone elective mammoplasty', *Gender & Society*, 16(6): 814–38.
Gaines, Jane (1986) 'White privilege and looking relations: Race and gender in feminist film theory', *Cultural Critique*, Fall: 59–79.
Gamman, Lorraine (1988) 'Introduction', in Lorraine Gamman and Margaret Marshment (eds) *The Female Gaze: Women as Viewers of Popular culture*, London: Women's Press, 1–11.
Gamman, Lorraine and Marshment, Margaret (eds) (1988) *The Female Gaze: Women as Viewers of Popular Culture*, London: Women's Press.
Gavey, Nicola (1989) 'Feminist poststructuralism and discourse analysis', *Psychology of Women Quarterly*, 13: 459–75.
Gerschick, Thomas J. (2005) 'Masculinities and degrees of bodily normativity in Western culture', in Michael S. Kimmel, Jeff Hearn and R. W. Connell (eds) *Handbook of Studies on Men and Masculinities*, Thousand Oaks, CA: Sage, 367–78.
Giddens, Anthony (1998) *The Transformation of Intimacy: Sexuality, Love and Eroticism in Modern Societies*, Cambridge: Polity.
Gill, Rosalind C. (2007) 'Critical respect: The difficulties and dilemmas of agency and "choice" for feminism. A Reply to Duits and van Zoonen', *European Journal of Women's Studies*, 14(1): 69–80.
Gilman, Sander L. (1998) *Creating Beauty to Cure the Soul: Race and Psychology in the Shaping of Aesthetic Surgery*, Durham, NC: Duke University Press.
Gilman, Sander L. (1999) *Making the Body Beautiful: A Cultural History of Aesthetic Surgery*, Princeton, NJ: Princeton University Press.
Gimlin, Debra (2000) 'Cosmetic surgery: Beauty as commodity', *Qualitative Sociology*, 23(1): 77–99.
Glucklich, Ariel (1999) 'Self and sacrifice: A phenomenological psychology of sacred pain', *Harvard Theological Review*, 92(4): 479–506.
Goddard, Kevin (2000) '"Looks maketh the man": The female gaze and the construction of masculinity', *The Journal of Men's Studies*, 9(1): 23–39.
Goffman, Erving (1968) *Stigma: Notes on the Management of Spoiled Identity* [1963], Harmondsworth: Penguin.
Goldberg, RoseLee (1995) 'Here and now', in Chrissie Iles (ed.) *Marina Abramovic: Objects, Performance, Video, Sound*, Oxford: Museum of Modern Art Oxford, 11–19.
Goldin, Nan (2003) *The Devil's Playground*, London: Phaidon.
Goodeve, Thyrza Nichols (1995) 'Travels in hypertrophia', *Artforum*, 33(9): 66–71.

Gooren, Louis (1999) 'Expert witness statement in the case of Elizabeth Bellinger', http://home.vicnet.net.au/~man/archives/99/gooren.html.
Grant, Michael (1998) 'Crimes of the future', *Screen*, 39(2): 180–5.
Green, Ian (1984) 'Male function: A contribution to the debate on masculinity in the cinema', *Screen*, 25(4–5): 36–48.
Green, Malcolm (ed.) (1999) *Brus, Muehl, Nitsch, Schwarzkogler: Writings of the Vienna Actionists*, London: Atlas.
Greenhalgh, Trisha and Hurwitz, Brian (1998) *Narrative Based Medicine*, London: BMJ Publishing Group.
Greer, Germaine (1971) *The Female Eunuch*, London: Paladin.
Greer, Germaine (2003) *The Boy*, London: Thames and Hudson.
Grice, Elizabeth (2007) 'Over the top', *The Daily Telegraph (Weekend)*, 6 January: 1–2.
Grimshaw, Jean (2003) 'The iconic body and the Crash', in Jane Arthurs and Iain Grant (eds) *Crash Cultures: Modernity, Mediation and the Material*, Bristol: Intellect, 143–52.
Grosz, Elizabeth (1994) *Volatile Bodies: Toward a Corporeal Feminism*, Bloomington and Indianapolis: Indiana University Press; Sydney: Allen & Unwin.
Grosz, Elizabeth (1995) *Space, Time, and Perversion: The Politics of Bodies*, St Leonards, NSW: Allen and Unwin.
Hagström, Charlotte (2006) *Man är vad man heter: Namn och identitet* (You are what you are named: Name and identity), Stockholm: Carlssons.
Haiken, Elizabeth (1997) *Venus Envy: A History of Cosmetic Surgery*, Baltimore: John Hopkins University Press.
Hall, Alex, Hockey, Jenny and Robinson, Victoria (2007) 'Occupational cultures and the embodiment of masculinity: Hairdressing, estate agency and firefighting', *Gender, Work and Organization*, 14(6): 534–51.
Hall, Stuart (ed.) (1997) *Representation: Cultural Representation and Signifying Practices*, London: Sage.
Hanke, Robert (1992) 'Redesigning men: Hegemonic masculinity in transition', in Steve Craig (ed.) *Men, Masculinity and the Media*, London: Sage, 185–98.
Hanmer, Jalna (1996) 'Women and violence: Commonalities and diversities', in Barbara Fawcett, Brid Featherstone, Jeff Hearn and Christine Toft (eds) *Violence and Gender Relations: Theories and Interventions*, London: Sage, 7–21.
Hark, Ina Rae (1993) 'Animals or Romans: Looking at masculinity in *Spartacus*', in Steve Cohan and Ina Rae Hark (eds) *Screening the Male: Exploring Masculinities in Hollywood Cinema*, London: Routledge, 151–72.
Hart, Lynda (1998) *Between the Body and the Flesh: Performing Sadomasochism*, New York: Columbia University Press.
Haug, Frigga, Andreson, Sünne, Bünze-Elfferding, Anke, Hauser, Kornelia, Lang, Ursel, Laudan, Marion, Lüdemann, Magret, Meir, Ute, Nemitz, Barbara, Niehoff, Erika, Prinz, Renate, Räthzel, Nora, Scheu, Martina and Thomas, Christine (1987) *Female Sexualisation: A Collective Work of Memory*, trans. Erica Carter, London: Verso.
Hausman, Bernice (1995) *Changing Sex: Transsexualism, Technology and the Idea of Gender*, Durham: Duke University Press.
Healey, Emma (1996) *Lesbian Sex Wars*, London: Virago.
Hearn, Jeff (1992) *Men in the Public Eye: The Construction and Deconstruction of Public Men and Public Patriarchies*, London: Routledge.
Hearn, Jeff (1998) *The Violences of Men: How Men Talk about and How Agencies Respond to Men's Violence to Women*, London: Sage.

Hearn, Jeff (2004) 'From hegemonic masculinity to the hegemony of men', *Feminist Theory*, 5(1): 49–72.

Hearn, Jeff (2006) 'The implications of information and communication technologies for sexualities and sexualised violences: Contradictions of sexual citizenships', *Political Geography*, 25(8): 944–63.

Hearn, Jeff and Jyrkinen, Marjut (2007) '"I could be talking about a porn flick": Television-Internet Media Companies' Policies and Practices, Young People and Pornographisation', in *Unge, kjoenn og pornografi i Norden – Mediestudier*, Copenhagen: Nordic Council of Ministers, TemaNord 2006: 544.

Hearn, Jeff and McKie, Linda (2008) 'Gendered policy and policy on gender: The case of "domestic violence"', *Policy and Politics: An International Journal*, 36(1): 75–91.

Hearn, Jeff and Melechi, Antonio (1992) 'The transatlantic gaze', in Steve Craig (ed.) *Men, Masculinity and the Media*, London: Sage, 215–32.

Hearn, Jeff and Morgan, David (eds) (1990) *Men, Masculinities and Social Theory*, London: Unwin Hyman.

Hearn, Jeff and Parkin, Wendy (1987/1995) *'Sex' at 'Work': The Power and Paradox of Organisation Sexuality*, London: Prentice Hall/Harvester Wheatsheaf; New York: St. Martin's.

Hearn, Jeff and Parkin, Wendy (2001) *Gender, Sexuality and Violence in Organizations: The Unspoken Forces of Organization Violations*, London: Sage.

Heathcote, Owen (1994a) 'Is there abuse in the text? Legitimate and illegitimate violence in *La Question, Les Chiens, Le Boucher* and *Mémoires d'une fouetteuse*', in Renate Gunther and Jan Windebaek (eds) *Violence and Conflict in Modern French Culture*, Sheffield: Sheffield Academic Press, 153–77.

Heathcote, Owen (1994b) 'Masochism, sadism and homotextuality: The examples of Yukio Mishima and Eric Jourdan', *Paragraph*, 17(2): 174–88.

Herd, Juliet (1996) '*Crash*: Art or erotic trash?' *Weekend Australian*, 30 November.

Herman, Judith L. (1992) *Trauma and Recovery*, New York: Basic.

Hicinbothem, Julie, Gonsalves, Sonia and Lester, David (2006) 'Body modification and suicidal behavior', *Death Studies*, 30(4): 351–63.

Hills, Matt (2002) *Fan Cultures*, London and New York: Routledge.

Hirsch, Susan F. (1995) 'Interpreting media representations of a "Night of madness": Law and culture in the construction of rape identities', *Law and Social Inquiry*, 19(4): 1023–58.

Hockey, Jenny, Meah, Angela and Robinson, Victoria (2007) *Mundane Heterosexualities: From Theory to Practices*, Basingstoke: Palgrave Macmillan.

Hodge, Robert and Tripp, David (1986) *Children and Television: A Semiotic Approach*, Cambridge: Polity.

Holliday, Ruth and Cairnie, Allie (2007) 'Man made plastic: Investigating men's consumption of aesthetic surgery', *Journal of Consumer Culture*, 7(1): 57–78.

Holliday, Ruth and Sanchez Taylor, Jacqueline (2006) 'Aesthetic surgery as false beauty', *Feminist Theory*, 7(2): 179–95.

Horne, John, Tomlinson, Alan and Whannel, Gary (1999) *Understanding Sport: An Introduction to the Sociological and Cultural Analysis of Sport*, London: Routledge.

House, Annabel (2003) 'Web of fantasy turns the boy wizard blue', *The Scotsman on Sunday*, 5 January, http://www.scotsman.com/entertainment/Web-of-fantasy-turns-the.2390999.jp.

Howells, Christina (2000) 'Sartre: Desiring the impossible', in Hugh J. Silverman (ed.) *Philosophy and Desire*, New York: Routledge, 85–95.

Hubert, Henri and Marcel Mauss (1964) *Sacrifice: Its Nature and Functions*, Chicago: University of Chicago Press.

Hughes, Donna M. (1999) 'The Internet and the global prostitution industry', in Donna M. Hughes and Christine Roche (eds) *Making the Harm Visible: Global Sexual Exploitation of Women and Girls. Speaking Out and Providing Services*, Kingston, RI: Coalition against Trafficking in Women, 64–86.

Hughes, Donna M. (2002) 'The use of new communication and information technologies for the sexual exploitation of women and children', *Hastings Women's Law Journal*, 13(1): 127–46.

Huxford, John (2001) 'Beyond the referential: Uses of visual symbolism in the press', *Journalism*, 2(1): 45–71.

Jarlbro, Gunilla (2006) *Medier, genus och makt* (The media, gender and power), Lund: Studentlitteratur.

Jasanoff, Sheila (2002) 'Science and the statistical victim: Modernizing knowledge in breast implant litigation', *Social Studies of Science*, 32(1): 37–69.

Jefferson, Tony (1998) 'Muscle, "hard men" and "Iron" Mike Tyson: Reflections on desire, anxiety and the embodiment of masculinity', *Body & Society*, 4(1): 77–98.

Jeffords, Susan (1994) *Hard Bodies: Hollywood Masculinity in the Reagan Era*, New Brunswick, NJ: Rutgers University Press.

Jeffreys, Sheila (1986) 'Sado-masochism: The erotic cult of fascism', *Lesbian Ethics*, 2)1: 65–82, reprinted in Sheila Jeffreys (1994) *The Lesbian Heresy*, London: The Women's Press, 210–34.

Jeffreys, Sheila (1990) *Anticlimax: Feminist Perspectives on the Sexual Revolution*, London: Women's Press.

Jeffreys, Sheila (1996) 'Heterosexuality and the desire for gender', in Diane Richardson (ed.) *Theorising Heterosexuality*, Buckingham: Open University Press, 75–90.

Jeffreys, Sheila (2000) '"Body art" and social status: Cutting, tattooing and piercing from a feminist perspective', *Feminism and Psychology*, 10(4): 409–29.

Jeffreys, Sheila (2003) *Unpacking Queer Politics*, Cambridge: Polity.

Jeffreys, Sheila (2005) *Beauty and Misogyny: Harmful Cultural Practices in the West*, London: Routledge.

Jeffreys, Sheila (2006) 'Judicial child abuse : The family court of Australia, gender identity disorder, and the "Alex' case", *Women's Studies International Forum*: 29: 1–12.

Jenkins, Henry (2006) *Convergence Culture: Where Old and New Media Collide*, London and New York: New York University Press.

Jolly, Margaretta (1992) 'The epistemology of pornography: Between images and acts', *Women: A Cultural Review*, 3: 167–80.

Jones, Amelia (1998) *Body Art/Performing the Subject*, Minneapolis: University of Minnesota Press.

Jones, Amelia (2000) 'Survey', in Tracey Warr (ed.) *The Artist's Body*, London: Phaidon, 16–47.

Jones, Lorelei 'Morality in fiction, or "Have you no decency?"', The Fanfic Symposium, http://www.trickster.org/symposium/ (accessed 9 August 2007).

Jones, Michelle (2004) '"A Fight about Nothing": Constructions of Domestic Violence', Unpub. PhD thesis, Adelaide: University of Adelaide.

Jowett, Lorna (2004) 'Shirtless and in chains?: The male body displayed in *Buffy the Vampire Slayer* and *Angel*', paper presented at the American Quality Television Conference, Dublin, Ireland, April.

Jowett, Lorna (2005) *Sex and the Slayer*, Middletown, CT: Wesleyan University Press.

Kaite, Berkeley (1988) 'The pornographic body double: Transgression is the law', in Arthur and Marilouise Kroker (eds) *Body Invaders: Sexuality and the Postmodern Condition*, Houndmills: Macmillan, 150–68.

Katz, Elihu and Liebes, Tamar (1984) 'Once upon a time in *Dallas*', *Intermedia*, 12(3): 28–32.

Kaufman, Michael (1993) *Cracking the Armour: Power, Pain and the Lives of Men*, New York: Viking; Toronto: Penguin.

Kaw, Eugenia (1998) 'Medicalization of racial features: Asian-American women and cosmetic surgery', in Rose Weitz (ed.) *The Politics of Women's Bodies: Sexuality, Appearance, and Behavior*, Oxford: Oxford University Press, 167–83.

Kaye, Richard A. (1996) 'Losing his religion: Saint Sebastian as contemporary gay martyr', in Peter Horne and Reina Lewis (eds) *Outlooks: Lesbian and Gay Sexualities and Visual Cultures*, New York: Routledge, 86–105.

Kelly, Liz, Burton, Sheila and Regan, Linda (1996) 'Beyond victim or survivor: Sexual violence, identity and feminist theory and practice', in Lisa Adkins and Vicki Merchant (eds) *Sexualizing the Social: Power and the Organization of Sexuality*, Houndmills: Macmillan, 77–101.

Kent, Julie (2003) 'Lay experts and the politics of breast implants', *Public Understanding of Science*, 12: 403–21.

Kermode, Mark, and Petley, Julian (1997) 'Road rage', *Sight and Sound*, 7(6): 16–8.

Kilby, Jane (2001) 'Carved in skin: Bearing witness to self-harm', in Sara Ahmed and Jackie Stacey (eds) *Thinking through the Skin*, London: Routledge, 124–42.

Kim, Taeyon (2003) 'Neo-Confucian body techniques: Women's bodies in Korea's consumer society', *Body & Society*, 9(2): 97–113.

Kimmel, Michael S. (2002) '"Gender symmetry" in domestic violence: A substantive and methodological research review', *Violence against Women*, 8(11): 1332–63.

Kimmel, Michael S. and Kaufman, Michael (1993) 'The new men's movement: Retreat and regression with America's weekend warriors', *Gender Issues*, 13(2): 3–21.

Kinnunen, Taina (2004) 'Bodybuilding et sacralisation de l'identité', *Ethnologie Francaise*, 2: 319–26.

Kinnunen, Taina and Wickman, Jan (2006) 'Pin-up warriors', *NORMA: Nordic Journal of Masculinity* Studies, 1(2): 167–81.

Kirkham, Pat and Thumin, Janet (eds) (1993) *You Tarzan: Masculinity, Movies and Men*, London: Lawrence & Wishart.

Kitses, Jim and Rickman, Gregg (eds) (1998) *The Western Reader*, New York: Limelight Editions.

Klein, Alan M. (1993) *Little Big Men: Bodybuilding Subculture and Gender Construction*, Albany: State University of New York Press.

Klesse, Christian (2000) '"Modern primitivism": Non-mainstream body modification and racialized representation', in Mike Featherstone (ed.) *Body Modification*, London: Sage, 15–38.

Klocker, Hubert (1989) 'Günter Brus – Biography and action chronology', in Hubert Klocker (ed.) *Viennese Aktionism Vienna 1960–1971: The Shattered Mirror*, Klagenfurt: Ritter Verlag, 113–83.

Kobrin, Sandy (2004) 'More women seek vaginal surgery', *Womensenews* 11(14), *http://www.womensenews.org/article.cfm/dyn/aid/2067/context/archive* (accessed 12 February 2007).

Kotarba, Joseph A. (1983) *Chronic Pain: Its Social Dimensions*, Beverley Hills, CA: Sage.
Krimmer, Elisabeth and Raval, Shilpa (2002) 'Digging the undead: Death and desire in *Buffy*', in Rhonda V. Wilcox and David Lavery (eds) *Fighting the Forces: What's at Stake in Buffy the Vampire Slayer?*, Lanham, MD: Rowman and Littlefield, 153–64.
Kulmala, Ilona, McLaughlin, Joseph K., Pakkanen, Matti, Lassila, Kai, Hölmich, Lisbet R., Lipworth, Loren, Boice, John D., Raitanen, Jani and Luoto, Riitta (2004) 'Local complications after cosmetic breast implant surgery in Finland', *Annals of Plastic Surgery*, 53(5): 413–9.
Kuppers, Petra (2007) *The Scar of Visibility: Medical Performances and Contemporary Art*, Minneapolis: University of Minnesota Press.
Laing, R. D. (1960) *The Divided Self*, Harmondsworth: Penguin.
Langdridge, Darren (2006) 'Voices from the margins: Sadomasochism and sexual citizenship', *Citizenship Studies*, 10(4): 373–89.
Langdridge, Darren and Butt, Trevor (2004) 'A hermeneutic phenomenological investigation of the construction of sadomasochistic identities', *Sexualities*, 7(1): 31–53.
Lasch, Christopher (1979) *The Culture of Narcissism: American Life in an Age of Diminishing Expectations*, London: W. W. Norton.
Lash, Scott (1993) 'Reflexive modernization: The aesthetic dimension', *Theory, Culture and Society*, 10: 1–23.
Lash, Scott (2000) 'Risk culture', in Barbara Adams, Ulrich Beck and Joost Van Loon (eds) *The Risk Society and Beyond*, London: Sage, 47–62.
Laviolette, Patrick (2007) 'Hazardous sport?', *Anthropology Today*, 23(6): 1–2.
Lawrence, Anne (n.d.) 'Transsexual surgery: Its pros and cons', www.annelawrence.com/twr/ (accessed 16 May 2005).
Lawrence, Anne A. (2006) 'Clinical and theoretical parallels between desire for limb amputation and gender identity disorder', *Archives of Sexual Behavior*, 35(3): 263–78.
Lehman, Peter (ed.) (2001) *Masculinity: Bodies, Movies, Culture*, London: Routledge.
Lemaire, Anika (1977) *Jacques Lacan*, trans. David Macey, London: Routledge.
Levenkron, Steven (1999) *Cutting: Understanding and Overcoming Self-Mutilation*, New York: Norton.
Levine, Martin P. (1998) *Gay Macho: The Life and Death of the Homosexual Clone*, New York: New York University Press.
Lévi-Strauss, Claude (1955) *Tristes Tropiques*, Paris: Librairie Plon.
Levy, Ariel (2005) *Female Chauvinist Pigs: Women and the Rise of Raunch Culture*, New York: Free Press.
Lewis, Wendy (2007) *Plastic Makes Perfect*, London: Orion.
Lilleaas, Ulla-Britt (2007) 'Masculinities, sport and emotions', *Men and Masculinities*, 10(1): 39–53.
Linden, Robin Ruth, Pagano, Darlene, Russell, Diana E. and Star, Susan Leigh (eds) (1982) *Against Sadomasochism: A Radical Feminist Analysis*, California: Frog in the Wall.
Lingis, Alphonso (1984) *Excesses: Eros and Culture*, New York: State University of New York.
Lingis, Alphonso (1985) *Libido: The French Existential Theories*, Bloomington: Indiana University Press.
Livholts, Mona (2001a) '"Women", Welfare, Textual Politics and Critique: Different categories of "women", the making of welfare states and emancipation

in a Nordic welfare state context'. Dissertation, nr 34, Department of Social Work, Umeå University.

Livholts, Mona (2001b) 'The making of Nordic "women-friendlyness" and the language of emancipatory politics', *NORA: Nordic Journal of Women's Studies*, 9(3): 191–209.

Livholts, Mona (2007) *'Vanlig som vatten': Manlighet och normalitet i mediernas berättelser om* våldtäkt ('As normal as water': Masculinity and normality in media representations of rape), Malmö: Gleerups.

Lloyd, Paul (1997) 'Crashing into sex', *Adelaide Advertiser*, 8 February.

Loe, Meika (2006) 'The viagra blues: Embracing or resisting the viagra body', in Dana Rosenfeld and Christopher A. Faircloth (eds) *Medicalized Masculinities*, Philadelphia: Temple University Press, 21–44.

Loughlin, Gerard (2004) *Alien Sex: The Body and Desire in Cinema and Theology*, Oxford: Blackwell.

Lucie-Smith, Edward (1972) *Sexuality in Western Art*, London: Thames and Hudson.

Lury, Celia (1993) *Cultural Rights: Technology, Legality and Personality*, London: Routledge.

Lyng, Stephen (1990) 'Edgework: A social psychological analysis of voluntary risk-taking', *American Journal of Sociology*, 95: 851–86.

Lyng, Stephen (2005) 'Edgework and the risk-taking experience', in Stephen Lyng (ed.) *Edgework: The Sociology of Risk-Taking*, London: Routledge, 3–14.

Lyotard, Jean-Franois (2004) *Libidinal Economy* [1974], trans. Iain Hamilton Grant, London: Continuum.

MacKinnon, Catharine A. (1987) *Feminism Unmodified: Discourses on Life and Law*, Cambridge, MA: Harvard University Press.

MacKinnon, Kenneth (1997) *Uneasy Pleasures: The Male as Erotic Object*, London: Cygnus Arts.

Maine, Margo (2000) *Body Wars: Making Peace with Women's Bodies*, Carlsbad, CA: Gürze.

Mains, Geoff (1984) *Urban Aboriginals: A Celebration of Leathersexuality*, San Francisco, CA: Sunshine.

Maley, Jacqueline (2006) 'Italians passed us by, says Everest rescuer', *The Guardian*, 9 June.

Mangan, John A. (2000) *Making European Masculinities: Sport, Europe, Gender*, London: Frank Cass.

Marcus, Sharon (1992) 'Fighting bodies, fighting words: A theory and politics of rape prevention', in Judith Butler and Joan Scott (eds) *Feminists Theorise the Political*, New York: Routledge, 385–403.

Marks, Laura (2000) *The Skin of the Film: Intercultural Cinema, Embodiment, and the Senses*, Durham NC: Duke University Press.

Markwick, P. (2002) 'Harming consent', *Res Publica*, 8(2): 157–62.

Martin, Adrian (1997) 'Sex, car and death', *The Age*, 11 January.

McCorquodale, Duncan (ed.) (1996) *Orlan: Ceci est mon corps, ceci est mon logiciel*. London, UK: Black Dog Publishing.

McEvilley, Thomas (1995) 'The serpent and the stone', in Chrissie Iles (ed.) *Marina Abramovic: Objects, Performance, Video, Sound*, Oxford: Museum of Modern Art Oxford, 45–53.

McKay, Jim, Messner, Michael and Sabo, Don (eds) (2000) *Masculinities, Gender Relations and Sport*, London: Sage.

Mead, Margaret (1977) *Sex and Temperament in Three Primitive Societies* [1935], London: Routledge & Kegan Paul.
MedicineNet.com (1996) www.medterms.com (accessed 6 June 2007).
Meredith T G (2007) 'The new bme personals: Body modification ezine', http: //iam.bmezine.com/pers4.exe?cmd=zoom&rec=7287 (accessed 15 June 2007).
Messerschmidt, James W. (2005) 'Men, masculinities and crime', in Michael S. Kimmel, Jeff Hearn and R. W. Connell (eds) *Handbook of Studies on Men and Masculinities*, Thousand Oaks, CA: Sage, 196–212.
Messner, Michael (1990) 'When bodies are weapons: Masculinity and violence in sport', *International Review for the Sociology of Sport*, 25(3): 203–20.
Messner, Michael (1992) *Power at Play: Sports and the Problem of Masculinity*, Boston: Beacon.
Messner, Michael and Sabo, Don (eds) (1990) *Sport, Men and the Gender Order*, Champaign, IL: Kinetics.
Messner, Michael and Sabo, Don (eds) (1994) *Sex, Violence and Power in Sports: Rethinking Masculinity*, Freedom, CA: Crossing Hart.
Meyerowitz, Joanne (2002) *How Sex Changed: A History of Transsexuality in the United States*, Cambridge, MA: Harvard University Press.
Midol, Nancy and Broyer, Gerard (1995) 'Toward an anthropological analysis of new sport cultures: The case of whiz sports in France', *Sociology of Sport Journal*, 12: 204–12.
Miglietta, Francesca Alfano (2003) *Extreme Bodies: The Use and Abuse of the Body in Art*, Milan: Skira.
Miller, Dusty (2005) *Women Who Hurt Themselves: A Book of Hope and Understanding*, New York: Basic.
Miller, Phillip and Devon, Molly (1995) *Screw the Roses, Send Me the Thorns: The Romance and Sexual Sorcery of Sadomasochism*, Fairfield, CT: Mystic Rose.
Minha, Trinh T. (1991) *When the Moon Waxes Red: Representation, Gender and Cultural Politics*, London: Routledge.
Miriam, Kathy (2007) 'Toward a phenomenology of sex-right: Reviving radical feminist theory of compulsory heterosexuality', *Hypatia*, 22(1): 211–28.
Moller, Michael (2007) 'Exploiting patterns: A critique of hegemonic masculinity', *Journal of Gender Studies*, 16(3): 263–76.
Monaghan, Lee (2005) 'Big handsome men, bears and others: Virtual constructions of "fat male embodiment"', *Body & Society*, 11(2): 81–111.
More, Kate and Whittle, Stephen (eds) (1999) *Reclaiming Genders: Transsexual Grammars at the fin de siecle*, London and New York: Cassell.
Morgan, Kathryn Pauly (1998) 'Women and the knife: Cosmetic surgery and the colonization of women's bodies', in Rose Weitz (ed.) *The Politics of Women's Bodies: Sexuality, Appearance, and Behavior*, Oxford and New York: Oxford University Press, 147–66.
Morley, David (1980) *The 'Nationwide' Audience: Structure and Decoding*, London: BFI.
Morris, David B. (1991) *The Culture of Pain*, Berkeley, CA: University of California Press.
Morris, Meaghan (1994) 'Introduction', in Paul Willemen (ed.) *Looks and Frictions: Essays in Cultural Studies and Film Theory*, London: BFI Publishing/ Bloomington: Indiana University Press, 1–23.
Mort, Frank (1996) *Cultures of Consumption: Masculinities and Social Space in Late Twentieth-Century Britain*, London: Routledge.

Moye, Andrew (1985) 'Pornography', in Andy Metcalf and Martin Humphries (eds) *The Sexuality of Men*, London: Pluto, 44–69.

Mulvey, Laura (1975) 'Visual pleasure and narrative cinema', *Screen*, 16(3): 6–18.

Mulvey, Laura (1989) *Visual and Other Pleasures*, Basingstoke: Macmillan.

Musafar, Fakir (1996) 'Body play: State of grace or sickness?', in Armando Favazza (ed.) *Bodies under Siege: Self-mutilation and Body Modification in Culture and Psychiatry*, Baltimore: Johns Hopkins University Press, 325–34.

Museum Moderner Kunst Stiftung Ludwig Wien (1997) *Split: Reality VALIE EXPORT*, Wien: Springer-Verlag.

Nader, Laura (1997) 'Controlling processes: Tracing the dynamic components of power', *Current Anthropology*, 38(5): 711–37.

Nead, Lynda (1992) *The Female Nude: Art, Obscenity and Sexuality*, London: Routledge.

Neale, Steve (1982) 'Images of men', *Screen*, 23(3–4): 47–53.

Neale, Steve (1983) 'Masculinity as spectacle: Reflections on men and mainstream cinema', *Screen*, 24(6): 2–16.

Negrin, Llewellyn (2000) 'Cosmetics and the female body: A critical appraisal of poststructuralist theories of masquerade', *European Journal of Cultural Studies*, 3(1): 83–101.

Nettleton, Sarah and Watson, Jonathan (1998) *The Body in Everyday Life*, London: Routledge.

Neuman, W. Lawrence (1997) *Social Research Methods: Qualitative and Quantitative Approaches*, Boston: Allyn and Bacon.

Nixon, Sean (1996) *Hard Looks: Masculinities, Spectatorship and Contemporary Consumption*, London: UCL Press.

Nixon, Sean (1997) 'Exhibiting masculinity', in Stuart Hall (ed.) *Representation: Cultural Representation and Signifying Practices*, London: Sage, 291–336.

Noyes, John, K. (1997) *The Mastery of Submission: Inventions of Masochism*, Ithaca: Cornell University Press.

Noyes, John K. (1998) 'S/M in SA: Sexual violence, simulated sex and psychoanalytic theory', *American Imago*, 55(1): 135–53.

O'Dell, Kathy (1998) *Contract with the Skin: Masochism, Performance Art, and the 1970s*, Minneapolis: University of Minnesota Press.

Ohshima, T. (2000) 'Forensic wound examination', *Forensic Science International*, 113(1–3):153–64.

Owen, Susan (1999) '*Buffy the Vampire Slayer*: Vampires, postmodernity and postfeminism', *Journal of Popular Film and Television*, 27(2): 24–32.

Palahnuik, Chuck (1996) *Fight Club*, New York: Hyperion.

Palm, Anne-Marie (1996) 'War against the body', in Susanne Lundin and Lynn Åkesson (eds) *Bodytime: On the Interaction of Body, Identity and Society*, Lund: Lund University Press, 85–110.

Palmer, Catherine (2004) 'Death, danger and the selling of risk in adventure sports', in Belinda Wheaton (ed.) *Understanding Lifestyle Sports: Consumption, Identity, Difference*, London: Routledge, 55–69.

Pateman, Carole (1988) *The Sexual Contract*, Cambridge: Polity.

Patton, Michael Quinn (1980) *Qualitative Evaluation Methods*, London: Sage.

Percy, Carol (1998) 'Feminism', in Karen Trew and John Kremer (eds) *Gender and Psychology*, London: Arnold, 27–35.

Perovic, Sava V., Stanojevic, Dusan S. and Djordjevic, Miroslav L. (2005) 'Vaginoplasty in male to female transsexuals using penile skin and urethral flap', *International Journal of Transgenderism*, 1: 43–64.

Pitts, Victoria (2000a) 'Visibly queer: Body technologies and sexual politics', *The Sociological Quarterly*, 41(3): 443–63.

Pitts, Victoria (2000b) 'Body modification, self-mutilation and agency in media accounts of a subculture', in Mike Featherstone (ed.) *Body Modification*, London: Sage, 291–304.

Pitts, Victoria (2003) *In the Flesh: The Cultural Politics of Body Modification*, Basingstoke: Palgrave Macmillan.

Plummer, David (1999) *One of the Boys: Masculinity, Homophobia, and Modern Manhood*, Binghamton, NY: Harrington Park.

Plummer, Ken (1995) *Telling Sexual Stories: Power, Change and Social Worlds*, London: Routledge.

Pope, Harrison G. Jr, Phillips, Katharine A. and Olivardia, Roberto (2000) *The Adonis Complex: The Secret Crisis of Male Body Obsession*, New York: Free Press.

Power, Charmaine (1998) 'Reconstituting Self: A Feminist Poststructural Analysis of Women's Narrative of Domestic Violence', Unpub. PhD thesis, Adelaide: Flinders University.

Pronger, Brian (1992) *The Arena of Masculinity*, Toronto: University of Toronto Press.

Prosser, Jay (2001) 'Skin memories', in Sarah Ahmed and Jackie Stacey (eds) *Thinking through the Skin*, New York: Routledge, 52–68.

Rajchman, John (2000) *The Deleuze Connections*, Cambridge, MA: MIT Press.

Randeberg, Lise Lyngsnes, Winnem, Andreas M., Langois, Niel E., Larsen, Eivind L. P., Haaverstad, Rune, Haugen, Olav A. and Svaasand, Lars O. (2007) 'Skin changes following minor trauma', *Lasers in Surgery and Medicine*, 39: 403–13.

Raymond, Janice (1994) *The Transsexual Empire* [1979], Boston: Teachers' College Press.

Rechy, John (1977) *The Sexual Outlaw: A Documentary*, London: W. H. Allen.

Reich, Wilhelm (1969) *Character-Analysis*, [1949] New York: The Noonday Press.

Reik, Theodor (1941) *Masochism in Modern Man*, New York: Grove.

Reimers, Eva (2005) "'En av vår tids martyrer" - Fadime Sahindal som mediehändelse' ("One of the martyrs of our time" - Fadime Sahindal as a media event), in Paulina De los Reyes and Lena Martinsson (eds) *Olikhetens paradigm: intersektionella perspektiv på (o)jämlikhetsskapande* (Paradigms of differences. Intersectional perspectives on (in)equality making processes), Lund: Studentlitteratur, 141–59.

Reinharz, Shulamit (1992) *Feminist Methods in Social Research*, Oxford: Oxford University Press.

Renshaw, Domeena C. (2003) 'Body dysmorphia, the plastic surgeon, and the counseler', *The Family Journal: Counseling and Therapy for Couples and Families*, 11(3): 264–67.

Reynaud, Emanuel (1983) *Holy Virility: The Social Construction of Masculinity*, London: Pluto.

Reynolds, Nigel (1996) 'Violent, nasty and morally vacuous', *Daily Telegraph*, 9 November.

Rhee, Jieun (2005) 'Performing the Other: Yoko Ono's *Cut Piece*', *Art History*, 28(1): 96–118.

Rinehart, Robert and Sydnor, Synthia (2003) 'Proem', in Robert Rinehart and Synthia Sydnor (eds.) *To the Extreme: Alternative Sports, Inside and Out*, Albany: State University of New York Press, 1–7.

Ritchie, Ani and Barker, Meg (2005) 'Feminist SM: A contradiction in terms or a way of challenging traditional gendered dynamics through sexual practice?', *Lesbian & Gay Psychology Review*, 6(3): 227--39.

Roberti, Jonathan W. and Storch, Eric A. (2005) 'Psychosocial adjustment of college students with tattoos and piercings', *Journal of College Counseling*, 8(1): 14(6pp.).

Robinson, Victoria (2004) 'Taking risks: Identity, masculinities, and rock-climbing', in Belinda Wheaton (ed.) *Understanding Lifestyle Sports: Consumption, Identity and Difference*, London: Routledge, 113–30.

Robinson, Victoria (2008) *Everyday Masculinities and Extreme Sport: Male Identity and Rock-Climbing*, Oxford: Berg.

Rodowick, David (1982) 'The difficulty of difference', *Wide Angle*, 5(1): 4–15.

Rossi, Leena-Maija (1995) 'Stunt shots or everyday violence', *Siksi*, 3: 35–7.

Rubin, Gayle (1984) 'Thinking sex: Notes for a radical theory of the politics of sexuality', in Carol S. Vance (ed.) *Pleasure and Danger: Exploring Female Sexuality*, London: Routledge & Kegan Paul, 267–319.

Russell, Diana (1982) 'Sadomasochism: A contra-feminist activity', in Robin Ruth Linden, Darlene Pagano, Diana Russell and Susan Leigh Star (eds) *Against Sadomasochism: A Radical Feminist Analysis*, Palo Alto, CA: Frog in the Wall, 176–83.

Saco, Diana (1992) 'Masculinity as signs: Poststructuralist feminist approaches to the study of gender', in Steve Craig (ed.) *Men, Masculinity and the Media*, London: Sage, 23–39.

Saco, Diana (1994) 'Feminist film criticism: The piano and "the female gaze"', guest presentation for the Minnesota Humanities Commission's Teacher Institute Seminar on *Screening Society: Film as Art and Culture*, Chaska, MN, 13–18 November, http://diana.saco.name/Female_Gaze.htm (accessed 28 July 2007).

Sahlin, Ingrid (1999) 'Diskursanalys som sociologisk metod' (Discourse analysis as sociological method), in Katarina Sjöberg (ed.) *Mer än kalla fakta: Kvalitativ forskning i praktiken* [More than cold facts: Qualitative research in practice], Lund: Studentlitteratur.

Salecl, Renata (1998) *(Per)Versions of Love and Hate*, London and New York: Verso.

Sandberg, David (2003) 'Riktig våldtäkt: En undersökning av våldtäkt i nyhetsrapporteringen' [Real rape: An investigation of rape in news media], Dissertation for Bachelor of Science, Ethnology: Stockholm University.

Sartre, Jean-Paul (1965) *Essays in Existentialism*, Secaucus, New Jersey: Citadel.

Sartre, Jean-Paul (2000) *Being and Nothingness* [1943], London: Routledge.

Sarwer, David B. (2002) 'Cosmetic surgery and changes in body image', in Thomas Pruzinsky and Thomas F. Cash (eds) *Body Images: A Handbook of Theory, Research, and Clinical Practice*, New York: Guilford Press, 422–30.

Savran, David (1998) *Taking It Like a Man: White Masculinity, Masochism, and Contemporary American Culture*, Princeton, NJ: Princeton University Press.

Saxey, Esther (2001) 'Staking a claim: The series and its fan fiction', in David Lavery (ed.) *Reading the Vampire Slayer*, London: IB Tauris, 187–210.

Schofield, Margot, Hussain, Rafat Loxton, Debbie and Miller, Zoe (2002) 'Psychosocial and health behavioural covarieties of cosmetic surgery: Women's Health Australia Study', *Journal of Health Psychology*, 7(4): 445–57.

Schor, Juliet B. (2004) *Born to Buy: The Commercialized Child and the New Consumer Culture*, New York: Scribner.
Schwartz, Ari J. and Ricci, Lawrence (1996) 'How accurately can bruises be aged in abused children? Literature review and synthesis', *Pediatrics*, 97(2): 254–7.
Scott, Linda M. (2005) *Fresh Lipstick: Redressing Fashion and Feminism*, Basingstoke: Palgrave Macmillan.
Screen (ed.) (1992) *The Sexual Subject: A Screen Reader in Sexuality*, London: Routledge.
Seidler, Victor (1997) *Man Enough: Embodying Masculinities*, London: Sage.
Sharp, Lesley A. (2000) 'The commodification of body and its parts', *Annual Review of Anthropology*, 29: 287–328.
Shainberg, Steven (2002) *Secretary*, Lionsgate Films.
Shaw, Sarah Naomi (2002) 'Shifting conversations on girls' and women's self-injury: An analysis of the clinical literature in historical context', *Feminism and Psychology*, 12(2): 191–219.
Shilling, Chris (1993) *Body and Social Theory*, London: Sage.
The Shorter Oxford Dictionary (1990) Oxford: Oxford University Press.
Silverman, Kaja (1992) *Male Subjectivity at the Margins*, New York: Routledge.
Silverman, Kaja (1997) 'Speak, body' Museum Moderner Kunst Stiftung Ludwig Wien (ed.) *Split: Reality VALIE EXPORT*, Wien: Springer-Verlag, 214–23.
Simpson, Mark (1994) *Male Impersonators: Men Performing Masculinity*, London: Routledge.
Simpson, Mark (1996) *It's a Queer World*, London: Vintage.
Sisson, Kathy (2005) 'The cultural formation of S/M: history and analysis', *Lesbian & Gay Psychology Review*, 6(3), 147–62.
Sjölander, Annika (2004) 'Kärnproblem: Opinionsbildning i kärnavfallsdiskuren i Malå' (Nuclear problem: Leading public opinion about nuclear waste in Malå), Dissertation nr 7, Department of Media and Communication, Umeå University.
Slattery, Dennis P. (1999) *The Wounded Body: Remembering the Markings of Flesh*, New York: SUNY Press.
Smelik, Anneke (1999) 'Feminist film theory', in Pam Cook and Mieke Bernink (eds) *The Cinema Book*, 2nd edn, London: British Film Institute, 353–65.
Smith, Charles W. (2005) 'Financial edgework: Trading in market currents', in Stephen Lyng (ed.) *Edgework: The Sociology of Risk-Taking*, London: Routledge, 187–200.
Smith, Marc (1999) 'Wound envy: Touching Cronenberg's *Crash*', *Screen*, 40(2): 193–202.
Smithers, Rebecca (2007) 'Knives, whips and a slap in the face: How complaints to the ad watchdog doubled', *The Guardian*, 19 November: 3.
Sobchack, Vivian (1991) 'Baudrillard's obscenity', *Science-Fiction Studies*, 18: 327–9.
Sobchack, Vivian (1998) 'Beating the meat / Surviving the text, or how to get out of this century alive', in Paula A. Treichler, Lisa Cartwright and Constance Penley (eds) *The Visible Woman: Imaging Technologies, Gender, and Science*, New York University Press, New York, 310–21.
Spector, Nancy (organiser) (2007) *All in the Present Must Be Transformed: Matthew Barney and Joseph Beuys*, Deutsche Guggenheim, Berlin.
Spivey, Nigel (2001) *Enduring Creation: Art, Pain, and Fortitude*, Berkeley, CA: University of California Press.

Stacey, Jackie (1994) *Star Gazing: Hollywood Cinema and Female Spectatorship*, London: Routledge.

Stanley, Liz (1995) *The Auto/Biographical I: Theory and Practice of Feminist Auto/*Biography, Manchester: Manchester University Press.

Steinberg, Marlene (1994) 'Systematizing dissociation: Symptomatology and diagnostic assessment', in David Speigel (ed.) *Dissociation: Culture, Mind and Body*, Washington, DC: APA Press, 59–90.

Steinman, Clay (1992) 'Gaze out of bounds: Men watching men on television', in Steve Craig (ed.) *Men, Masculinity and the Media*, Newbury Park, CA: Sage, 199–214.

Stephens, Elizabeth and Lorentzen, Jørgen (2007) 'An introduction', *Men and Masculinities*, 10(1): 5–8.

Stevens, Katy (2003) 'Sex, spectatorship and the surface of the body: Spike as Buffy's "dolly"', paper presented at Staking a Claim: Exploring the Global Reach of Buffy conference, University of South Australia, Adelaide, July.

Stofman, Guy M., Neavin, Timothy S., Ramineni, Praful M. and Alford, Aaron (2006) 'Better sex from the knife? An intimate look at the effects of cosmetic surgery on sexual practices', *Aesthetic Surgery Journal*, 26(1): 12–7.

Stoller, Robert J. (1991) *Pain & Passion: A Psychoanalyst Explores the World of S & M*, New York: Plenum.

Stone, Lawrence (1977) *The Family, Sex and Marriage 1500–1800*, London: Weidenfeld & Nicolson.

Stranger, Mark (1999) 'The aesthetics of risk': A study of surfing', *International Review for the Sociology of Sport*, 34(3): 265–76.

Strong, Marilee (2000) *A Bright Red Scream: Self-Mutilation and the Language of Pain*, London: Virago, 1st pub. New York: Viking.

Sullivan, Deborah A. (2002) *Cosmetic Surgery: The Cutting Edge of Commercial Medicine in America*, New Brunswick, NJ: Rutgers University Press.

Sullivan, Nikki (2001) *Tattooed Bodies: Subjectivity, Textuality, Ethics and Pleasure*, Westport, CT: Praeger.

Sullivan, Nikki (2004) 'It's as plain as the nose on his face': Michael Jackson, modificatory practices, and the question of ethics', *Scan: Journal of Media Arts Culture*, 1(3): 6.

Sweetman, Paul (2000) 'Anchoring the (postmodern) self? Body modification, fashion and identity', in Mike Featherstone (ed.) *Body Modification*, London: Sage, 51–76.

Szymczak, Julia E. and Conrad, Peter (2006) 'Medicalizing the aging male body: Andropause and baldness', in Dana Rosenfeld and Christopher A. Faircloth (eds) *Medicalized Masculinities*, Philadelphia: Temple University Press, 89–111.

Taft, Angela, Hegarty, Kelsey and Flood, Michael (2001) 'Are men and women equally violent to intimate partners?', *Australian and New Zealand Journal of Public Health*, 25(6): 498–500.

Talle, Aud (1993) 'Transforming women into "pure" agnates: Aspects of female infibulation in Somalia', in Vigidis Broch-Due, Ingrid Rudie and Tone Bleie (eds) *Carved Flesh/CS Selves*, Oxford: Berg, 83–106.

Tasker, Yvonne (1993a) 'Dumb movies for dumb people: Masculinity, the body, and the voice in contemporary action cinema', in Steven Cohan and Ina Rae Hark (eds) *Screening the Male: Exploring Masculinities in Hollywood Cinema*, London: Routledge, 230–44.

Tasker, Yvonne (1993b) *Spectacular Bodies: Gender, Genre and the Action Cinema*, London: Routledge.

Taylor, Gary and Ussher, Jane (2001) 'Making sense of S&M: A discourse analytic account', *Sexualities*, 4(3): 293–314.

Tea, Michelle (2002) 'Love bites' http://www.sfbg.com/36/52/cover_sexhickey.html 25 September, (accessed 10 January 2008).

Theweleit, Klaus (1989) *Male Fantasies II* [1977–78], Minneapolis: Polity.

Thomas, Calvin (2002) 'Reenfleshing the bright boys: Or how male bodies matter to feminist theory', in Judith Kegan Gardiner (ed.) *Masculinity Studies and Feminist Theory*, New York: Columbia University Press, 60–89.

Thompson, Bill (1994) *Sadomasochism: Painful Perversion or Pleasurable Play*, London: Cassell.

Thompson, Denise (2001) *Radical Feminism Today*, Thousand Oaks, CA: Sage.

Tolson, Andrew (1977) *The Limits of Masculinity*, London: Tavistock.

Tookey, Christopher (1996) Review of *Crash*, *Daily Mail*, 6 June.

Trosell, Aino (1999) *Ytspänning* (Surface tension), Stockholm: Prisma.

Trotman, Nat (2007) 'Ritual space/sculptural time', in Nancy Spector (organiser) *All in the Present Must Be Transformed: Matthew Barney and Joseph Beuys*, Berlin, Deutsche Guggenheim, 140–59.

Truscott, Carol (1991) 'Gender role reversal and the violated lesbian body: Towards a feminist hermeneutic of lesbian sadomasochism', *Journal of Lesbian Studies*, 3(3): 61–72.

Tulloch, John and Lupton, Deborah (2003) *Risk and Everyday Life*, London: Sage.

Turner, Bryan S. (1996) *The Body and Society: Explorations of Social Theory*, London: Sage.

Turner, Bryan S. (2000) 'The possibility of primitiveness: The sociology of body marks in cool societies', in Mike Featherstone (ed.) *Body Modification*, London: Sage, 39–50.

van Dijk, Teun (1995) 'Power and the news media', in David L. Paletz (ed.) *Political Communication and Action*, Cresskill, NJ: Hampton, 9–36.

Vance, Carol S. (ed.) (1984) *Pleasure and Danger: Exploring Female Sexuality*, London: Routledge & Kegan Paul.

Vergine, Lea (2000) *Body and Performance: The Body as Language*, Milan: Skira Editore; London: Thames and Hudson.

Vettel-Becker, Patricia (2002) 'Destruction and delight: World War II combat photography and the aesthetic inscription of masculine identity', *Men and Masculinities*, 5(1): 80–102.

Vidal, John (1999) 'Call of the wild', *The Guardian*, 9 June: 2–3.

Von Krafft-Ebing, Richard (1886) *Psychopathia Sexualis: A Medico-Forensic Study*, New York: Bell.

Von Krafft-Ebing, Richard (1965) *Psychopathia Sexualis: A Medico-Forensic Study* [1886], New York: G. P. Putnam's Sons.

Walker, Alexander (1996a) 'A movie beyond the bounds of depravity', *Evening Standard*, 3 June.

Walker, Alexander (1996b) 'Porn goes into overdrive', *Evening Standard*, 6 June.

Walsh, Barent W. and Rosen, Paul M. (1988) *Self Mutilation: Theory, Research and Treatment*, New York: Guilford.

Wardle, Claire (2007) 'Monsters and angels: Visual press coverage of child murders in the USA and UK, 1930–2000', *Journalism* 8(3): 263–84.

Warr, Tracey (ed.) (2000) *The Artist's Body: A Survey of the Use of the Artist's Body in 20th-Century Art*, London: Phaidon.

Warriors for Innocence (2007) 'It's just fiction', www.warriorsforinnocence.org/2007/06/its-just-fiction.html (accessed 3 August 2007).

Waterhouse, Ruth (1993) 'The inverted gaze', in Sue Scott and David Morgan (eds) *Body Matters! Essays on the Sociology of the Body*, London: Falmer, 105–21.

Watney, Simon (1987) *Policing Desire: Pornography, AIDS and the Media*, London: Comedia.

Watson, A. (2005) 'You don't have to be crazy', *The Telegraph*, 28 May: 15.

Watson, Jonathan (2000) *Male Bodies: Health, Culture and Identity*, Buckingham: Open University Press.

Weille, Katharine-Lee H. (2002) 'The psychodynamics of consensual sado-masochism and dominant-submissive sexual games', *Studies in Gender and Sexuality*, 3(2): 131–60.

Weinberg, Thomas S. (1995) 'Sociological and social psychological issues in the study of sadomasochism', in Thomas S. Weinberg (ed.) *S&M: Studies in Dominance and Submission*, New York: Prometheus, 289–303.

Weiss, Gail (1999) *Body Images: Embodiment as Intercorporeality*, New York: Routledge.

Weiss, Margo (2006) 'Mainstreaming kink: The politics of BDSM representation in US popular media', *Journal of Homosexuality*, 50(2/3): 103–32.

Wheaton, Belinda (2000a) '"New lads"? Masculinities and the "new sport" participant', *Men and Masculinities*, 2(4): 434–56.

Wheaton, Belinda (2000b) 'Just do it: Consumption, commitment and identity in the windsurfing subculture', *Sociology of Sport Journal*, 17(3): 254–74.

Wheaton, Belinda (ed.) (2004a) *Understanding Lifestyle Sports: Consumption, Identity and Difference*, London: Routledge.

Wheaton, Belinda (2004b) '"New lads"? Competing masculinities in the windsurfing culture', in Belinda Wheaton (ed.) *Understanding Lifestyle Sports: Consumption, Identity and Difference*, London: Routledge, 131–53.

Wheaton, Belinda and Tomlinson, Alan (1998) 'The changing gender order in sport? The case of windsurfing', *Journal of Sport and Social Issues*, 22: 252–74.

Wheelywitch (2007) 'The new bme personals: 7kmp-wheelywitch Body Modification ezine' http://iam.bmezine.com/pers4.exe?cmd=zoom&rec=7344 (accessed 15 June 2007).

Whitehead, Stephen M. (2002) *Men and Masculinities*, Cambridge: Polity.

Widerberg, Karin (1995) *Kunskapens kön: Minnen, reflektioner, teori* (The knowledge of gender: Memory, reflections, theory), Stockholm: Norstedts förlag.

Willard-Traub, Margaret K. (2007) 'Scholarly autobiography: An alternative intellectual practice', *Feminist Studies*, 33(1): 188–206.

Willemen, Paul (1981) 'Anthony Mann: Looking at the male', *Framework*, 15, 16, 17.

Willemen, Paul (1994) *Looks and Frictions: Essays in Cultural Studies and Film Theory*, London: BFI Publishing; Bloomington: Indiana University Press.

Williams, Gareth H. (1984) 'The genesis of chronic illness: Narrative reconstruction', *Sociology of Health and Illness*, 6: 175–200.

Williams, Linda (1989) *Hard Core: Power, Pleasure, and the 'Frenzy of the Visible'*, Berkeley CA: University of California Press.

Williams, Rowan (1979/1990) *The Wound of Knowledge: Christian Spirituality from the New Testament to St John of the Cross*, 2nd edn, London: Darton Longman and Todd.

Williams, Simon J. and Bendelow, Gillian (1998) *The Lived Body: Sociological Themes, Embodied Issues*, London: Routledge.

Williamson, Milly (2005) 'Spike, sex and subtext: Intertextual portrayals of the sympathetic vampire on cult television', *European Journal of Cultural Studies*, 8(3): 287–311.

Wilson, Tamar Diana (2002) 'Pharaonic circumcision under patriarchy and breast augmentation under phallocentric capitalism', *Violence against Women*, 8(4): 495–521.

Winokur, Mark (2004) 'Technologies of race: Special effects, fetish, film and the fifteenth century', *Genders* 40, http://www.genders.org/g40/g40_winokur.html.

Winter, Bronwyn, Thompson, Denise and Jeffreys, Sheila (2002) 'The UN approach to harmful traditional practices: Some conceptual problems', *International Feminist Journal of Politics*, 4(1): 72–94.

Wiseman, Jay (1997) *SM 101*, 2nd rev. edn, San Francisco: Greenery.

Woods, Chris (1995) *State of the Queer Nation: A Critique of Gay and Lesbian Politics in 1990s Britain*, London: Cassell.

Woodward, Kath (2006) *Boxing, Masculinity and Identity: The 'I' of the Tiger*, London: Routledge.

Yalom, Marilyn (1998) *A History of the Breast*, New York: Ballantine.

Young, Iris Marion (1998) 'Breasted experience – The look and the feeling', in Rose Weitz (ed.) *The Politics of Women's Bodies: Sexuality, Appearance, and the Behavior*, New York and Oxford: Oxford University Press, 125–36.

Young, Kevin and White, Philip (2000) 'Researching sports injury: Reconstructing dangerous masculinities', in Jim McKay, Michael Messner and Don Sabo (eds) *Masculinities, Gender Relations and Sport*, London: Sage, 108–26.

Young, Kevin, White, Phillip and McTeer, William (1994) 'Body talk: Male athletes reflect on sport, injury and pain', *Sociology of Sport Journal*, 11(2): 175–94.

Zeiler, Barbie (2008) 'Why memory's work on journalism does not reflect journalism's work on memory', *Memory Studies*, 1(1): 79–87.

Zell, Andrea (2000) *Valie Export: Inszenierung von Schmerz: Selbstverletzung in den frühen Aktionen*, Berlin: Dieter Reimer Verlag GmbH.

Zimbardo, Phillip (2007) *The Lucifer Effect: How Good People Turn Evil*, London: Rider.

Zubriggen, Eileen, Collins, Rebecca L., Lamb, Sharon, Roberts, Tomi-Ann, Tolman, Deborah, Ward, L. Monique and Blake, Jeanne (2007) *Report of the APA Task Force on the Sexualization of Girls*, Washington, DC: American Psychological Association.

Index

GPSR Compliance
The European Union's (EU) General Product Safety Regulation (GPSR) is a set of rules that requires consumer products to be safe and our obligations to ensure this.

If you have any concerns about our products, you can contact us on

ProductSafety@springernature.com

In case Publisher is established outside the EU, the EU authorized representative is:

Springer Nature Customer Service Center GmbH
Europaplatz 3
69115 Heidelberg, Germany

www.ingramcontent.com/pod-product-compliance
Ingram Content Group UK Ltd.
Pitfield, Milton Keynes, MK11 3LW, UK
UKHW041913040925
462611UK00003B/242
97813-9361823